Justice

Justice

The Memoirs
Of Attorney General
Richard Kleindienst

Richard G. Kleindienst

Jameson Books
Ottawa, Illinois

Library of Congress Cataloging in Publication Data

Kleindienst, Richard G., 1923-
   Justice: the memoirs of Attorney General
Richard Kleindienst.

   1. Kleindienst, Richard G., 1923-
   2. Attorneys-general—United States—Biography.
   I. Title.
   KF373.K55A33   1985   353.5 [B]   85-5182
   ISBN 0-915463-15-6

Copies of this book may be purchased directly from the publisher for $16.95. All inquiries should be addressed to Jameson Books, 722 Columbus St., Ottawa, IL 61350. (815) 434-7905.

Printed in the United States of America

ISBN: 0-915463-15-6

To Marnie

Contents

PART III

Preface

I have written this book for two primary reasons. First, so many friends who have known me, my wife Marnie, and our four wonderful children—Alfred, Wallace, Anne, and Carolyn—have constantly urged that, for the record, I chronicle my experiences as a politician and as an officer of the U.S. Department of Justice. Whether these experiences will interest the reading public remains to be seen. It is important, however, to attempt the task for so many friends.

Second, since controversy has surrounded my service in the Department of Justice, I would like to leave for my children and grandchildren a record of these controversies from my point of view. Perhaps they and other young Americans will not only gain an insight into the realities of the government of their country, but also be encouraged to participate to some degree in government themselves.

This book is not a judgment of Richard Nixon. He has written extensively about himself, and many others have written about him in a judgmental way. Enough is enough. Nevertheless, President Nixon weaves his way in and out of my life from September 1956 to April 1973, when I as the attorney general walked out of my last meeting of the cabinet. That was the last time I saw him. To the best of my ability, and as fairly as I know how, I have described the many incidents in politics and government that brought us together. The reader may draw his own conclusions as to what those incidents suggest about us.

Whether for good or ill, I may be the only person to have attained the high position of attorney general of the United States for no other reason than my involvement in the organizational politics of the Republican party. Consequently, Part I explains why I found myself in the Department of Justice in 1969 as the deputy attorney general. Part II recounts some of my experiences during the some four and a half years I was at Justice. Part III contains a chapter on my experience with the office of the special prosecutor after I left Justice in May 1973, and a chapter setting forth my views of the role of the presidential counselor in our government.

Unfortunately, much of this book is autobiographical. Since I, as an individual, am not the important thing, but the events themselves, I have chosen to describe my participation in those events by talking about them through other individuals. I hope this method will permit a broader and more meaningful perspective. I hasten to add that none of these individuals has asked to be so utilized, and most, if not all, may not like or agree with what I have said about them. I apologize in advance to them, but hold fast to my First Amendment rights. They are all heroes of mine, and I trust they will become heroes to you.

Politics, I believe, is a noble pursuit in our blessedly free society and service in our government is a great privilege. Thus, if even a handful of young American men and women are idealistically motivated to become citizen-volunteer politicians or to seek public office, a reward of great magnitude will be mine.

Although it is sometimes unpleasant, even traumatic, to recall unpleasant experiences, writing this book has been the most enriching experience of my life. No matter that no one else will benefit by it. I have. Because it has forced me repeatedly to remind myself how fortunate I have been to be a free person and a citizen of the United States of America.

Acknowledgments

This book could not have been written without the friendship, support, love, and affection over a lifetime of hundreds of persons. Without regard to the relative importance to me of such bonds, I list alphabetically those who come to mind, knowing full well in advance that there are others who should be included:

John Alexander, Jesse Allen, Vivian Allen, John S. Andrews, Robert E. Anderson, Esq., Hon. Mark Andrews, Hon. Leslie C. Arends, Hon. William Armstrong, John S. Autry, Rev. Margaret Babcock, Francis J. Bagnell, Kenneth W. Ball, Tracy Balogh, Hon. James Baker, Dr. B. J. Barber, Hon. William J. Bauer, Hon. George Beall, Hon. Louis C. Bechtle, Dr. William Becker, Hon. James M. Beggs, Mary Beggs, Hon. Henry Bellmon, K. G. Bentson, William T. Birmingham, Esq., Brice I. Bishop, Esq., Margorie Borodkin, Marvin Borodkin, Esq., Fred I. Brown, Keith Brown, Hon. Herbert Brownell, Jr., Hon. James Buckley, Hon. William F. Buckley, George M. Bunker, Hon. Dean Burch, Hon. Warren E. Burger, John Burke, Hon. Richard K. Burke, Hon. George Preston Bush.

Plato Cacheris, Esq., Richard L. Callaghan, Esq., Jameson Campaigne, Jr., Joan Cannon, George Read Carlock, Esq., Peter Carlsen, Hon. Norman A. Carlson, John Joseph Cassidy, Esq., Harry J. Cavanagh, Esq., Gene Cernan, Hon. John Chaffee, Hon. Richard H. Chambers, S. Thomas Chandler, Esq., Donald P. Charles, Elmer Clark, Robert M. Clark, Hon. William F. Clayton, Oscar Collier, Hon. Walker B. Comegys, Hon. John B. Connally, Hon. Clarence M. Coster, Frank Coy, George L. Cornell, Hon. Elaine Crane, Daniel Cracchiolo, Esq., Hon. Scott Crampton, Timothy Creedon, Albert Culbertson, Shirley Culbertson, John Charles Daly, Mary Lou Davidson, Phil Davidson, Dr. Charles Davis, Charles E. Davis, Hon. Dennis DeConcini, Hon. Evo DeConcini, Lt. Gen. Joseph R. DeLuca (Ret), Hon. Cartha deLoach, Edward Delph, David P. Dolgen, Trixie Landsberger Dorsett, John Duffner, Clarence J. Duncan, Esq., Helen Edwards, Max Elbin, Pete Elliott, Hon. Ralph Ericson, Lt. Col. James Ervin, Gen. Howell M. Estes, Jr. (Ret), Hon. Richard M. Fairbanks, III, Alma Fannin, Hon. Paul J. Fannin, Hon. Raymond F. Farrell, Hon. Gerald D. Fines, Harry S. Flemming, George A. Fogarty, Pres. Gerald R. Ford, Hon. John G. Fox, Edward A. W. Franklin, Esq., David R. Frazer, Esq., Hon. Kent Frizzell, Hon. Donald F. Froeb.

Paul Garbler, Hon. Oliver Gasch, Wm. A. Geoghagan, Esq., Hon. Brian P. Gettings, Rev. Charles Glaenzer, Abe Gibron, Maj. Gen. Roland Gleszer (Ret), Peggy Goldwater, Robert W. Goldwater, Rev. Billy Graham, Otto Graham, Kermit Greer, Wilbur Griffin, Hon. Erwin N. Griswold, Max Grullon, Robert W. Haack, Robert C. Hackett, Esq., Phil B. Hammond, Esq., Hon. George L. Hart, Jr., Rt. Rev. Joseph L. Harte, Hon. Stan Hathaway, Hon. William D. Hathaway, Hon. John Haugh, Hon. John W. Haynes, Jr., Priscilla Hays, Horton H. Heath, Hon. A. Sydney Herlong, Jr., Peggy Herman, Richard L. Herman, Frank Higgins, Esq., Hon. James D. Hodgson, Edwin K. Hoffman, James V. Holcombe, Hon. Benjamin F. Holman, Pliny G. Holt, Rodger Howard, Hon. Roman Hruska, William Hundley, Esq., Hon. Evan L. Hultman, John W. Hushen, Patricia Hutchinson, Hon. John E. Ingersoll, Claude J. Jasper, Esq., Hon. Howard Jenkins, Hon. Wallace H. Johnson, Dolores Johnston, William N. Johnston, Dr. Karl C. Jonas, Frank P. Jones, Jr., Sheila Joy, Joe Juan.

Howard H. Karman, Esq., Hon. Shiro Kashiwa, Hon. Thomas E. Kauper, Hon. Donald Kendall, Robert L. Keuch, Hon. Walter Kiechel, Jr., Lewis Kinslow, Hon. Henry Kissinger, Hon. Dennison Kitchell, Betty Kitchell, Sam Kitchell, Dr. Jack Kleh, Axel Kleiboemer, Esq., Anne Lucile Kleindienst, Esq., Alfred D. Kleindienst, Jane Barrett Kleindienst, Jo Anne Kleindienst, Robert A. Kleindienst, Sharon Pandak Kleindienst, Esq., Wallace H. Kleindienst, Esq., Howard E. Kraft, Hon. Melvin R. Laird, Cy Laughter, Hon. Frank J. Lausche, Hon. Paul Laxalt, N. Warner Lee, Esq., Edward J. Le Fevre, L. G. Lefler, Hon. Jerris Leonard, Robert O. Lesher, Esq., Hank Leiber, Sol Lindenbaum, Esq., Joseph P. Lynch, William S. Lynch, Esq.

David Mac Donald, Esq., Hon. George E. MacKinnon, Forbes Mann, Charles T. Marck, Dorothy Mardian, Hon. Robert C. Mardian, Rodney W. Markley, Hon. William P. Mahoney, Jr., Kevin T. Maroney, Esq., Anne Marshall, Gordon Marshall, J. Pat Madrid, Edward A. McCabe, Esq., James R. McDonald, William H. McGee, Charles W. McWhorter, John M. McGowan, II, Esq., Dorothy McMullen, Joaquin Meyer, Rev. William Meyers, Hon. Robert H. Michel, Hon. Herbert J. Miller, Jr., John F. Mills, Richard Minne, Esq., Douglas G. Mode, Esq., Hon. Philip H. Modlin, Hon. Rose Mofford, Gordon Mohr, Esq., Hon. Luke Moore, Powell A. Moore, Richard A. Moore, Esq., Edward P. Morgan, Esq., Reg T. Morrison, Warren S. Mount, Mikel Narten, Janet Narten, William Naumann, Richard E. Norling, Esq., William O'Brien, Hon. Sandra Day O'Connor, Hon. A. William Olson, John Ourisman, Robert Ourisman, Mandell Ourisman, Hon. David Packard, Hon. Hubert B. Pair, J. Snead Parker, Everett M. Parkinson, Hon. David J. Perry, W. Theodore Pierson, Esq., Robert H. Pitt, Hon. Pete Pitches, Hon. Glen E. Pommerening, Thomas G. Pownall, Bertha Prouty, John L. Quebedeaux, Lucille Quebedeaux.

Hon. Thomas F. Railsback, A. Raymond Randolph, Esq., J. Donald Rauth, John U. Raymond, Hon. Gerard D. Reilly, Hon. William Rehnquist, James T. Rhind, Esq., Betty Rhodes, Hon. John J. Rhodes, Gene Rice, J. A. Riggins, Jr., Esq., Joseph H. Riley, Darryl Rogers, Edwin L. Roome, Jr., H. Chapman

Rose, Esq., Maurice Rosenberger, Harry Rosenzweig, Sandy Rosenzweig, Hon. Donald R. Ross, John L. Rotunno, Esq., Hon. William D. Ruckelshaus, Hon. Eldon Rudd, Hon. Donald Rumsfeld, Carl W. Ruppert, Hon. Kenneth Rush, Neille Mallon Russell, John F. Ryan, Sidney Sachs, Esq., William Safire, Hon. Donald E. Santarelli, Hon. William B. Saxbe, Hubert A. Schneider, Michael B. Scott, Esq., Jill Seibert, Hon. John H. Shaffer, Carolyn Kleindienst Sherman, Herbert Sherman, Helen Shimmel, J. Frank Shoaf, Hon. George P. Shultz, Susan Shultz, James Simpson, Esq., Hon. William B. Simon, Hon. George A. Smathers, Donald E. Smiley, William C. Smitherman, Esq., Hon. Dean C. Smith, Michael A. Smith, Hon. William French Smith, Harry D. Steward, Esq., Charles L. Strouss, Jr., Esq., Jacob Struble, Jess W. Sweetser.

Hon. Edward A. Tamm, Maurice Tanner, Henry C. Thomas, Esq., Hon. Richard L. Thornburgh, Hon. Strom Thurmond, Hon. James Tobin, Hon. Ozell M. Trask, Al Turner, Cynthia Turner, Hon. William C. Turner, Keith Turley, Hon. Thomas F. Turley, Jr., Hon. Harold R. Tyler, Jr., Hon. Morris Udall, Hon. Stewart Udall, Hon. Fred B. Ugast, Sanford Ungar, Hon. Richard W. Velde, Hon. Fred M. Vinson, Jr. (Dec), Billy D. Vessels, Philip Von Ammon, Esq., Hon. Charles E. Walker, John H. Walker, Robert Wallace, Hon. Johnnie M. Walters, Robert Ward, Horace Webb, Vincent T. Wasilewski, Esq., Hon. John W. Warner, Dr. F. V. Wedel, Robert Wells, Richard S. Wheeler, John L. Wheeler, Esq., Preston White, Dwight Milton Whitley, Gail Whitley, Mark Wilmer, Esq., Claud C. Wild, Jr., Hon. Jack Williams, Charles Bud Wilkinson, George S. Will, Ann Wyatt, Darryl L. Wyland, Esq., J. Hillman Zahn, Lawrence Zimmerman, Esq., Henry G. Zipf, Esq.

PART I

The *Oxford Universal Dictionary*, 3d ed.,
gives seven definitions of *politics*.

The first is:
"the science and art of government."

The seventh is:
"factional scheming among members of a group."

Introduction

After the demonstration had ended following Richard Nixon's nomination for the presidency on the night of July 27, 1960, in Chicago, Ray Bliss of Ohio, the Republican chairman, located me in the Arizona delegation on the floor of the convention. "You are supposed to be in Vice President Nixon's suite in the Blackstone Hotel at midnight."

"Why me?"

"Goldwater was invited. He doesn't want to go and requested that you attend as his representative."

"Okay by me."

Looking at my watch, I noticed I had only thirty minutes to get from the convention hall to the hotel and I pointed that out to Bliss.

"Don't get excited, Kleindienst; a car is waiting outside for you."

As I made a rather fast trip downtown to the hotel I couldn't help wondering to myself what this was all about. I soon found out. Upon arrival at the Blackstone I inquired at the Nixon desk in the lobby where I might find the vice president's suite. My arrival was obviously anticipated because when it was learned who I was, I was immediately escorted to the meeting by a Nixon aide.

Within a minute or two I was entering a large conference room in which twelve or fourteen men sat around a large rectangular table. All were neatly dressed in typical Republican blue suits. I felt uncomfortable. I was dressed in a sports jacket and slacks, and having just been a part of a demonstration on the floor of the convention, I looked the part. I recognized only four of the persons at the table. Thomas Dewey, the former governor of New York and twice the Republican nominee, was easy to identify, as was John Bricker, a former senator of Ohio, with his wavy white hair. William Stratton, the governor of Illinois, was not a nationally recognized political figure, but I recognized him as the person who welcomed the delegates to the convention in Chicago. I knew Fred Seaton, the former governor of Nebraska and then the secretary of the interior, but only casually. Part of my embarrassment went away when he recognized me and pointed to the chair next to him. I still recall feeling awkward as I walked past the assembled group and sat down. And well I might have. I, a thirty-six-year-old unknown lawyer and political functionary of a small state, was now seated among the leaders of the Republican party.

Seconds later Nixon walked in with a big smile. Everyone immediately stood up and began clapping. When this little demonstration ended, the nominee sat down and everyone else followed. After expressing his appreciation for everyone being there at such a late hour—a needless sentiment under the circumstances —Nixon then informed the group why he had asked them to be there.

"I want your advice and help in the selection of a vice presidential running mate. I personally have come down to three possibilities: Dr. Walter Judd, Thruston Morton, and Henry Cabot Lodge. Unfortunately, Dr. Judd has informed me that for reasons of health he would prefer not to be considered. So, I want you to help me decide between Thrus and Cabot." He then stated that he would like to go around the table and ask each person to speak for a minute or two, giving his reasons as to which of the two should be the next vice president of the United States. William Stratton, seated at Nixon's left at the head of the table, was asked to lead off. At that instant I asked myself, "How in the hell did I wind up here?"

In the short interval before it would be my turn to speak, I not only agonized over what I was going to say, but also saw flashing vividly before my eyes the three persons in my life who were responsible for my presence here—my grandfather, Joseph Ernest Kleindienst; my high school teacher of government, Verla Oare; and Barry Morris Goldwater.

We will return to that meeting in Chicago later. However, because my life was thereafter to be so deeply involved in the political career of Richard Nixon, let me show how those three persons were responsible for my presence at that Chicago meeting.

1

Verla Oare

Embryonic Politics

Winslow, Arizona, is situated on a brown dirt plateau in northern Arizona near the southern tip of the Navajo Indian Reservation. On a clear day the outlines of the sandstone monuments, which are peculiar to the Navajo country, can be seen in all their silent mystery. But when the wind blows, you cannot see your hand in front of your face. And when the wind blows in the winter, the only thing between you and the North Pole is a barbed-wire fence, it is said.

In 1909 my grandfather, Joseph Ernest Kleindienst, arrived from Washington, D.C. Winslow then had a population of about eighteen hundred and had become a division point of the Atchison, Topeka & Santa Fe Railroad. It was so selected because of the existence of a water supply six miles south of town. Without ample water, those magnificent steam locomotives of days gone by would be stopped in their tracks.

Granddad was a carpenter in Washington before migrating west. I think the last job he worked on before heading for Arizona was the tunnel between the Capitol and the old House of Representatives office building.[1] He was a short man—grandmother towered over him—but he was as strong as a bull. Many men in that frontier town would learn the hard way of the dynamite he packed in his fists and forearms.

He never picked a fight. However, his small stature and strong personality not infrequently tempted a bigger man to a physical encounter. In one fight grandfather lost an ear, which they say he carried in his hand to the doctor's office to be sewed back on. When in his seventies, with one blow he knocked a large young railroader through a drugstore's glass display case because he had been pushed away from the cash register. He was absolutely fearless.

At the same time, he was highly respected. A hard worker, he had accumulated by the 1929 crash a substantial estate, for those times. He was nearly broke when he arrived in Winslow, and not long after had to survive the failure of the local

---

1. My great-grandfather, John Henry, was born in Washington, D.C., in 1845; grandfather in 1866; and my father in 1893. Who says "chickens don't return home to roost"—at least for a while?

bank. This tough little man of German descent was also a strict disciplinarian with his four sons and his many grandchildren. None ever showed disrespect, or even thought it. He demanded respect, but gave unstinting care and loyalty in return. Grandmother, a saintly and devoted Christian, was married to him for sixty-three years. It was only after she died peacefully in her sleep of an unexpected heart attack on Christmas Day 1949 that his unrelenting spirit began to wane.

Granddad also brought to Arizona the deep conviction that the preservation of freedom in America depended solely upon the Republican party, and that its destruction would surely occur if a Democrat were ever elected president. Although his lack of a formal education and his trade as a carpenter prevented him from being a political activist in sophisticated Washington, D.C., neither was a detriment in a frontier town in territorial Arizona. As a building contractor in Winslow, he was an equal among the equals. By 1912—the year Arizona became the forty-eighth state of the Union—he was deeply involved in the bitter internecine Republican warfare between William Howard Taft and the Bull Moosers of Teddy Roosevelt. Although Woodrow Wilson became president that year, as a consequence of that campaign, grandpa was launched as an active and established Republican politician.

Because of his absolutely unshakable conviction in the righteousness of his party, because of his fearlessness, and because of his ability to articulate in the vernacular of the West, he gained recognition as an organization regular. At a state convention in Phoenix before 1920 the regulars needed time to work out a strategy. Granddad was selected to delay the proceedings by giving a speech. By the time he finished, the convention had turned into fisticuffs. The needed time was obtained and the regulars won the day.

Granddad's political efforts paid off. His political status made it possible for my father to be appointed postmaster of Winslow under Harding, Coolidge, and Hoover—a coveted and prestigious position in those days.

For some strange reason granddad and Carl Hayden were good friends. Hayden was elected to the Congress as a Democrat in 1912 and remained there for sixty years, the longest continuous service in the history of Congress. Their friendship and mutual respect were such that when I graduated from law school in 1950, Senator Hayden, whom I had never met, sent me a wire inviting me to join his staff in Washington. I respectfully declined. Thereafter, when I would see him in Arizona and Washington he always referred to granddad with affection and in the same way: "I liked Joe Kleindienst because you always knew what he was and where he stood." That was good enough for me, and until 1982, Senator Hayden was the only Democrat seeking federal office for whom I ever voted.

We lived next door to granddad. I guess I was the favorite grandchild. As a little boy, I would sit by the hour in the kitchen and listen to him talk about politics, as he "saucered and blowed" his coffee. I'm sure he had decided I was going to be a politician because of three incidents that happened before I entered high school.

The first was in 1930. George Wiley Paul Hunt was the first governor of Arizona. He was brilliant and successful. He was a "populist" Democrat. But he was also the reincarnation of the devil as far as granddad was concerned.

One evening granddad came over to our house and said to me, "Come on!" Everybody in the family responded at his command and I, without hesitation, said, "Yes, sir."

We got in his car and drove off. "Where are we going, granddad?" I asked. "Never mind, just do as I say."

In those days, a political rally near election time, with a statewide politician the speaker, was an event of significance for a little railroad town 250 miles from Phoenix. Before I knew it, we found ourselves in a vacant lot on Main Street, sitting in the front row of an audience waiting for the speaker to appear. To my amazement the principal speaker turned out to be Governor Hunt.

"Granddad," I exclaimed, "what are we doing here?"

"Be quiet and listen to the old son-of-a-bitch, because he is *not* what you are going to be."

I listened and solemnly resolved that night that I wasn't ever going to be like George Wiley Paul Hunt—whatever that was supposed to mean.

The next incident was in the 1936 presidential campaign. Needless to say, Franklin Delano Roosevelt was the ruination of America as far as granddad was concerned. Alf Landon's campaign train had to stop in Winslow to change operating crews, take on water, and be serviced. The hour was early morning and granddad came next door to take me to see him. After Landon had offered some bland remarks to a few Republicans from the platform of the candidate's car, granddad shoved me forward and insisted that Mr. Landon give me his autograph. I can still see Landon's kindly and understanding eyes and feel the pat on my head as he obliged with the words: "Good luck, young man."

The incident that I could never forget, however, occurred on the night of the 1936 election. By 1936 there was only a handful of Republican families in Winslow. The Great Depression had taken its toll. The railroaders were unionized and vociferous in their support for Roosevelt. At the same time, granddad's Republicanism on the one hand and his hatred for President Roosevelt on the other hand were well known in the town. I was listening with him to the late election returns on his radio when a boisterous group of people appeared in his front yard. We went out on the front porch to hear victorious Democrats shout: "Get out of Arizona, Joe Kleindienst. Get out of the United States. You're not an American!"

Granddad went back into the house, quickly returned with his .45 revolver in his hand, and shouted, "Any son-of-a-bitch out there thinks he is big enough to run me and my family out of this town, come on up and try!"

As the happy victors began to depart, I started to cry. "Don't cry, Dickie," granddad soothed; "remember, in politics there is always another day."

That night, without knowing it, I was prepared for Verla Oare, whom I would meet next September when I entered Winslow High School as a freshman. Most of us are indeed fortunate if one or two individuals—other than members of our family—take the time and interest to help us on life's way. For reasons unknown to me, my life has been so touched by several people. Verla Oare is one such person.

Verla was a teacher until her retirement in 1970. She was born in Herrick, Illinois, and arrived in Winslow with her family in 1921. She graduated from Winslow High School the next year. In 1926 she received her bachelor's degree from the University of Arizona and returned to Winslow as a teacher that year. In 1938 she received her master's degree in history from Stanford University.

At Winslow High, Verla, a Republican, taught the Constitution, government, and history. She was a stern disciplinarian and the only standard she knew was excellence. She also taught speech and debating. Debating was an elective for everybody except myself.

Verla was waiting for me, I guess, because she put me on the debating team in the first month of my freshman year. She also assumed the responsibility for my dress and deportment. This had become painfully necessary as a result of the death of my mother one month after I entered high school.

Every spring a debate tournament was held among the high schools of northern Arizona at the then Teacher's College at Flagstaff, sixty miles due west of Winslow. A debate topic was assigned each year. Preparation for the tournament began in September. Three of the topics during the four years I was involved were: (1) Resolved, the U.S. and Great Britain should have a permanent alliance. (2) Resolved, the railroads should be owned and operated by the federal government. (3) Resolved, the Constitution should be amended to provide for a unicameral legislative body.

Reading, research, preparation, and practice were, it seemed, all I did for five months. I nearly flunked Latin, algebra, and chemistry, but I knew a lot about railroads. Verla won the tournament four years straight.

The American Legion sponsors a National High School Oratorical Contest. Verla determined that I must enter it in my senior year. Then, the contestant would write the principal oration (she wrote mine), and be required to give an extemporaneous speech on a topic given to him, immediately after the first speech was delivered. The subject matter of the contest was the Constitution. To get to the state finals one had to win the Northern Arizona Tournament, which I did. To be sure that the extemporaneous speech wasn't really extemporaneous, Verla picked about twenty topics that had previously been used, wrote twenty more speeches, had me memorize them and then relentlessly beat me over the head for weeks and weeks to keep me practicing.

She came in second in the state finals. Some say she was cheated out of first place. When we drove to Phoenix the day before the tournament—in those days that drive of 250 miles took all day—a flooding rainstorm was in process. The out-of-Phoenix judges couldn't make the event. An all-Phoenix panel was substituted. You guessed it. The Phoenix kid won. Politics? Sour grapes? Not really. He went on to win the national championship.

Because Verla wanted to win the debate tournament the fourth year, she had to persuade the superintendent, Dr. Zimmerman, to rescind his decision to kick me out of school. I was elected student body president in my senior year. I defeated the captain of the football team, Jimmy Upchurch, by one vote. He was the establishment. Our organization was a coalition of the Spanish-speaking (30 percent of the class), Navajo Indians (15 percent), blacks (2 percent), Japanese (5 percent), and the Anglos jealous of Jimmy Upchurch (7 percent).

At the first meeting of the student body council, I proposed a radical change in the manner in which committees were determined and members selected. This was a campaign pledge. Dr. Zimmerman disapproved of the "factional scheme." When I politely informed him that I was running the show he promptly kicked me out of school. Verla got to me that night, wrung my neck, made me promise I wouldn't pull anything like that again, and got me safely back into school to begin working on the year's debate topic.

The second event was even more critical to Verla because it occurred a week before the debate tournament the following spring. Some of us used to sneak certain forms of grain spirits into the building at the time of school dances. A few of us got caught and Dr. Zimmerman called me into his office, closed the door, and informed me that because of us, there would be no senior hop that year.

I pleaded for my class. "Dr. Zimmerman, we are wrong and I know who they are. Let me talk to them, and get their solemn pledge that it won't happen again."

"All right, but it had better not happen again," he reluctantly responded.

The agreement was kept at the next dance by everyone—except the student body president. Out the door again. Verla got me back into school the day before the debate tournament. (Dr. Zimmerman was a dear friend. He also wanted to win the tournament.)

I graduated in May 1941, thirteenth in a class of fifty-five. I was glad to leave. I was still sore about the licking Willkie took from Roosevelt the previous November, and even more resentful of the fact that a couple of Jimmy Upchurch's establishment friends slapped me around after school the day I gave a speech for Willkie to the student body assembly. They were, in my humble opinion, bad losers and bad winners.

The year and a half spent at the University of Arizona and the two and a half years in the air force in World War II were dead years, as far as politics were concerned. But because of Verla (with an assist from Dr. Zimmerman) the heavens opened in January 1946, and I found myself in Harvard College.

Why Harvard? Let me digress a moment. My mother, Gladys, was born in Dracut, Massachusetts, on June 11, 1893. In 1921 she took a vacation trip to the West and, as fate would have it, met my father in Needles, California. Dad was then a brakeman on the Santa Fe, a not unusual occupation if you grew up in Winslow. Although he had not graduated from high school, he was a bright, articulate, handsome, and engaging young man. He swept mother off her feet, and without returning to Massachusetts, mother married him in Needles. They returned to Winslow to live.

In October 1937, my freshman year of high school, she died as a result of an infection following an operation. I was alone with her for a few hours shortly before and I'll always remember her saying: "Hitch your wagon to a star, Dickie, and if possible, someday try to go to Harvard."

All the frustrations of soldiering and war and all the suppressed desires to be involved in politics were relieved at Harvard. No one talked politics in the Fifteenth Air Force in Italy. When President Roosevelt died, the day was cold and overcast in northern Italy. I wondered how granddad was reacting. Truman succeeded. Wasn't he the nondescript haberdasher senator from Missouri whom Roosevelt put on the ticket in 1944? Didn't Roosevelt have some kind of a problem with Vice President Henry Wallace in 1944 and wash his hands of him? Didn't Roosevelt then, in effect, leave the selection of the vice president up to the convention, with, however, the admonition, "Clear the nominee with Sidney"? (Sidney Hillman was a top labor leader.) What a hell of a time to have something like this happen![2]

Harvard will never again be as it was when the veterans began to return in 1945 and 1946. The usual rules for admission didn't quite apply. There weren't enough "preppies" and "grotties" around; and because of the GI bill of rights, many could think of Harvard who before the war could not afford it. A passel of eager but intellectually starved veterans turned loose on old John Harvard makes for an interesting situation. They studied hard, played hard, drank hard, and argued hard. I argued about politics.

To me politics at Harvard in 1946 was really economics. My first class was in beginning economics. James Tobin[3] was the instructor. There were no assignments, but he asked everybody in the class to state his political or economic philosophy. One said he was a socialist, another said he was a Waldensian, a third said he was a Keynesian, and so on. By the time he came to me I was so frustrated that I blurted out, "By damn, I'm an American!" The kindly, understanding Tobin, with his characteristic half grin, gently responded, "We're all Americans. The purpose of this course is to try to determine what kind of America we are going to have."

That wasn't difficult for me to figure out, especially after taking a course in public finance from Harold Hastings Burbank, the chairman of the economics department. I became his disciple the first day of class—"If you are not a socialist when you are twenty-one, you have no heart; if you are still one when you are fifty, you have no brain."

Professor Burbank was also anti-Keynes, and was involved in a running debate

---

2. At Harvard I was a Truman antagonist. Many years later, as I stated to his daughter at a dinner in Washington, D.C., I had come to the conclusion that he was our fifth or sixth greatest president. His daughter was incensed that I did not put her father in first place.

3. He subsequently became a member of the Council of Economic Advisers to President Kennedy and the recipient of the Nobel Prize in economics in 1981.

with Alvin Hansen, one of Keynes's leading proponents. When I opened my examination chapter in public finance with the rather presumptuous sentence, "I come to bury Professor Hansen," it was calculated, of course, to prove my discipleship. It apparently worked. Professor Burbank selected me as his "undergraduate tutee" for the purpose of supervising the writing of my undergraduate thesis. What a stroke of luck to be able to meet once a week for an hour for an entire semester with Burbank!

Burbank gave me all the information and inspiration I needed for political debate and activity during 1946 and 1947. Naturally, I joined the debating team. A group of us formed the Harvard Conservative League, of which I became president in '47. (The group wasn't very large.) Our favorite sport was debating the John Reed Society. The debate usually devolved into a yelling contest. Neither side, at that time, ever yielded an inch.

By the fall of '47, the haberdasher president had become the object of all political discussion. We had to defeat him. Who could? Harold Stassen was my man. I remembered his stirring keynote speech at the 1940 Republican convention in which he so vividly described how "the lights of Europe are going out." We began to recruit other like-minded activists and formed the "Harvard Stassen for President Club." (Twenty years later—in 1968 at the Republican convention in Miami Beach, and when Stassen, the perennial presidential candidate, was seeking the nomination—I told him of our effort. What a sparkle came to his eye.)

That effort was blown out of the water in May 1948, when Tom Dewey eliminated Stassen in the Oregon primary. Even though Dewey had lost to Roosevelt in 1944, anything was better than Truman. We therefore insinuated ourselves into the Dewey camp, and by November we were pretty much in control.

The night of the 1948 election remains unforgettable. The prestigious political commentator H.V. Kaltenborn was intoning in the early evening hours that "when the upcountry vote comes, Dewey would be a shoo-in." We had taken over "Old Main" for a gigantic celebration. Optimism was everywhere. America would have a change! The only problem was, the upcountry vote never came in. Dewey, who had been proclaimed elected in September, conducted one of the most lackluster campaigns in history. The little haberdasher, however, gave 'em hell. He gave the do-nothing Republican Congress hell. He gave Strom Thurmond, who headed the States' Rights ticket, hell. He gave Henry Wallace, who headed the Progressive ticket, hell. But most of all, he gave Dewey hell. With his own party split in three parts, President Truman accomplished the biggest upset in American politics. He had a fighter's heart. Neither party since 1948 has felt secure enough to put on a 1948 Dewey campaign.

Because I had to get home and go to work for the summer, I missed my college graduation and also missed hearing Secretary of State Marshall enunciate the Marshall Plan for Europe—one reason I later altered my opinion of Truman.

The year 1948 was not, however, a complete disaster. About six weeks before

Easter, I met Margaret Elizabeth Dunbar through her cousin, Gardner Clark. "Gardie" was in the Business School. I was in the Law School and we were both proctors of freshman dorms. His cousin had graduated from Radcliffe during the war and had returned to Radcliffe for a graduate degree. Gardie asked me whether I would like to take his cousin out for a cup of coffee. I did. Six weeks later, on Easter Sunday, we became engaged and were married on September 3 in Cleveland.

With America perched on what I deemed the brink of disaster because of the Truman catastrophe, I was quite content to knuckle down and finish the Law School.

They were long hard days. When we were married, Marnie had a job with the editor of *The Letters of Theodore Roosevelt*, Elting Morrison. Shortly after our wedding, however, unmistakable signs indicated approaching parenthood. Her employment soon ended. The last year and a half of school found me clerking forty hours a week for a Boston firm then known as Ropes, Gray, Best, Coolidge, & Rugg. That employment and the rigors of my law studies left little time to think about the sorry state of the country.

The day after my last exam in the Law School, Marnie and the infant Kleinie went to Cleveland to stay with her parents, and I took off for Arizona to take the bar exam and look for a job. I passed the bar and became employed by Jennings, Strauss, Salmon & Trask in Phoenix.[4] There I was when Barry Goldwater came into my life.

---

4. Our daughter, Kiki, became an associate of that firm in 1983.

2
Goldwater

Arizona Politics and the 1964 Campaign

The name *Goldwater* I first heard in the winter of 1936, one of the severest winters of record in northern Arizona. For weeks the temperature hovered around sixteen to twenty degrees below zero. That winter my brother, Bob, and I delivered the *Albuquerque Journal* to Winslow homes at four in the morning.

The Navajos on the reservation were especially hurt by the cold. Their sheep, upon which they so much depended, were dying for want of feed. Goldwater and others in Phoenix had organized relief teams to fly hay and feed to the reservation in an emergency response. That's really something for a rich guy in Phoenix who has a plane to be doing for those poor Navajos, I thought at the time. I didn't know then that such wasn't unusual for that "rich guy" to do, nor did I begin to imagine the impact he would have upon his country.

Goldwater was elected to the United States Senate in 1952; it was one of the great political upsets of the time. The registration of voters was against him six to one, and his opponent was majority leader of the Senate. His election, however, was no accident. It was the byproduct of two forces: the politics of Arizona from 1912 to 1950 meeting face to face with an unusual person. When the antecedents of these forces are understood, the result is not surprising.

Arizona became the forty-eighth state of the Union on Valentine's Day, February 14, 1912. Only Texas and California then exceeded it in geography. In population, however, it was the smallest state of the Union. That only 20,289 voters cast their ballots for the office of governor in Arizona's first statewide election reveals how thinly populated this vast western expanse really was. If Arizona was the frontier when my grandfather arrived in Winslow in 1909, imagine what kind of a frontier it was when Barry Goldwater's grandfather, Mike, began to develop trade in Arizona in 1860. When he first came to Arizona there were only five thousand non-Indian inhabitants. Many a time Mike Goldwater drove wagons across the southern Arizona desert, from California to the tiny communities of the Arizona territory. Even today, with modern air-condi-

13

tioned automobiles, driving across this forbidding Sahara-like desert is an awesome experience to sightseers from the East.

Those wagon trips enabled Barry's father, Baron, to receive a good education in San Francisco. In 1882 Baron went to Prescott, the territorial capital. He was sixteen, and remained in Arizona the rest of his life. Baron and brother Morris later started in Prescott a trading business that eventually became known throughout the country as Goldwater's. By 1890 Morris Goldwater was recognized as one of the leaders of the Democratic party in the territory. On the eve of statehood he was elected vice president of the constitutional convention.

In the early years Prescott was a gold-mining center. By 1896, however, its heyday had passed and Baron Goldwater, the more sophisticated of the two brothers, moved to Phoenix and opened Goldwater's store. Deemed the most eligible bachelor around the town, he seemed content to remain so. Josephine Williams, however, changed that.

It is one thing to have a rugged pioneer grandfather, an able merchant and politician as an uncle and an educated personable father, but quite another to have a legend for a mother. "Mum," as she was affectionately known by family and intimate friends, arrived in Phoenix in 1903. She was young, alone, a trained nurse, and suffering from tuberculosis. The dry climate of the Southwest had attracted many others who were afflicted with this disease. Her first housing was a tent on the outskirts of Phoenix where other "lungers" were living.

This remarkable woman soon captured the attention, admiration, and affection of the ten thousand inhabitants of Phoenix, and shattered Baron Goldwater's dream of idyllic bachelorhood. The next thing he knew, the forty-one-year-old comfortable Jewish merchant was being married in an Episcopal church in Prescott to a twenty-nine-year-old woman of courage, compassion, and determination. Barry Morris Goldwater was born on January 1, 1909.

In 1909 the politics of Arizona were based upon two competing forces. The principal economic interests were the copper mines, cotton farmers, and cattlemen. Known as the 3 Cs, they combined their efforts and resources to establish and maintain a state government that would be supportive of their vested interests. Opposing the 3 Cs, however, was the populism of William Jennings Bryan.

Bryan had a natural appeal to the frontier inhabitants of a sparsely populated, vast, and forbidding area of little economic wealth or resources. The Populists had their doubts about capitalism, believed strongly in the public ownership of utilities and railroads, and were convinced that only by the increase of paper money and the free coinage of silver would the workingman be able fully to share the wealth of the nation. After Bryan failed in 1908, for the third time, to win the presidency on behalf of the Populist party, the Progressive party of Theodore Roosevelt became the natural haven for the party's supporters. It at least promised to regulate big business and to extend the democratic controls of government.

When in 1911 it was necessary to write a constitution in preparation for Arizona's statehood, these two forces met head on. The catalyst was George Wiley Paul Hunt.

A short portly man, with balding round head, large mustache, and steel-rimmed glasses, Hunt was instantly recognizable by nearly every Arizonan. His typical dress was a white linen suit. Tobacco juice adorned his mustache and suit. Although elected governor of his state more times (seven) than any other person in any other state, he wasn't a great speaker. Even in his later years in office he would confess to nervousness before speechmaking. His unprepossessing figure and costume counted for nothing, however, when he did begin to speak. He was very bright and well read, and conveyed to the workingman a sincere zeal and conviction. George Wiley Paul Hunt was for wage earners first, last, and always. They knew it, and gave him their support until the day he died.

Hunt was a delegate to the constitutional convention in 1911. Everyone assumed he would be a candidate for governor. The 3 Cs approached the drafting of the new constitution with that in mind. I daresay that no state constitution in the history of our nation was ever drafted to circumvent the potential power of one man.

The Arizona Constitution did just that. All statewide offices, including that of governor, were for a term of only two years. Incurring a budgetary deficit was prohibited. The essential functions of the government were discharged by several boards and commissions. The governor was given the power to appoint the members of the boards and commissions, but such appointments were subject to the "advice and consent" of the state senate. Once appointed, they were beyond the control of the governor. The real control of the power of the governor was hidden in the advice-and-consent function of the senate. This vast geographical area was divided into fourteen counties, each named after an Indian tribe. Thus, Phoenix is in Maricopa County, Tucson is in Pima, and I was born and raised in Navajo County. Each county, however, would have two senators. The ease by which the copper, cotton, or cattle interests could dominate the election of two senators from a sparsely populated county is not difficult to understand. The state house of representatives would be selected from each county on the basis of population. Not surprisingly, the senate dominated the legislature until the U.S. Supreme Court proclaimed its one-man, one-vote decision in 1962.

From the beginning Arizona was predominantly Democratic in registration and would remain so for sixty years. Because of the strident populism of Hunt, however, there were in reality two Democratic parties: the Hunt party and the anti-Hunt party. (In modern times, what with the emergence of organized labor as a political force, such division would be described in liberal and conservative terms.) That alignment of the Democratic party Barry Goldwater would later utilize.

The Republican party, on the other hand, had only about one third of the registered voters. In election after election, however, the Republicans were joined by the anti-Hunt Democrats in the general election. As a result, Hunt would be elected by the narrowest of margins. Thus, in the 1911 election, Hunt only won by less than two thousand votes. In the 1916 election the Republican, Thomas

Campbell, thought he had defeated Hunt by thirty-six votes only to have the victory taken away by the Arizona Supreme Court. In 1922 Campbell received 10,050 votes in the Republican primary, Hunt 38,634 in his primary; but Campbell received 30,599 votes in the general election and narrowly lost. In 1924, with a turnout of 77 percent of the registered voters in the general election, Hunt defeated Republican Dwight B. Heard by only 801 votes. In 1926, when there were 75,012 registered Democrats and only 30,408 Republicans, Hunt received 39,979 to 39,580 votes for his Republican opponent. In 1928, a national Republican landslide year, John Phillips, with better than a two-to-one registration against him, defeated Hunt by 3,264 votes; he lost to Hunt, then seventy-one, by 2,644 votes two years later.

By 1932 many Republicans had decided they had had enough of this old populist and registered as Democrats to get rid of him once and for all in the primary election. Hunt described his primary opponent, Dr. B. B. Moeur, as an "atheist who was in the KKK." This bitter reference delighted the Republicans who joined to give Hunt his first and only defeat by his party. As the *Arizona Republic* observed, "The dissolution of the Macedonian Phalanx" had occurred.

But the Republicans had not anticipated the Roosevelt landslide in 1932. Whatever the Republican party was in 1932, it was virtually wiped out. Those Republicans who had registered as Democrats to retire Hunt had no incentive to reregister as Republicans. As a consequence, through the 1930s and the '40s, the Democrats outregistered the Republicans by about six to one. With George Wiley Paul Hunt resting peacefully in his grave, the franchise of the Democratic party was securely held in the hands of the 3 Cs. For the next two decades, a rather static and essentially conservative political environment characterized Arizona. The election of Ernest W. McFarland[1] in 1940 to the U.S. Senate symbolized this environment. At the time of his election, he was a superior-court trial judge in the cotton-growing county of Pinal. But forget not those Republicans hidden in the rolls of registered Democrats. The day would come when they would join with the antipopulist or conservative Democrats and their fellow Republicans to make Barry Goldwater a household word in America.

As Arizona politics were evolving, Goldwater was growing up in Phoenix. Parents and environment greatly determine the kind of person we become. No better environment could be found to produce a future presidential nominee than the streets, alleys, and schools of Phoenix in the 1920s and '30s. In his childhood there was no social separation based on economic conditions. The Goldwater family owned a successful business, but Barry's closest friends came from the entire community. One of his best friends was John Henry Lewis, a black who became the world's light-heavyweight champion. "I had to go to school in Virginia before I learned anything about segregation," said Barry.

Barry camped all over the state, boxed, played football and basketball, attended the public schools, and served as an acolyte in the Episcopal church. Because

---

1. Ernest W. McFarland is one of the great sons of Arizona. If I'm not mistaken, he is the only American to have served as a U.S. senator, governor, and chief justice of his state's supreme court.

of his wide range of interests, one finds it hard to believe that he did not excel in formal studies. When radio was in its infancy he spent hours tinkering with a crystal set. In the midthirties he learned to fly without his mother's knowing of it, and went on to fly almost every kind of airplane, including jet fighters. Developing an early interest in photography, he became the foremost photographic artist of the Navajo Indian and his reservation. He floated the rapids of the Grand Canyon and walked its trails. "The sand and dirt of Arizona are in my bones," he was wont to say in his campaigns.

But it was Goldwater's warm manner that distinguished him from the beginning. Harry Rosenzweig, to this day his closest personal friend, recalls that none of his contemporaries could resist his friendly smile, piercing blue eyes, the strong cut of his square jaw, and his handsome head of wavy hair. When Barry entered the freshman class in high school, his popularity gained him the presidency of his class. At the University of Arizona he qualified as the substitute center of the varsity football team in his freshman year, and was elected president of the freshman class. In short, Barry Goldwater liked everything about life, and life liked him.[2]

One year before Pearl Harbor, Barry volunteered to use his reserve infantry commission as a second lieutenant at the newly established Luke Air Force Base near Phoenix. Within a year he had logged more than two hundred hours in the North American AT-6 training plane, doing so as "a completely unofficial student." In May 1942 Captain Goldwater was directed to open a new air force training school in Yuma, Arizona. Considered "an older pilot" at the age of thirty-three, Goldwater was assigned to the Far Eastern theater as chief pilot, ATC. This service found him constantly shuttling everything from ammunition to surgical supplies to all theaters of war. As a lieutenant colonel he returned to the United States at the end of the war.

The Phoenix Goldwater returned to after the war was not the small community he had left. The area had grown economically because of the many air force training fields, and thousands of young men who had been trained on these fields returned to Phoenix to live. One would become the first Republican from Arizona elected to the U.S. House of Representatives, and because of his great ability and character, John J. Rhodes would eventually become its minority leader.

The domination of the state government and legislature by the sparsely populated rural counties had come to be irrelevant to a growing metropolitan area of diverse economic interests. Before 1946 Phoenix had a ward type of city government, which was controlled by Democrats. This didn't augur well for a vibrant young postwar city seeking to flex its muscles. Goldwater and other progressive Phoenicians, Democrats and Republicans alike, took care of the problem by bringing about a charter form of city government. They might not have been able to amend the state constitution, but they could do something about their city government. Under their charter form of government, the political

2. The best account of Goldwater's early days that I have read is Stephen Shadegg's *Barry Goldwater: Freedom Is His Flight Plan* (New York: Fleet Publishing, 1962).

wards were abolished and the mayor and city councilmen must run on a citywide slate without party designation.

After the charter was adopted, Goldwater and his friend Harry Rosenzweig were assigned the task of putting together the first charter slate of candidates. After a diligent effort had been made to persuade good civic-minded citizens to run for the new city council, they found themselves two candidates short. They solved that problem by simply naming themselves. They won. If they hadn't, this and any other book about Barry Goldwater wouldn't exist.

That first charter government did much to upset many applecarts. One of the first things the new city council did was to terminate the racial segregation of the city airport facilities, public eating places, and the Air National Guard—something unheard of in the South and Southwest then.

By the end of 1948, Goldwater's name was associated in Phoenix with something more than a department store—change.

Change was what the thousands of young newcomers to Arizona were demanding. A sleepy one-party domination of state politics and government might have been satisfactory before, but it was not adequate for the challenges of the future. Goldwater, more than any other Arizonan, sensed this and therefore believed the time was ripe to do the impossible—elect a Republican governor in 1950. That had not happened since 1928. All he had to do was find a person who shared his convictions to such an extent that he would be willing to be the candidate even in the face of a six-to-one registration against him.

The popular Howard Pyle was one of Arizona's best known citizens. His resonant and articulate voice was a daily must to thousands of Arizonans on radio station KOY in Phoenix. He was also highly respected for his untiring and prodigious efforts in behalf of civic enterprises. While flying Pyle back to Phoenix from the Grand Canyon where Pyle had been the principal speaker at a woman's club convention, Barry persuaded him to make the run for the governorship. Characteristically, Pyle responded, "I will do anything to help the Republican party in Arizona." He did have one condition—Goldwater must become his campaign manager.

The timing could not have been better, as it turned out, for electing a Republican governor for the first time in twenty-two years. Not only was Pyle a strong candidate, but the desire for change was evident, as were the internal problems of the Democrats.

One of the Democrats, and a great public servant, was Anna Froehmiller. She had been elected state auditor repeatedly. Usually she was the leading vote-getter on the Democratic ticket. Dan Garvey was the Democratic governor, a result of the death of Governor Osborne; Garvey assumed that office because he was the secretary of state. But Garvey was ineffectual and lightly regarded. Anna's friends persuaded her the time was ripe for her to take advantage of her popularity and become the first woman governor of Arizona. The votes cast in the primary tell the story: Froehmiller—42,143; Garvey—32,495; Harless—31,118; Smith—19,912; Watkins—17,931; Sprouse—514. Pyle, the unopposed Republican, received 19,107 votes, 14 percent of the total Democratic vote. Traditional Democratic Arizona, however, wasn't quite ready for a woman governor. Pyle was qualified and therefore an acceptable alternative for the conservative Democrat. He was elected.

Marnie and I arrived in Phoenix in midsummer 1950. After taking the bar examination, I went to work for the firm of Jennings, Strauss, Salmon, & Trask. My wife and I promptly registered as Republicans and I joined the Maricopa County Young Republican organization. During the 1950 general election campaign we met Goldwater, Pyle, and John Rhodes. Rhodes was the Republican candidate for attorney general. Pyle's election thrilled us. Granddad was right, as usual: "There will always be another day."

National political change was also in the air. By the end of 1951 the national Democratic party was in serious trouble. Richard Nixon had nailed Alger Hiss; Joe McCarthy had people believing there was a communist under every desk at the State Department; and inflation, inevitable after a great war, had gripped the land. President Truman, now testy and defensive, signaled he would not seek reelection. Republicans sensed a new beginning in 1952. And Arizona Republicans, with their popular Republican governor in office, were ready and anxious to take advantage of what seemed to be a golden opportunity.

In this atmosphere Governor Pyle repaid Goldwater in kind by compelling him to run for the U.S. Senate against Ernest McFarland, the majority leader of that chamber. Barry agreed—reluctantly. With a six-to-one registration against him, his chances of defeating the majority leader of the U.S. Senate were minuscule.

When Pyle ran for governor in 1950, there was only a handful of Republicans on the ticket. If that situation prevailed in a national election year, the straight-ticket vote of the Democrats would make it almost certain that no Republican would be elected. Barry knew that, and, typically, did something about it.

First, he sought to fill the Republican ticket. John Rhodes was persuaded to run for Congress. All statewide offices were filled. Most county offices found themselves with Republican candidates for the first time in modern memory. The big problem was the state legislature. In 1951–52, even with a Republican governor, only two of ninety members of the house were Republican; in the senate, only one of twenty-eight. The legislative candidate is, however, the grass-roots, door-to-door candidate. Goldwater persuaded some forty persons—mostly Young Republicans—to run for the Arizona House of Representatives. I was one of them.

At the Arizona Republican convention in May 1952 to select delegates to the national convention, circumstances emerged that preview the national political figure Goldwater would become.

Taft and Eisenhower were seeking the presidential nomination that year. Taft was the overwhelming favorite among the delegates to the Arizona convention. Eisenhower was the favorite of the Young Republicans, primarily because we thought he could win. Barry was for Taft.

Before the balloting to select the fourteen Arizona delegates, Barry, in an effort to have a unified party for the general election campaign ahead, had persuaded the Taft managers to agree to give Eisenhower two delegates to the national convention and, in addition, to send two uncommitted delegates. Just before the balloting, however, the Taft leader indicated he would dishonor the agreement and send a full slate of delegates committed to Taft. When Barry heard of it, he immediately grabbed the mike on the floor of the convention and made a few direct and scathing statements. The original agreement was quickly reinstated. However, many Taft partisans tore up Barry's nominating petitions for the Senate and vowed they wouldn't vote for him for dogcatcher.

When Goldwater asked me to run for the state legislature to help fill the ticket, I asked the senior partners of my law firm if it would be all right. I assured them that I would do it on my own time. "Sure, go ahead," they said, knowing that my district was registered four to one against me, and that therefore I would have little chance of success.

From Easter Sunday to the night before the election, I went door to door every evening after work, and all day Saturday and after church on Sunday. My elderly incumbent opponent did nothing. The Eisenhower landslide descended on American politics. Goldwater's victory by some fifteen hundred votes was one of the nation's big upsets. Rhodes became the first Arizona Republican congressman by a similar margin. Statewide officeholders were elected. Thirty-five of us were elected to the Arizona House of Representatives. A new era had arrived in national and Arizona politics. At twenty-nine, I think I was the youngest member of the house. We Republicans joined with about twelve Democrats and formed a coalition by which we organized the house. I became vice chairman of Ways and Means and chairman of the Labor Committee. However, since my senior law partners decided—and I agreed—that little law work could be done on the floor of a legislative body, one two-year term was all the fun I was going to have.

Occasionally I visited Washington, D.C., on law business between '52 and '56, and always looked up Barry and Rhodes. One such afternoon I was in Barry's office. Somebody came in and informed him that Senator McCarthy had either said something or done something—what I cannot now recall. It meant something to Goldwater because he retorted angrily, "Get that SOB on the phone!" That day Barry tore up the sheets with McCarthy. Not long after, Joe McCarthy became one of those temporary aberrational events that come and go in politics.

Senator McCarthy became the symbol of McCarthyism. To me, that represents the basest side of politics and government. It appeals to our fears and prejudices, and when we respond to these forces we find ourselves committing against others trespasses that we ultimately come to regret. I remember when the senator was to be the speaker at a rally in Phoenix in 1952. A party worker called to ask me to buy a ticket and attend. When I said I wouldn't walk across the street to hear him even if I was paid to, he yelled, before slamming down the phone, "What are you, a f—— communist?" That *is* McCarthyism. And let us never deceive ourselves that there will be only one Joe McCarthy. He shows up every time we have times of stress and challenge. He was everywhere during the sad days of Vietnam. He reappeared in Watergate. When economic times become severe, he is on the street corner preaching fear, hatred, and despair. McCarthyism is also found in great universities. Harvard experienced it in the latter 1960s and early '70s, in the form of a brood of radical students, who, in the name of anti-Vietnam sentiments, prohibited the appearance of top government speakers.

The year 1954 saw political setback for the Republicans across the country. Ike's landslide in '52 gave him a Republican Congress; it was lost in two short years. We lost Governor Pyle, and all statewide offices and state legislators. Only John Rhodes survived, and that by an eyewink.

Defeats like that are traumatic to a political party. No one person is really responsible. Yet, if you are in a position of party leadership when it comes about, and if you don't have a loyal base of personal support, your head will roll. That's what happened to Col. James Wood, one of the finest men I ever knew. He was the Republican chairman in Arizona in 1954. From the night of the election until September '56, the time of the next state convention, the chief question among the Republican politicians was, Whom will we get to replace Jim Wood?

As a practical matter, Barry had to agree. A national election was coming up in '56 and two years later he would have to run for reelection, against McFarland again, who was then the governor of Arizona.

Counties caucus in Arizona before a state convention to pick their delegates to the state convention. They are noisy events. Politicians like to talk to each other. I was walking down the back aisle when two senior veterans of the party—Jim Beaman and Dick Fennimore—hollered at me, "Hey, kid, come over here."

They were good friends and I retorted, "What the hell do you want?"

To my amazement, they informed me that tomorrow I was going to be elected state chairman of the party.

"You've got to be kidding."

"Barry wants it, so shut up and do what you are told," they replied, saying no more.

Many years later Barry informed me that the night before, he had met with Fennimore, Beaman, and other senior leaders of the party and persuaded them that the future of Republicanism in Arizona depended to a great extent upon the involvement of its younger members.

The next day when I arrived at the Westward Ho Hotel for the convention, I couldn't find Goldwater. The reason became obvious later. In any event, my name was placed in nomination and I was elected the chairman of a party that had been decimated in 1954 and that didn't have a dime in the bank.

Shortly after I was elected and had given what I thought was a stirring extemporaneous speech (good old Verla) of acceptance and challenge, I found myself in a closed room in the back of the convention hall with Barry and the vice president of the United States, who was to be the principal speaker at the Arizona convention.

What was Nixon doing in Phoenix, in September of an election year, speaking to politicians already committed to Ike and himself? There are two very simple reasons. First, Goldwater asked him to be there. Barry, in three short years, had begun to make his mark on the Senate and, to some extent, on the country. Because of his forthright manner, his vote in the Senate couldn't be taken for granted by the White House.

The second reason bears on the nature of the office of vice president, generally, and on Richard Nixon, specifically. All vice presidents should be, by appearances at party functions, the link between the party and the president. Nixon worked harder at it and did a better job at it than any other vice president the Republican party has had (with perhaps the exception of George Bush), in my opinion. He was also one of the best extemporaneous speakers in the party. So far as I was concerned then—and I believe it to this day—Richard Nixon better articulated the middle-of-the-road approach to government, domestic or foreign, than anyone else I have ever heard.

In addition, in 1960 the party would nominate a new presidential candidate. Nixon probably was thinking of that in 1956. If so, then speaking to the party faithful would earn chips and brownie points, collectible at the national nominating convention. He got a chip and a handful of brownie points from me that day.

As Barry and I started to walk down the aisle with Nixon, the vice president turned to Barry and said, "Are things so bad in Arizona that you have to rob the cradle?"

"The Republican party in Arizona is the best damned cradle you'll ever see," retorted Barry, typically.

Nixon, with a temperature of 101 degrees, delivered his usual motivating call-to-arms for President Eisenhower. Afterward, as was his custom, he shook hands with the several hundred present.

That chore accomplished, he turned to me and asked whether I would like to accompany him to the airport. In those days vice presidents popped around the country on commercial airlines. Luckily for me (or unluckily, as the case might be) his flight was delayed and I had the opportunity to chat with him for an hour in the back seat of his car. Just before he got out of the car to board his plane, he turned to me and said, "Dick, I want you to be my man in Arizona." With stars in my eyes, I returned to the hotel to participate in the statutory obligation of the party to write its platform for filing with the secretary of state. Because of the kind of platform we wrote that year, the Democratic party leaders publicly threatened to disenfranchise the Republican state committee. It was a one-page document concisely setting forth a ten-item political "bill of rights" for the people of Arizona. Although it received much attention from the media, it didn't achieve the intended impact. Later platforms returned to the usual something-for-everyone content.

In November we were shellacked—except for John Rhodes—notwithstanding a full slate of outstanding statewide candidates. Eisenhower and Nixon easily carried the state, however.[3]

After the election, Barry got a group of us together: "Don't waste your time worrying about what went wrong in November. If you really believe in what we are trying to do in the state and the nation, then get off your hind ends and go to work for '58." When Goldwater thrusts out that square jaw, looks at you with those piercing eyes, and tells you to do something, your only response is assent.

The most important task was to find a candidate for governor. Governor McFarland had already indicated he was going to try to win back the Senate seat which Goldwater had snatched out of his hands in 1952. However, that decision set the stage for a bitter and divisive Democratic primary battle for the governorship.

In early spring 1958 Barry called me and said that "Fanny" is willing to run for governor. "He doesn't know a thing about party politics and he is probably the worst speaker I have ever heard," he said, "but he has friends all over the state, he's got the time and the money, and, most important, he wants to do it."

Paul Jones Fannin was thrice governor of Arizona and for twelve years a U.S. senator. He is one of those persons who, if you are fortunate to become involved with them, make the whole business of politics not only worthwhile, but rewarding.

As Fanny stumbled around in the early months of 1958, everyone asked me, "Where in heaven's name did you find him?" I have had few occasions to flatter myself as to my instinctive judgments in politics. I do flatter myself that I knew in my heart that Paul Fannin would be not only governor but the best governor Arizona ever had.

Barry, Paul, and John won in '58 in Arizona, a year when the party took its usual whipping around the country. New York's Nelson Rockefeller was the only other new Republican governor elected that year. In view of what was to occur in 1964 between Goldwater and Rockefeller, the '58 election has to be one of the most significant, if not fateful, events in the history of the Republican party.

Under the rules of the Republican party, the Republican National Committee is composed of a national committeeman and a committeewoman from each state. If a state votes for a Republican candidate for president in a presidential year, the state chairman of the party also becomes a member. Hence, in December 1956 I became a member of the national committee. I attended my first national committee meeting at the time of the second Eisenhower inaugural, January 1957.

3. Ike was never able to transfer his enormous popularity to the state candidates down the line. As I recall, we even lost Republican congressional seats in 1956.

Ray Bliss, the Ohio chairman and a superb and realistic politician, had put together an informal organization of state chairmen around the country who qualified to be on the national committee. National committee members usually find themselves on the committee for "past services" rendered, such as money raising, candidate support, and the like. The state chairmen, on the other hand, are on the active battlefront of political organization. They are also usually much younger. For some reason, Bliss took a special interest in me. I suppose he recognized that I needed help more than the others. We became fast friends—the friendship would assume some significance in 1968 after Nixon was nominated by his party for the second time.

One of the byproducts of being on the national committee is the opportunity to befriend politicians throughout the country. The actual committee meetings are usually dull, but in the evenings the politicians do what they do best—talk and drink. Before long, friendships begin to form. And these friendships enable a person involved in a presidential nomination to put together a national organization recruiting delegates for his candidate.

When vice president, Nixon was always available to meet with the national committee when it met in Washington, D.C. He would always take the time to chat with me personally. This flattery (or attention, if you will) naturally increased my admiration and allegiance. Over a period of years such attention paid by a vice president to eager young Republicans will produce delegates at a national nominating convention.

That Vice President Nixon's attention paid dividends is illustrated by the first face-to-face meeting I had with Nelson Rockefeller. In the early part of 1959 I attended the National Governors' Conference in Puerto Rico; I was there as the aide of the new governor of Arizona, Paul Fannin. George Hinman was the national committeeman from New York and was, in my opinion, the best political lieutenant Rockefeller ever had. He was warm and friendly and had that rare ability to relate to all segments of the Republican party. At a large reception Hinman introduced me to the new governor of New York. Rockefeller, with the TV lights all about him, immediately asked if I would like to chat with him in private the next morning. I accepted. Hinman correctly surmised how flattered I would be to receive such an invitation in that august public gathering.

I arrived at his suite at the appointed time the next day. The room was full of advisers. As soon as I walked in they departed. After the usual amenities, Rocky got down to business. "We are thinking of running for president in '60, and we would like to have you be part of our team. If you are willing, we can make arrangements to permit you to take the necessary time."

The meeting ended quickly when I said, "Thank you, Governor, but I'm a Nixon man." This was an impulsive reaction to an encounter that made me feel uneasy. Perhaps, because of my relationship with Nixon, my mind was predisposed. Perhaps I shouldn't have accepted the invitation in the first place. Nevertheless, I left with the feeling that I had been offered employment to work for his candidacy, an offer made without any discussion about him and his candidacy or about me and my attitudes and beliefs.

The presidential nomination of the Republican party always eluded Nelson Rockefeller. It did so, in my opinion, because of his great inherited wealth. Such a condition of life is not so disadvantageous in the Democratic party if the person becomes a sensitive liberal. It is, however, a handicap in the Republican party, the basic core of which is middle class. The middle class is a little leery about anybody who never had a mortgage on his house, who never had a debt, who never had to save for his retirement, or who never had to sacrifice to educate his children.

The nomination eluded Rockefeller for another reason. Rocky was always able to secure the best political talent for his campaign organizations. If, however, the best is paid for, it probably isn't the best for political effectiveness. National candidates are won by an army of enthusiastic and dedicated volunteers who believe in a candidate personally and for what he stands. This doesn't mean that Nelson Rockefeller did not have hundreds and hundreds of dedicated volunteers around the country supporting him. To intimate such would be an injustice to them. Most of his key people, however, seemed to be employed, either directly by Rockefeller or indirectly by entities that he and his family could influence. An employed political organizer can never be a match for the volunteer in a national campaign. The volunteer can secure the participation and efforts of other volunteers; the organizer on the payroll is subject to the suspicion that his zeal derives from his employment rather than his conviction.

Great wealth can also spoil people. If you are accustomed to getting or having everything you want, you can appear to be a poor sport when you lose. Nelson Rockefeller was a poor sport when he lost to Goldwater in 1964, at the Republican nominating convention in San Francisco. Ordinary people in politics have long memories and those memories of 1964 forced President Ford twelve years later to drop Vice President Rockefeller as his running mate in favor of Robert Dole of Kansas. In view of Dole's poor performance as a vice presidential candidate, Rockefeller on the ticket might have made the difference.

Finally, a disadvantage of great wealth in national politics is, strangely, the mere fact that a candidate requires less in voluntary contributions to cover the expenses of his campaign. When a citizen contributes to a candidate's campaign—whether the contribution is ten dollars or ten thousand—he is a worker in the vineyard. I don't know how many small contributions Rockefeller ever received but I suspect there weren't many, and I can't remember any one-thousand-dollar-a-plate dinners for Rockefeller in either 1964 or '68.

Notwithstanding this, and my efforts in 1964 and '68 to prevent his nomination, I personally liked and respected Nelson Rockefeller.

The 1960 Republican National Convention in Chicago was one for the books as far as I am concerned. Goldwater and Fannin let me be the chairman of the Arizona delegation, usually an honorary position. The chairman is the delegate who uses the mike on the convention floor on behalf of the delegation. By the time we got to Chicago in July, Nixon's nomination was a foregone conclusion. The convention opened on July 25, Nixon was to be nominated on the 27th, and adjournment would be the next day. There was some grumbling from the eastern establishment, and the emerging southern Republicans were dreaming of a bona fide conservative who, for once, would give the country a "choice and not an echo." Yet, on the morning of July 27, the inevitable was accepted, if grudgingly.

On that morning Nixon did something that seemed to be an act of betrayal to his western and southern supporters. He flew to New York City and met with Nelson Rockefeller. What had been accepted as a formality was transformed in a matter of hours into an organized protest, and a needless one at that. For an experienced politician, Nixon acted in a manner that was difficult to understand. It wasn't necessary and it created doubts and suspicions.

By way of response that afternoon, the South Carolina delegation determined to place in nomination the name of Senator Goldwater. This, however, was the last thing Barry wanted. To him, it was one thing to seek the nomination and to be supported; it was quite another thing to be used to satisfy parochial resentments. Every effort was made by Fannin, myself, and others to persuade the delegation not to do so. To no avail. What was supposed to have been a routine convention agenda that night was upset to make time available for the Goldwater nomination. Confronted with a fait accompli, Paul Fannin made the nomination speech, and Barry Goldwater was introduced to America on national television.

When a person is nominated to be president of the United States, it is customary for his supporters to demonstrate their support by marching around the convention floor and waving placards. Ordinarily, considerable planning is necessary for an effective demonstration. Ours for Barry was organized in a matter of hours, and was the shortest on record. All of us were in the back of the hall and started down the main aisle with our placards, anticipating a few runs around the convention floor. I was in the lead and followed the directions of the uniformed floor adjutants. In less than three minutes we found ourselves out the back door and in the parking lot.

We returned to our seats to witness Nixon's nomination and a real demonstration, replete with rockets, songs, hats, placards, and all the rest. Some thirty minutes later the roll call of the states began. By prearrangement with Barry, the chair was to recognize the chairman of the Arizona delegation for the purpose of moving that Nixon's nomination be unanimous. I intoned, "Mr. Chairman, I move that the nomination of the next president of the U.S. be made unanimous by this great convention." It was almost unanimous. Nixon received 1,321 votes, but Goldwater received the vote of ten of the twenty-six Louisiana delegates.

The foregoing explains how I found myself, at midnight, July 27, 1960, at the end of a table in a room with Richard Nixon, Thomas E. Dewey, John Bricker, Fred Seaton, William Stratton, and several others.

Nixon, you will recall, wanted each person to express, in a minute or two, his opinion as to whether Senator Thruston Morton from Kentucky (and chairman of the Republican National Committee) or Ambassador Henry Cabot Lodge of

Massachusetts, should be his choice for vice president. Walter Judd had asked to be excluded from consideration for health reasons.

Governor Stratton of Illinois led off with a strong endorsement of Thruston Morton. His reasons were typical of those in the room who would also recommend Morton: he was an experienced campaigner, a distinguished senator, and as party chairman would be a unifying force for the party. In addition, with Morton as a running mate, Nixon could take the high road and leave the "knee gouging" to Morton. The next two participants echoed these sentiments. Governor Dewey was next up; however, Nixon interrupted by saying he would like to pass over "Governor Dewey" for the moment. Two more came down for Morton. It was then my turn. Except for Secretary of the Interior Seaton sitting next to me, no one else except Nixon had the slightest idea who I was. The nominee smilingly informed those present of our friendship and of my presence there as Goldwater's surrogate. Smiles all around. I was even more emphatic for Morton. So were Seaton and the next two. It was now Senator Bricker's turn. Again, Nixon said he would pass over Bricker for the moment. The remaining three endorsed the Kentuckian.

"Now, Governor Dewey, what is your opinion?" Nixon asked.

There followed one of the most eloquent and best prepared discourses I've ever heard. If Dewey had given a speech like that in 1948, he would have been elected president. To him Cabot Lodge had to be the man. He was a household word to every housewife in America who watched his outstanding performance on TV as ambassador to the United Nations as he revealed the chicanery and espionage of the Russians. He had been a great senator. He was a great American. He was a man of proven merit who, if fate decreed, would be a great president.

"Senator Bricker, what do you think?" Nixon queried.

The Ohio senator allowed that while he and Dewey had often been on the opposite sides of the fence in party matters, in this instance he had to agree "100 percent" with Governor Dewey. His remarks also had the distinct characteristics of advance preparation, unlike the impromptu comments of the rest of us.

When Bricker finished, Nixon announced, "That does it. It's got to be Cabot!"

It really isn't worth much time speculating as to why presidential candidates decide on one person as opposed to another to be their running mate. "If you win, everything you did was right; if you lose, everything you did was wrong," runs the political axiom. Ambassador Lodge, however, turned out to be a temperamental aristocrat in the ensuing campaign. His reputed daily 3:00 P.M. nap seasoned many a conversation. How much Morton or Judd could have done to convert the eye-squeakers of Illinois and Texas to Nixon—the states by which he lost—is anyone's guess.

My own opinion is that Nixon went to New York on the morning of July 27 to secure Rockefeller's (and Dewey's) support and the *quid pro quo* was Lodge. If I'm correct, then what happened in that room at midnight is clear. If Nixon was to deliver his side of the bargain, he, of course, could not permit the choice of his running mate to be left up to the convention delegates. If that alternative was pursued, Walter Judd would have received the vice presidential nomination by acclamation. Judd's stirring keynote address on July 25 had set the delegates on fire. At the same time, it was a common practice for a presidential nominee to consult with party leaders and then announce his preference to the delegates. President Eisenhower twice employed this means before selecting Nixon to be his running mate. By announcing that Judd had taken himself out of the running for reasons of health, Nixon was able to pay proper tribute to him and at the same time eliminate him from consideration. By selecting Senator Morton as the alternative to Lodge, the prearranged endorsements of Governor Dewey and Senator Bricker would make it relatively easy to come down in favor of Lodge. I learned years later, however, that this was not the complete story.

Walter Judd is a great American. He was born in a small town in Nebraska, worked his way through medical school, and in 1925, under the Foreign Mission Board of Commissions of the Congregational church, went as a medical missionary to South China, where he survived bandits and communists. Malaria forced him home. He returned to China in 1934 and soon found himself under the control of Japan's invading armies. Upon his return to the U.S. in 1938, he stumped the country warning against our building up of Japan's military machine. After Pearl Harbor he was elected to Congress and served for twenty years, sixteen of those being on the House Committee on Foreign Affairs. Twenty-eight universities and colleges have conferred on him honorary doctorates. President Reagan presented to him in October 1981 the Presidential Medal of Freedom, America's highest civilian award. He has no peer as a public speaker. Some sixty million Americans heard him give the keynote address at the 1960 convention. I still shiver as I so vividly recall those stirring words that night: "We must develop a strategy for victory. . . . To save freedom! Freedom everywhere!"

On January 12, 1964, a Sunday, it was my privilege to introduce Dr. Judd to the congregation of Temple Beth Israel in Phoenix. Before the program began, I expressed to Judd my sincere regrets that he had, for health reasons, asked Nixon not to consider him as running mate.

"I asked him not to do what, for what reason?" he responded with surprise and incredulity.

The program was just about to begin at the temple and all Judd could say to me was that he had not requested his name be withdrawn but that he was ready and able to accept the challenge. Circumstances didn't permit me to pursue the matter further that evening. Because of Judd's surprised reaction to my comments, however, I always believed there was more to the story than met the eye. My belief was confirmed in August 1982, as a result of a conversation I had with Dr. Judd. According to him, here is what occurred on the evening of July 27, 1960, at the Republican nominating convention.

Between ten-thirty and eleven o'clock, while the roll call of states was in progress for the presidential nomination, Judd was invited to meet with Nixon in Nixon's hotel suite. Nixon informed him that the selection of his running mate was down to two persons, Lodge and himself. Judd was surprised. Just a few minutes before, on the convention floor, John Lodge, Cabot's brother, had confided to Judd that Cabot had been chosen and that he was preparing his acceptance speech. When Judd responded that he believed Nixon had already made up his mind in favor of Lodge, Nixon intimated that his mind was still open and asked Judd to set forth his reasons as to which of the two it should be. In substance, Judd advised that the ultimate decision should be based upon which person would better enhance Nixon's election. Judd sincerely believed that he himself would be the best choice for that reason. Nevertheless, Judd left that meeting with Nixon with the belief that the decision in favor of Lodge had been made. As indeed it had been.

National political conventions, in addition to nominating future presidents, serve to introduce those who will become contestants for the nomination at future conventions. President Kennedy is a good example. Adlai Stevenson left the choice of his 1956 running mate to the convention floor. Kennedy and Estes Kefauver of Tennessee wound up in a photo finish. Indeed, many feel that Kennedy actually won, but the tote board officially gave it to Kefauver. Kennedy's 1960 campaign for president began that night. The Goldwater 1964 campaign began the night of July 27, 1960, at the Republican convention in Chicago.

The South Carolina delegation knew what it was doing when it insisted upon placing Barry's name before the '60 convention. If he wasn't yet a household word in America, he was with the Republican party workers throughout the country. And deservedly so. Two years after his election to the Senate in 1952, his Republican colleagues selected him to be chairman of the Republican Senatorial Campaign Committee. He served in this capacity for four years, resigning in 1958 to undertake his own reelection campaign against Ernest McFarland.

In those four years Goldwater exerted more time and effort as chairman than anyone had before, or has since. He appeared on behalf of every Republican senatorial candidate who ran in '54, '56, and part of '58. Every candidate—liberal, moderate, conservative—requested his help and support. He traveled over twenty-five thousand miles, often on "redeye" specials to return to his senatorial duties in Washington, D.C. He gave 911 speeches in 36 states, and appeared at 125 fundraising events that produced over $6 million for Republican senatorial candidates. His book *The Conscience of a Conservative* had sold 10,000 copies by March 1960, 10,000 more by April, and an additional 50,000 by May.

Barry Goldwater, then, was the only other viable nominee of the Republican party on the night of July 27, 1960, in Chicago. The magnanimity with which he acknowledged his nomination and withdrew his name raised him to national prominence and endeared him to the hearts of the delegates of the convention, most of whom would be present in San Francisco four years later.

Marnie and I were returning from the 1964 New Year's Day Rose Bowl game in Pasadena where we had been guests of Bob and Dorothy Mardian—Bob being like a brother to me. When we got to the Arizona Border Inspection Station on the Colorado River a highway patrolman came up to our car.

"Are you Dick Kleindienst?"

"Yes, sir."

"You are to proceed directly to Senator Goldwater's home in Phoenix."

"Why, is there anything wrong?"

"Don't ask me—that's all I know."

In less time that it lawfully should have taken, we arrived at the senator's house to find bedlam. TV crews, vans, reporters, and electrical conduits were all over the place. We were casually dressed and felt a bit conspicuous.

Within moments I found myself in a back bedroom of the Goldwater home in the presence of Barry, Denison Kitchel, and Dean Burch.

"What is going on, you guys?" I blurted.

They all laughed at me and Barry announced, "In an hour or so, I'm announcing my candidacy for the Republican nomination."

"Great, but what does that have to do with me?"

To my amazement, Goldwater did not ask me, but informed me that I was to be the national director of field operations for the campaign, that Kitchel would be the campaign chairman, that Burch was to be deputy campaign manager, and that Ann Eve Johnson,[4] the Arizona Republican national committeewoman, would head the women's division of the campaign.

"No kidding," I said. "What am I supposed to do as—what did you call it—director of field operations?"

Barry then informed me that my job was to get 668 delegates for him on the first ballot.

"You've got to be crazy, Barry!"

"You're right, Kleindienst. If I wasn't crazy I wouldn't be doing it!"

"Barry, there is no one in the world who wants you to be president more than I, but you shouldn't structure a campaign organization with only Arizonans at the top. You need loyal qualified persons from around the country," I instinctively replied.

"Listen, and get this straight," Barry retorted with animation. "I'm not going to turn my life over to people I don't know and trust if I'm going to go through with this. Either the four of you agree to go through this with me or I'm not going to do it!"

By 1964 the struggles for the soul of the Republican party had been going on for twenty-two years. To many Republicans—especially those who lived in the Midwest and the West and who made up the great middle class—big government, big business, and big labor had combined to diminish their individuality. Except for the nomination of Alf Landon of Kansas in 1936, every four years the eastern

---

4. The victim of a tragic illness, she had no peer in lifetime dedication to her country and party.

establishment of business and finance dominated the nominating conventions of the Republican party. To these Republicans, Wendell Willkie in 1940, Thomas Dewey in 1944 and 1948, and even Dwight Eisenhower in 1952 and 1956 offered no clear-cut alternative to the "tax and tax, spend and spend" philosophy of the Democratic party. When Richard Nixon, a westerner, made his pilgrimage to New York City in 1960 and subsequently lost, many leaders of this wing of the party resolved that 1964 would be different. The country finally would be given a "choice and not an echo."

Because of his dynamic energy, his winning personality, and his forthright articulation of what came to be known as conservatism, Barry Goldwater was regarded by many as the only national political figure available who would bring about this long sought objective. For three years following the 1960 Republican convention, wherever he went he was besieged with demands that he seek the presidency. Although this was flattering to the junior senator of a small western state, I have always believed that the basic humility of Barry Goldwater prevented him from actually seeking his party's nomination. I've always sensed that when Barry thought of the American presidency he thought of Washington, Jefferson, Jackson, and Lincoln, and not Grant or Harding. Consequently, he vacillated.

By late fall 1963, however, two Republican members of the United States Senate—Norris Cotton of New Hampshire and Carl Curtis of Nebraska—and a former senator, William Knowland of California, all of whom Goldwater admired and respected, finally had persuaded him that, whether he desired to do so or not, he had a higher duty to his country and party. The session opened with Knowland and Curtis stating, "Barry, the time has come to either fish or cut bait." Cotton, tears in his eyes, ended it by appealing to Barry's patriotism—the one appeal Barry Goldwater could not resist.

Denison Kitchel in 1963 was a senior partner in one of Arizona's leading law firms. He had a national reputation as a lawyer and scholar. Although he had not been involved in the organizational politics of the Arizona Republican party until 1958, when he became its general counsel, he was an intimate friend and adviser of Goldwater. In summer 1963 Goldwater asked Kitchel to manage his forthcoming campaign for reelection to the Senate. Kitchel took a leave of absence from his law firm and moved to Washington, D.C., to work with Barry in preparation for the campaign.

Kitchel was present when Knowland, Curtis, and Cotton met with Goldwater. Denison was an ideal person for Barry to discuss the matter with after they had departed. An adviser to a politician must have one quality—absolute honesty. Kitchel had that, and many other qualities. Without personal ambition and with a maturity and toughness of mind, he was able to help Goldwater make the difficult decision that had been avoided for many months.

Asked what he thought, Kitchel, without emotion, simply said two things: "Barry, you have to make a decision for their sake. In addition, because of what you have come to mean to them and so many others, you have to do it."

A long silence followed. Finally Goldwater said, "I can't make it, but, all right, I'll run. Contact Bill Knowland, Carl Curtis, and Norris Cotton."

At that instant one of the most unusual presidential campaigns in the nation's history was set in motion. Goldwater, Kitchel, and many others would find themselves calling upon every ounce of strength and conviction they possessed in the months ahead.

Ten days after this fateful meeting, Dean Burch took a leave of absence from his Tucson law firm and joined Kitchel in Washington as his deputy. This was not mere happenstance. Burch had previously served Goldwater as an aide in his Washington Senate office. As a result, Barry was able to observe those same qualities in Burch that everybody who has ever known him has also observed. He has a wisdom that belies his age, is levelheaded in crises, and has a knack of communicating with everybody. That he ultimately became chairman of the Republican National Committee, chairman of the Federal Communications Commission, and counselor and adviser to Presidents Nixon and Ford tells us why Goldwater summoned him for the presidential campaign.

I left the January 1964 meeting with Goldwater, Kitchel, and Burch and went home to discuss this unexpected challenge. I then met with some of my law partners. With generous understanding, they all not only urged me to undertake the assignment, but also insisted that I had the duty to do it. I thus agreed to take on the responsibility, but did so feeling gravely uncertain and profoundly inadequate.

I had little time, however, to worry about such doubts. Kitchel and Burch had informed me at the senator's home that the Republican National Committee was meeting in Washington, D.C., and that I should leave for Washington immediately. They informed me that the one "sticky" problem I would have when I got there would be Clif White. "He hasn't been consulted about the announcement and your role. However, he will have learned of it from the media today."

Sticky indeed.

Clif White was a nationally known and respected professional pol in the Republican party, had been a leader in the National Young Republicans, and, most significantly, had put together a national Draft Goldwater for President Committee. The role I was to play is the role that was made to order for White.

He and I met each other for the first time the next day in my room at the Mayflower Hotel. I've never in my life had a more sympathetic feeling for another person in politics than I had for Clif that morning. After all he had done to launch Barry for president, not to mention his acknowledged experience and national reputation, he was literally crushed and on the verge of deserved tears.

"Clif, I can sympathize with how you feel. I didn't ask for this job. However, as long as Barry wants me to do it, I'm going to do my best. I desperately need and want your help and friendship. I'll understand if you don't want to give either. You will have to accept the fact, however, that as long as Barry says so, I'm in charge and you will have to accept me as such."

"If I stay on, what will my role be?" he asked.

"Why not as the codirector of field operations, Clif?"

"Okay, I'll do it."

That was a mistake on my part. It was just too much to expect from a man of White's caliber to accept the fact that he would be "directed" by a person of far less ability and experience. "Who in the hell ever heard of Dick Kleindienst from Arizona?" was a question to be raised time and time again by loyal supporters of Goldwater in the months ahead. Occasionally, I learned, Clif would cause the question to be raised himself. Not infrequently I would breakfast with a senator or a congressman and be implored to resign my post so that Clif or someone of his experience and national reputation could take over the delegate operation. My reply was always the same, "I don't disagree with you one bit, and you can tell Barry I said so. When he asks me to leave, I will. Until then I'm going to stay."

I stayed until Barry gave his acceptance speech on the night of July 16, 1964, at the Cow Palace in San Francisco. In the intervening months I estimate that I traveled several hundred thousand miles. Although I talked to Marnie and the children without fail every day on the phone, I didn't step into our house in Phoenix until June, following the California primary. Learning from scratch the business of nailing down delegates was at once the most fatiguing and exhilarating experience I've ever had.

In 1964 most delegates were chosen at state conventions, rather than in primaries. Today the reverse is true, and it is a nightmare for the candidate. The New Hampshire, Oregon, and California primaries were really all that mattered then. The balance of delegates would be found at the state convention.

The prime objective was to secure a Goldwater chairman in each state as soon as possible. A state's priority was dictated by the date of its primary or state convention. New Hampshire was the first primary so it got first attention as a primary state. Oklahoma had the first convention, and thus topped the list, whereas the state of Washington was on the bottom of the list, having its convention in late June.

No other candidate ever had such full, effective commitment from a volunteer political organization in a presidential campaign as did Barry Goldwater. Our efforts and organization were so effective that by the conclusion of the California primary in June, the nomination of Goldwater was in the bag. Had there been a floor fight, we were primed and ready.

That such a fight was in the offing derived from the personal bitterness and animosity that Rockefeller publicly manifested for Barry from the day the latter announced. The hostility contributed to the Johnson landslide. In the New Hampshire and California primaries it was most apparent. So intense was it at the convention in San Francisco that its effects were evident twelve years later, in 1976, when President Ford was forced to replace Rockefeller as the vice presidential candidate.

The explanation for the animosity is not easy. In 1959 Barry and Rocky had been in close communication with each other. Peggy and Barry had visited the

Rockefellers' home on Foxhall Road in Washington. When Rockefeller married Happy, Peggy was one of the first to call her with best wishes. Rockefeller's feelings toward Goldwater probably stemmed, however, from his attitude toward a number of persons who were highly vocal in their support of Barry. Many who found themselves involved in the '64 nomination in behalf of Goldwater had deep feelings about divorce in general and about Rockefeller's divorce in particular. In many ways they were a detriment to Barry and the party. With a fundamentalist approach to religion, and a similar attitude about what they perceived to be a deterioration of the basic "American" values in government, they made Rockefeller their target. Rockefeller's having divorced a wife of over three decades for a younger married woman, his wealth, which appeared to make it possible, and his being the embodiment of the eastern establishment were just too much. The anti-Rockefeller folk made their feelings known in no uncertain way. Rockefeller, understandably resentful, blamed Goldwater for their conduct. Thus followed one of the most bitter quests for the party's nomination.

We in the delegate operation likewise found those anti-Rockefeller activists to be a detriment to Goldwater's effort. In several states, these "true conservatives" came out of the woodwork and became involved in politics for the first time in their lives under the banner of Goldwater. No matter that their brand of conservatism was really not his. In state after state, particularly in the West, by virtue of diligent grass-roots organization, they arrived at their conventions to select delegates with a majority of the votes. If you weren't one of them, you weren't going to be a delegate to the national convention, even if you were a U.S. senator, a congressman, or a governor who openly supported Goldwater. We had the distressing task of confronting them in Oklahoma, Wyoming, and Colorado. Time and again it was necessary to invoke the name of Goldwater personally, to ensure that those elected officials who were his friends and early supporters could go to San Francisco as delegates. The presence of a large number of these well-intentioned but strident delegates at the convention contributed to the debacle that was to occur.

The Rockefeller bitterness, however, was manifestly most intense in the New Hampshire and California primaries.

By the latter part of 1963 Goldwater was far ahead in the polls as the Republican nominee in many midwestern, western, and southern states. This was also true in New Hampshire. Senator Cotton was the Goldwater chairman in New Hampshire. Early in the campaign an event occurred which ultimately determined the outcome of the primary. Goldwater had allowed at a press conference, that while he was 100 percent for social security, some thought should be given to making the program voluntary for those who so chose. That afternoon, the headline in the *Concord Monitor* shrieked: "Goldwater Opposes Social Security." A retraction was demanded by Goldwater and immediately given. (I understand the employee responsible was dismissed.) The matter was buried and forgotten—so we thought.

On the Saturday before primary day, Tuesday, the polls showed Barry and

Rockefeller neck and neck. Goldwater's last appearance was at a big rally in Manchester. He, Kitchel, and Burch departed for Washington that night. Senator Cotton, Marnie, and I remained in Concord. Commencing early the next morning, Sunday, one of the most dirty radio and TV campaign blitzes ensued that I have ever witnessed. Hour by hour, all day Sunday and Monday, the statement "Goldwater Is Against Social Security; Vote for Rockefeller" was seen on TV. The retracted headline of the *Concord Monitor* was shown repeatedly.

Astounded, I called Barry, Kitchel, and Burch and warned that something unexpected was emerging. It did. Notwithstanding a terrible winter storm on Tuesday, voting day, there was a record turnout. Cabot Lodge, then in Vietnam as our ambassador, won by write-in votes; Nixon came in second, in the same way; Rockefeller was third; and Barry fourth. Why such a crazy result? At that time New Hampshire had the highest proportion of retired persons on social security of any state in the nation. The stage was now fully set for a bitter campaign that nearly destroyed the Republican party.

During the next two months, I think Goldwater cared little whether he won the nomination. Kitchel, Burch, and I would comment nearly every evening that we had everything going for us—money, delegate support, organization—except a candidate. The decision was even made to sidestep the Oregon primary, one of the three musts in those days.

The California primary was June 6. Around May 1 Barry decided to make a fight out of it with Rockefeller. The prize was worth it—some eighty-six delegates.

Bill Knowland, former minority leader of the Senate, was Barry's California campaign manager. He assured Goldwater that he would have no problem defeating Rockefeller in June. Barry, however, had heard that old song before. "Kleindienst, get your tail out to California and find out what's going on," Goldwater ordered. The next day I departed for northern California, and spent the next four days in a car visiting what was supposed to be the Goldwater organization in every county and major city of the state. Just as Barry suspected, the organization was paper-thin. When I reported my findings to Barry, he immediately called an emergency meeting at the International Hotel at the Los Angeles airport with Knowland, Kitchel, Burch, and myself. I there gave my report.

"What is some arrogant, upstart kid from Arizona doing trying to tell me about California?" retorted Knowland.

Goldwater intervened: "Sorry, Bill; we're taking over the campaign from here on out."

"Okay, have it your own way. Good luck," replied Knowland.

The next day the entire Goldwater team in Washington invaded Los Angeles. We took over what was up to then a nice residential hotel—the Los Altos, next to Perino's restaurant—and turned it into a madhouse.

Three events within a week of voting day determined the outcome. The first was the cancellation by the archbishop of Los Angeles of a speech scheduled by Rockefeller at Villanova University. Reason: the Rockefeller divorce. The next was a press conference called by leaders of several of the largest Protestant denominations in California. Purpose: to condemn divorce in general and Rockefeller's in particular. The third event was one of those things that only fate determines. Happy Rockefeller was pregnant, and with much publicity had to return to New York the weekend before primary day, Tuesday, to have her baby. Barry won by a slim majority.

The California primary determined the outcome of the nomination. Before June 6, Goldwater and Rockefeller each had about the same number of committed delegates—450. Many state delegates were sitting on the sidelines awaiting the outcome in California. Could Goldwater win the popular vote in a large state? Within ten days following June 6, Illinois and Ohio caucused and publicly announced for Goldwater. Those delegates plus the eighty-six from California cinched it for Barry. Rockefeller's people knew this. If they had gone home to New York and taken their whipping in good style, Rockefeller might have been the Republican nominee in 1968 instead of Nixon.

But Rockefeller and followers showed up in San Francisco to do two things: discredit Goldwater and make a last-ditch attempt to find someone who could seize the nomination from Goldwater. They perfectly fulfilled their first purpose; they failed miserably in their second.

Governor Scranton of Pennsylvania was the hoped-for alternative. President Eisenhower's name was even bandied about—without his permission—to suggest that only Scranton could save the party and the country from Goldwater. Milton Eisenhower, the president's brother, made the nominating speech for Scranton. It was a masterpiece of innuendo. Scranton shouldn't have lent himself to such an effort. Had he not, he might have been the nominee for president of the Republican party at a future time. A man of great ability, he could perhaps have been a great president.

The frantic effort to stop Goldwater and the attendant divisive atmosphere created a real problem for the party when it came to the selection of a vice presidential nominee. The selection of a running mate is difficult even when there is an atmosphere of harmony and unity. We have seen the steps Nixon felt it necessary to take four years before when he selected Henry Cabot Lodge to be his running mate.

Goldwater, however, was confronted with a bitterly divided party, and as a consequence was severely limited in his choice of a running mate. It should have been a person of stature from the opposite wing of the party, such as Governor Scranton. He and others like him had taken themselves out of consideration. It was, therefore, not until noon of Thursday, July 15, one day before the convention would come to a close, that Goldwater turned to William E. Miller of New York. Miller was the chairman of the Republican National Committee, an able congressman, and a Roman Catholic, and was respected by his colleagues in the Congress and by party workers throughout the country. Small in stature physically, he was a man of courage, dedication, and patriotism. Barry asked me to get Miller on the phone for him. When Miller came on the line, I wrote down Barry's end of the conversation:

"Bill, you don't have to say yes or no right now. It could be a lonesome road, but I would like to have somebody who will go down the road with me. Will you do it?"

Miller, to his credit, accepted without hesitation. The road would be lonesome indeed.

When the speeches were over, Goldwater received 883 votes, Rockefeller 114, and Scranton 214. Political debris littered the floor.

I still shudder when I recall the boos and noes of the eastern establishment when, in his acceptance speech on July 16, Goldwater intoned: "I would remind you that extremism in the defense of liberty is no vice. And let me remind you also that moderation in the pursuit of justice is no virtue.[5]" I never quite understood the reason for such a negative reaction to this statement by the press, as well as by the so-called liberal wing of the party. It seems to me that in today's troubled world, that statement pretty much sums up the case.

In light of the Lyndon Johnson landslide in November 1964, it has been easy for political writers to conclude that Goldwater was too far ahead of the nation and the times. Ronald Reagan, however, became a national political figure as a result of his televised support of Goldwater during the election. Two years later he was elected governor of California, and in 1980 was elected president by an even larger landslide over President Carter than that of Johnson's over Goldwater. Unlike Rockefeller, Romney, and Scranton, Richard Nixon stumped the country for Barry Goldwater and was nominated and elected president in 1968. Had it not been for Goldwater, I believe that neither Richard Nixon nor Ronald Reagan would have become president of the United States.

In the great marketplace of the body politic in America, it can never be said that the presidential candidate who introduces new concepts is ahead of his times. He has been but the vehicle of meaningful change, and whether a particular election is won or lost is unimportant.

Barry Goldwater was able to articulate what many Americans had come to feel about their country. As a result of the Great Depression and World War II, the individual had become submerged in an increasingly complex, collectivistic society. That such a concept of the individual came to be labeled conservatism always troubled me. It is the essence of the liberal ideas espoused by William Jennings Bryan and Theodore Roosevelt. Franklin Roosevelt appropriated the liberal label to characterize his New Deal. Whether in the long run the American citizen will be better off because of the massive intervention in his life by the federal government, remains to be seen. By the end of the Carter administration

---

[5]At that moment, Bob Mardian and I left the convention floor. I returned to Phoenix that night to begin my campaign in the Republican primary for governor of Arizona. This was the most arduous physical experience of my life. I won the primary handily but lost the general election to Sam Goddard. On the night of the election I swore to myself that I was through with politics. As they say, "Never say never."

in 1980, the dismal results of excessive government were visible everywhere. Goldwater had warned his fellow citizens about what to expect. By spending more money out of our federal treasury than the productive capacity of the country would produce in taxes, ever mounting federal deficits would lead to inflation, unemployment, and recession. Unfortunately, those who would suffer the most would be the very ones the so-called liberal programs were designed to benefit—the aged, the poor, the minorities, and the uneducated. At the same time, the initiative of the individual to work, produce, invest, and save would be stifled.

For decades to come, America will debate the causes of its problems and their solutions. The point of view Barry Goldwater enunciated in his book *Conscience of a Conservative* will be part of that debate.

Goldwater's candidacy also paved the way for the emergence of the Republican party in the South. Alabama, Georgia, Louisiana, South Carolina, and Mississippi broke nearly a hundred-year tradition by giving him their electoral votes. Today Republicans from Virginia, North Carolina, South Carolina, Georgia, Florida, Alabama, and Mississippi find themselves in the U.S. Senate. No party can now take the South for granted.

For me, however, it is Barry Goldwater's basic qualities that I will always remember and admire. Politicians come and go and political movements ebb and flow. But the enduring qualities that mark great men and women remain. Goldwater was endowed with more than his share of such qualities and he has generously shared them with his fellow man all his life. To those of us who have the privilege to know him well, two characteristics overshadow all his others: there isn't a vindictive bone in his body; and he is loyal.

Retaliation is a natural human response when others publicly condemn us. In 1964 Barry was subjected to the grossest personal abuse by segments of the media. It would have destroyed a lesser man. He took it in stride and had the wisdom to recognize that it was nothing more than the dark side of political debate and expression. Vitriolic cartoons of himself adorn the walls of his study and evoke in him chuckles instead of hate.

Through loyalty to principles and people, however, a politician earns the right to lead. Barry Goldwater has always been loyal to the principles in which he has believed, even if such loyalty was at times politically inexpedient. He has also been loyal to his friends. I am one such, and for that I will always be grateful to this unique man from Arizona.

3
Mitchell
The 1968 Campaign

I was in a hurry to finish repairing a hole in the roof of our summer cabin in the Bradshaw mountains, an old gold-mine site among magnificent huge ponderosa pines outside Prescott. Teeoff time for the first day of the Hassayampa Mountain Club Labor Day Golf Tournament of 1967 was 12:20 P.M. My golf game sharpens with practice during my August vacation and I was ready to demonstrate that fact to my opponents.

The telephone rang. I started down the ladder. Just as I picked up the phone it stopped. Back up the ladder. I was descending the ladder after finishing my chore when the phone rang again.

"Mr. Kleindienst, please," a very efficient eastern voice demanded. "One moment for Vice President Nixon."

"Well, I'll be an SOB," I said to myself. It had been some time.

Nixon greeted me in the light pleasant voice I remembered from our first meeting some eleven years before. "We're giving some thought to running for president again next year. You have always been my man in Arizona, and, well, could you take charge out there—you know, keep the franchise to yourself—see to it that somebody we don't know doesn't get hold of it—you know what I mean. . . ?"

"If you have any concern about carrying Arizona, no matter who has the franchise, you shouldn't even be thinking about running," I advised. "But, yes, I'll mind the store in Arizona—that will be a snap. Arizona's already inclined to go your way."

"Good, Dick. We'll be in touch soon."

I shot a ninety-two and was eliminated from the tournament on the first day.

About a month later I was sitting in my office, discussing a rather urgent legal matter with a new client when my loyal friend and secretary, Helen Edwards, put a note in front of me: "Mr. Nixon is holding on line two."

"Dick, sorry to interrupt. I know it's Friday and very short notice. But we are having a little strategy meeting at 9:00 A.M. Sunday in New York City. Could you possibly make it?"

I suppose I paused only a second, but it seemed longer. To myself, I said, "Here we go again." To Nixon, "I'll be there. Where's the meeting place?"

Rose Mary Woods, Nixon's personal secretary of longstanding and a lovely and decent person with whom to work, came on the phone and gave me the address.

New York City was overcast when I left my hotel for the meeting. As I recall I was the last participant to arrive. Just a few men were there. I recognized Senator Henry Bellmon of Oklahoma. He was elected Republican party chairman in his state in 1956 and we had served on the national committee together. I also recognized Herbert Brownell, Ike's attorney general, who had been a quietly constructive party leader ever since. And next to him a pleasant-looking man, a little younger than I, with sandy hair and a strong face. He was introduced to me as Linwood Holton of Roanoke, Virginia, a moderate Republican, in the near future to be elected Virginia's governor.

Another was there to whom I was introduced for the first time—rather stocky, in his early fifties, receding straight hair, full cheeks, aquiline nose, and shrewd and humorous eyes that surveyed me over his pipe tamper. Unknown to me then, I was to work closely with this man for the next five years and would develop an abiding affection and admiration for him.

Nixon's candidacy was then being spurred by this small group of personal and political associates; they were gambling on a man who had apparently been shelled conclusively from the political mound in the California gubernatorial election of 1962. John Mitchell was the chief author of that gamble. One evening in spring 1968 my wife, Marnie, came to town to renew our acquaintance, since my absence from home was chronic that year. Having already developed a friendship with this man, I asked him to join us for dinner at a restaurant. We asked John about Richard Nixon and his estimate of him.

Vividly I recall John saying, "When Dick Nixon first came back here to practice law in my firm he was a beaten man. But I have watched him grow in self-confidence over the last months. I have seen him slowly realize that he is the mental equal of any of the most high-powered international business figures with whom he has dealt recently on legal matters. He has acquired a new maturity and balance, and the resentments of the early sixties have been put behind him."

I submit that those of us who began that fateful campaign with John Mitchell were similarly convinced, and most of us working in the government departments under Richard Nixon maintained that belief until the firings began the morning after the 1972 election.

John, in those early days, was profoundly excited, I felt, by the solemn importance of fostering a major candidacy for the presidency of the United States. His confidence in Nixon's ability to be a great president was deeply felt. I believe in later years this deep sense of responsibility contributed to his sacrificial behavior during the Watergate period. John, more than anyone else in the country, knew that his personal evaluation of Richard Nixon in 1967 and his decision to put his law firm's prestige, manpower, and money behind the nomination drive were fundamental to placing Nixon in the White House.

Thus John did everything he could during the White House years to enable Nixon to govern. He covered up what he termed the "White House horrors," which he learned of only after the break-in. And he was able not only to tolerate callous treatment, by advisers like Ehrlichman, who wanted to offer him up, as well as by Nixon himself, but also to maintain with Nixon a close friendship, which persists as I write this.

From the beginning of the Nixon presidency, John Mitchell was cast by members of the press as a "tough guy." At first he almost acquiesced in this portrayal, since he felt he had to serve as a point man in the many real struggles for policy change the administration faced. The misrepresentations fostered by press observers only accumulated.

The man I met in New York City that Sunday morning, though, proved to be a quiet man, with a constantly operative sense of humor. He could produce some wonderfully funny, and perceptive, one-liners. Mitchell was a man with whom men liked to work, who inspired loyalty among his associates. I will speak further about his political abilities later. One asset he brought to Nixon's campaign was a portfolio of friendships garnered from all sections of the United States during his work on sponsoring municipal-bond issues. Men with whom he had worked on legal matters invariably, it seemed, became his devoted friends.

One aspect of John's character soon became evident to all but one or two intimates—his immense reserve about his inner emotions and his private life. He was, and is, an unusually self-contained person. I knew John had a grown son and a daughter whom he adored. I have met Jill, his daughter, two or three times, but not his son. They seemed never to intrude on his political life, and those of us who were close to him in Washington were rarely aware when they visited John.

John, I heard, had been married a second time and had a little girl, Marty. His wife was reportedly less than happy with John's diversion from the prosperous life of a successful New York corporate lawyer to a speculative adventure into national politics. She and John then lived near the Rye Country Club, and Martha Mitchell was apparently highly desirous of conserving that suburban existence, and the annual vacation-conventions where her driving social instincts had full play. I never met Martha during the 1968 campaign, and John rarely mentioned her. Near the end, when it was increasingly forecast that Nixon might win and John be needed in Washington, I heard a rumor that Martha was hospitalized with nervous problems, perhaps partly because of these forecasts.

John's restraints concerning his personal affairs, including his life with Martha later, I believe, worked an injustice upon him. The press coverage of Martha Mitchell, and especially of John's relationship with her in the Watergate years, varies greatly from the reality I knew. Let me digress further from the campaign opening and look ahead.

As I recall, I first met Martha Mitchell at a meeting of the Republican National Committee near the end of 1968 and shortly after the campaign victory. I saw a short blonde woman, rather fussily dressed, inclined to make strong statements in a coquettish manner. At this meeting, like any other gathering where numerous men circled her, Martha was at her best—in high humor, enjoying the fun and the flattery.

But another side of Martha I, to my astonishment, soon saw. Immediately after the inauguration I moved into a little house in Bethesda with Marnie and three of our four children, our oldest then a student at Harvard. A day or two later, after eleven one night, Marnie nudged me awake and handed me the phone.

"Kleindienst, I think that SOB Landau [Jack Landau, newly appointed head of public information at the Department of Justice] is saying bad things about John behind his back! I want you to call J. Edgar Hoover tomorrow and have him put a tap on Landau's phone!"

I was now wide awake. I stared incredulously at the cabbage roses on the bedroom rug we'd inherited, and protested to Martha Mitchell that I couldn't quite do that.

She called two or three more times, as I recall, usually somewhere between midnight and three in the morning. The next morning after each call I would tell John what had taken place. And I advised Martha that I intended to do just that, that I worked for her husband and not for her. The calls became more embittered and eventually stopped.

We had received the first hint of a difficulty that would pursue us through the Nixon presidency. Martha Mitchell's temperament was always a matter of concern, whether she was arriving dramatically late to join a Washington luncheon head table that included a patiently smiling Mrs. Nixon, or drunkenly refusing to preside over a fashion show whose sponsors had been counting on her for months.

As I look back, this was the sequence of events with Martha. At first, in early 1969, she still acutely regretted the loss of her New York way of life and was somewhat apprehensive both of the press and of her new responsibilities. At a "ladies' retreat" she announced, after a small formal dinner, that she "would not have had anything to do with all these crooked politicians if John didn't have to come to Washington to save the country." Then she was discovered by the press, which saw her as a colorful and, I believe, vulnerable adjunct to a rather taciturn group. Her fan mail piled up, requests for personal appearances multiplied, and Martha Mitchell had at last the public attention she craved.

A few months of this treatment and she became convinced she was by far the most important administration wife. Her only disappointment, she told intimates, was that the White House seemed not to realize this fully. John, I think, felt at first that his wife's witty barbs were funny, and that they seasoned press coverage. But he too came increasingly to realize that Martha's immaturity and irresponsibility were becoming a general burden.

The difficulties intensified as 1972 approached. Martha believed her spotlight was permanent. I remember a night at El Chorro restaurant in Paradise Valley outside Phoenix, where Marnie and I had accompanied the Mitchells to the first Fiesta Bowl football game. Our group was seated at a long table.

"Kleindienst," Martha called, "I know how we can work out this campaign. John can go over to run the Committee to Reelect the President, and you can be acting attorney general. Then, when it's over, he can come back and be the attorney general again."

That of course was John's problem in 1972. He was being pulled in both directions, not only by Martha but by the president. Her suggestion was unethical and would have compounded his problem a hundredfold. But Martha believed that John was prepared, in fact, to follow her advice. When he told her otherwise the very morning his appointment as campaign chairman was announced, she went into a paroxysm of hysteria, from which, it seemed, she never fully recovered. Her emotional state was later tragically compounded by the tensions of Watergate.

Back to the beginning. The strategy proposed to me that Sunday morning in the fall of 1967 was that I put together a "Nixon for president" committee to secure nomination delegates in all the western states except California, a primary state which then had Ronald Reagan as governor. My objective should be to have this group of states organized by the end of the year and to get as much publicity as possible from this fact before the New Hampshire primary in early 1968. I guess I protested the assignment a little, but I wasn't really serious. Here was a chance for involvement in a national campaign with a good chance of success—and for a man in whose candidacy I believed. I was hooked again.

What were Nixon's assets on the eve of that election drive? They were many. After the nationwide defeat of 1964 the Republican party had only one direction to go—up. Nixon had not been involved in the Rockefeller-Goldwater intraparty bloodletting. In 1966 he reestablished himself as a force within the party as a result of his prodigious and frequently successful campaigning for Republican candidates for Congress. He was now Nixon at his best—mature, articulate, optimistic as to the party's future, encouraging to the new candidate, a happy, confident warrior. This is how chips are earned in politics, and Richard Nixon once again earned his. I had always liked him and had greatly admired his ability. I felt, as John Mitchell did, that it took courage to overcome the effects of his bitter and petulant exit out the back door from California to New York after his 1962 defeat for the California governorship.

This time around, in spite of lonely hotels and endless plane travel, I had fun serving as a regional chairman for the delegate operation. The candidate was confident, and camaraderie characterized the small staff back in New York City. My objective was first to recruit a Nixon chairman in each western state. The chief requisite, of course, was an individual truly committed to the candidate. But especially important to me and to the rest of the campaign staff was finding a person who was not objectionable to either faction of the Republicans, the conservatives or the liberals. We felt that it was of little avail to secure the delegates of a state as a result of a pitched party battle, only to lose that state in the general election because of rankling divisions. With bitter memories of 1964 in mind, I personally determined that I would leave a state open rather than settle for a divisive Nixon state chairman. The little girl by the railroad track with the sign saying "Bring Us Together" was sincerely anticipated by the Nixon nomination committee. We built our campaign on accumulated goodwill.

By the end of December 1967 the Nixon for President Committee in the West was, with but one or two open slots, in place. I could now turn my attention to planning a meeting of the entire group of chairmen with Nixon himself. The place we selected was Denver, and the Brown Palace Hotel.

Amid these arrangements the unexpected happened, premonitory perhaps of campaign changes in both attitude and technique. I received a call from a young Phoenix attorney by the name of Edward Morgan, of a fine Phoenix law firm. Having never met him, I was astonished when he informed me that he would be in charge of all arrangements for the Denver meeting.

"What do you have to do with Nixon?" I shot back in my usual direct fashion.

Morgan courteously explained that he knew Bob Haldeman (then a relative stranger to me) and John Ehrlichman as a result of having been an advance man for Nixon in either 1960 or 1962 (I don't remember which).

"Don't do anything further, Ed, until you hear from either me or New York," I instructed, and then called New York.

I had just spent three months flying all over the West to put together a political organization, many members being close friends and coworkers in the past. Now a former advance man, whom I didn't even know, was going to be in charge of the arrangements for my Denver meeting. I guess I made my point with New York. Ed Morgan didn't show up in Denver. But apparently Ehrlichman and Haldeman were already moving in.

A word about the persons who get involved in contemporary national politics in the U.S. The most common is, like myself, the volunteer or avocational politician. Unpaid, such politicians take time from their usual employment and participate in party organization and in the selection and election of candidates. (I had worked since 1950 at party jobs in Arizona without pay.) They have a fairly well defined political philosophy and a pretty clear idea as to the general course the country should take. Often, perhaps, they are enticed by the excitement and complexity of mounting a nationwide political drive. But most, I believe, are motivated by constructive and often idealistic purposes. The role of citizen-politician has deep roots in the United States; it is not antithetical to honorable subsequent government service but can enhance that service by an intimate knowledge of the American psyche. For me, my appointment as deputy attorney general under Richard Nixon was not a springboard to *any* other office but the end of a long journey of conviction. By the way, during the next presidential campaign, in 1972, I refused all requests to make political speeches, and John Mitchell and I saw little or nothing of each other.

Then there are the professional politicians. These are highly skilled managers. They know demographics, public relations, the media, polling, and all the other facets of a campaign. They are well paid and they should be. Without these pros many a new aspirant to local, state, or federal office would never get off first base. Their only limitation is their necessity, for their continued employment, to preserve a record of successes. The pros' loyalty may thus be divided between their own career and the welfare of candidates. For that reason most serious presidential hopefuls do not use pros. They turn instead to loyal and time-tested friends.

An advance man is in a different category. He may have a general interest in politics. But usually he has not been involved before, and it is a glamorous new world for him. His function usually concerns logistics—getting the candidate from one place to another, putting him up in a hotel, working out precise arrangements for appearances, and working with local backers for the best possible attendance at functions and for advantageous press, radio, and TV coverage. It is hard work. It can also be exciting. He sees the great man from time to time and he works with those who likewise are in personal contact with that man. If, as happens more often than not, the individual is young, if his only previous experience in the game of politics is having been an advance man, and if he suddenly finds himself on the White House staff and in the middle of government, strange things can happen. (Nixon's administration was by no means unique in employing advance men. But I do think Ehrlichman and Haldeman had too many running around the town doing errands for them. I can remember one slightly disgusted friend of mine calling them "the White House Brownies." The appointed officers of Nixon's Department of Justice were apparently less aware than other department heads of some of the pressure tactics used by the White House liaison personnel—until John Mitchell left. He had the political strength to ward off interference and did so, I believe, more than will ever be known.)

Dick Nixon was at his best at that meeting in Denver. He inspired his new organization. He was jovial, friendly, upbeat. Everyone got a photograph of himself and the candidate. The press was fair and the TV coverage couldn't have been better. It was an ideal PR event on the eve of the New Hampshire primary and the 1968 national campaign for the Republican nomination.

After that meeting of the state delegates was over, I dropped by to say goodbye to my friend. My assignment was concluded and I had to get back to gainful employment. Nixon was appreciative of my effort, and as he said goodbye, added, "Let's keep in touch."

"Sure," I replied as I went out the door, uncertain about the future employment of my talents. But shortly thereafter Mitchell called me and asked me to visit him in New York. By the time that visit was concluded I was on my way home to say goodbye to the family once more, and return to New York to begin my responsibility as national director of field operations for the Nixon presidential campaign under John Mitchell, campaign manager.

The Nixon general operation was as different from the Goldwater 1964 effort as day is from night. To begin with, the country was restless for change. Whether

President Johnson ran for reelection or not, the war in Vietnam had begun to exact its political price of personal bitterness and loss. On the domestic front, Johnson's guns-and-butter policy was creating the inevitable economic consequences of inflation and uncertainty. Second, we had an eager and optimistic contender, unlike Goldwater in the sad early spring months of his primary races. (Barry, I think, intuitively foresaw the campaign's conclusion at its outset.) Most of all we had in John Mitchell an amiable and subtly effective director. Working with John Mitchell in the 1968 presidential campaign was the most pleasant and rewarding political experience of my life.

John Mitchell was ideal to be Nixon's campaign manager. At the outset he was compared frequently to Denison Kitchel, Barry's manager in 1964. There were similarities. They were both fine men. Neither had prior experience in managing a campaign for even a candidate for sheriff, let alone for president. Neither was known to the politicians of the Republican party. Both were unswervingly loyal to the man they served and both were low key publicly. Neither Kitchel nor Mitchell had the desire or need for public attention, a highly desirable quality in a presidential campaign manager, indeed.

Mitchell, however, brought to national politics a dimension few others ever have, Democrat or Republican. In 1968 he was regarded as one of this nation's most effective practitioners of public law, a specialty that concerns itself with assisting municipal and state governments in securing financing for their major needs. The lawyer's clients are the governors, mayors, legislators, and councilmen who direct those governments. By 1968 Mitchell had personally practiced his specialty in every one of the fifty states. He knew elected officials everywhere, well. Although not previously involved in organizational politics, he knew the end product, the men elected. These state and city officials certainly had as much influence in the selection of convention delegates as the regular politician, if not more.

Mitchell's greatest strength as a manager derived from his personal character. He had a superior intellect and a retentive mind, and was a good listener. Most politicians like to talk, particularly about themselves. As a listener, John Mitchell wound up knowing what the talker knew. He could relate to and communicate with everyone. If it was a finance matter, he could talk about bankers, contributors, and budgets. If a media problem, he just happened to know most of the dominant figures in that industry. If a staff problem, he had the sensitivity to make those on both sides of an argument feel they were right. He was an able manager.

The one "limitation" that I observed in John—an asset during a political campaign, but a detriment during Watergate—was his soft-spokenness and his tendency to understate his view. Even if he strongly disagreed, he seldom raised his voice. When I was his deputy at the Department of Justice I frequently found it necessary, after a staff meeting, to interpret in unequivocal language what Mitchell really intended. I can imagine what may have happened in the reelection campaign. Many, recently delegated by the White House, were unused to this aspect of John's behavior. If, say, Gordon Liddy or Jeb Magruder presented a harebrained proposal, Mitchell, instead of rejecting the idea in strong, angry terms, would dismiss it in a manner inoffensive to its author. Such could be interpreted as a neutral stand or perhaps as tacit approval. This may well have happened with Jeb Magruder in Miami.

The initial headquarters for the nomination campaign the winter of 1967–68 was in New York City at 450 Park Avenue, in the old and vacant Bible Society Building, on the fourth floor. At the very beginning there were five of us—John Mitchell; Peter Flannigan, a young and quietly sophisticated investment banker; Leonard Garment, then head of the trial department at Mitchell's firm; Ed Nixon, who had taken leave from his job as a geologist in Washington State to further his brother's candidacy; and myself. We were all quite different. Peter went home at night to an elegant townhouse in Manhattan or to lovely rolling acres in Purchase, north of the city in Westchester County. Len, now a successful lawyer, had been born and reared in Brooklyn and worked his way through law school as a jazz musician. (John Mitchell had furthered his education by playing professional ice hockey—and acquiring painful hip injuries as a result.) Len's friends were many of the creative New Yorkers, writers, and advertising men, as well as amateur and professional musicians. Ed Nixon was slim, amiable, quiet, and intelligent. His work was out of affection and admiration for his brother.

The team's offices consisted of several small cubicles of glass and green-painted wood, lined up next to each other on the fourth floor. Our quarters in that echoing building placed us in close proximity and we all grew to be good friends. Ed Nixon's domain was below us. He presided over Xeroxing, mailings, and matters of that sort. I set my boys to work for Ed during the summer, and they found him a kindly and reasonable employer. During June and July 1968 my wife and four children came to keep me company, and the campaign rented us an apartment at Ninetieth Street and Park. But until they came I stayed at the Drake Hotel, next door.

Nixon had a small office beyond our cubicles. He came in and out of our offices quite frequently and informally. He was readily accessible to us and usually invited me in for a pleasant chat when I would return from a field trip. This closeness was inhibited only once. Herblock, the *Washington Post* cartoonist and inveterate Nixon hater, drew what I thought was a funny cartoon after George Romney quit the race for the nomination. The cartoon showed Nixon dressed as an undertaker in black clothes shoveling dirt over the graves of all his contenders for the nomination. I rushed into Nixon's office with the cartoon and said, "Want to see something really funny, Dick?" A cold hard look came over his face when he saw it. Since Goldwater has similar cartoons of himself hanging all over his house, I was somewhat surprised at my candidate's reaction to what I thought was a "plus" political cartoon.

In putting together the delegate field force I turned to my former coworkers in the 1964 Goldwater delegate campaign. I chose those I thought the most effective. First on board were Dick Herman from Omaha and Bob Mardian from Pasadena. In addition to taking over the Midwest and the western regions for us, they were responsible for recruiting other regional directors and state chairmen. It wasn't long before the whole field organization was in place. For some strange reason the *New York Times* and the *Washington Post*—not exactly Nixon or Goldwater supporters—never picked up the fact that the Nixon delegate operation was composed mainly of persons who were part of the Goldwater field operation.

We were certainly visible. In fact, I think my most effective innovation of the 1968 effort was our in-house newspaper. I selected Frank Leonard as publisher of the "Nixon Nominator," which became the "Nixon Elector" after the convention, and finally the "Nixon President" after the election and before the inaugural. Frank did an excellent job. His newspaper proved the best possible means of communication for the whole operation. When someone was added to the team a feature story would be written. The paper also reprinted each week the names of those already on board. Then, as delegates committed themselves to Nixon, headlines would advertise the fact. Leonard also regularly featured good pictures of the candidate and his wonderful family.

This happy, carefree environment came to a screeching halt about May 1, 1968. Mitchell assembled the headquarters staff early on a Monday morning and informed us that Bob Haldeman and John Ehrlichman were coming aboard. Haldeman would manage the personal life of the candidate and Ehrlichman would be in charge of the convention in Miami Beach in July. "In order to make the best and most effective use of Richard Nixon's time and energy," we were instructed, all contacts with Nixon thereafter had to go through Haldeman.

At the time I thought it was a good idea. I recalled an exhausted and ill Nixon when running for president in 1960, voluntarily but foolishly trying to fulfill his campaign pledge to visit every one of the fifty states before the night of the general election. This approach argued for a better and more efficient use of Nixon's time. Believe me, it was efficient. I seldom saw or talked to Nixon thereafter. I didn't really have to, but the general atmosphere changed.

Of the two men, I personally preferred Haldeman. He was always available, and though very busy and businesslike at all times, he would listen attentively and intelligently. If he agreed with a suggestion, it would be implemented; if he did not, he always had a good reason why. I liked and respected him.

Ehrlichman, however, was a different kettle of fish. As I listened to Mitchell's announcement that day, I thought of my first encounter with John, in fall 1967, when I was trying to secure state chairmen for the delegate drive in the West. At that stage the state of Washington presented us with probably our most difficult staffing problems. Seattle's county, King County, was, of course, critical, not only to garnering delegates to the national convention but also to winning for a Republican candidate in the general election. That county's Republican party leadership was "true conservative" in contrast to the party's leadership in the rest of the state, which was closer to the middle or left of the Republican spectrum. Even after I had made three visits to the state and met with both factions, I was unsuccessful in my effort to come up with a Nixon chairman acceptable to both sides.

As I recall, I reported this problem to the New York office—I think to Mitchell—and was informed that I should make no final decision for Washington without first talking to John Ehrlichman. "Who is he?" I asked. It turned out he was a friend of Nixon and was a lawyer in Seattle. Before I left Phoenix for my fourth trip to Seattle I talked to Ehrlichman and arranged to meet him at the Olympic Hotel. We had a pleasant conversation about my dilemma. As we discussed and eliminated all the candidates for chairman on my list, I finally, out of frustration, turned to him and blurted, "John, why don't you do it yourself?"

"Not me. I don't want to get involved in politics."

I was astonished. "Aren't you involved in politics right now in behalf of a person who you say is your friend? Why in hell do you think I've been here four times at the expense of *my* law practice? Politics is the only way we are going to be able to nominate and elect this man!"

Ehrlichman, unmoved, left for home, and I returned to Phoenix the next day, disgruntled.

I next differed with John Ehrlichman before and during the Republican convention the following summer. A party convention is a political event. It nominates a candidate and expounds the political program of the nominee and his party. For an aspiring nominee, his nomination there is his first priority.

The logistics of presenting a major candidate to a national convention are enormous. The expense can, and usually does, run into millions of dollars. A good manager is an absolute must. John Ehrlichman was a good manager, make no mistake about that. But from a political standpoint, he was a fish out of water. Too much of my time in a rushed and fatiguing period for me was spent arguing with Ehrlichman about the "politics" of the forthcoming convention and the practical necessities, necessities that might change from minute to minute and from hour to hour. Ehrlichman, on the other hand, wanted every situation inscribed on paper in advance, and that was that. Two examples of our differences during the convention come to mind.

Shortly after coming on board, John Ehrlichman sent the head of each division of the organization a memo requesting a budget for his requirements at the convention. On the surface, good planning. My particular problem, however, was that there was no possible way to project the logistical needs of the field force in the middle of May for a July event. If we had the nomination sewed up before the convention opened, our needs would be negligible. If, on the eve of the convention, the outcome would be uncertain, our needs would be enormous.

I couldn't get this across to Ehrlichman. He still insisted on a budget. I related my problem to Mitchell. Apparently he was having his own problems with John, and in his affable, almost joking way, merely admonished me to work out my own problems. The upshot was that I submitted two budgets, one for a few thousand dollars and one for a million. That set the tone of my relationship with John Ehrlichman, a relationship that was to endure until that fateful Monday in April 1973, when President Nixon announced my resignation as attorney general, along with those of Haldeman and Ehrlichman.

The best—or worst, as you will—example of our differences occurred during the week before the convention opened in Miami Beach. The Nixon hotel headquarters was the Doral. The top floors were set aside for the staff. The very top floor was reserved for the some sixty people in the delegate operation. Everybody who had business on the top floors was given a baldheaded eagle pin to wear for identification. Without a pin, no one was allowed on the top floors—no matter what.

To show off the proficiency of the Nixon organization, I invited Ray Bliss, the national Republican party chairman, and Senator Bellmon of Oklahoma, both longtime friends of mine, to come over for a tour. Bliss would be talking to everybody in town and I wanted to impress him.

They showed up at the receptionist's desk in the hotel lobby at the appointed hour and asked to be escorted to my office, a room on the top floor.

"I'm so sorry, gentlemen, but no one is allowed up there," the little girl with the pretty little Nixon hat sweetly informed them.

Bliss and Bellmon asked her to call me. I came down immediately.

"Don't worry, sweetie-pie, I'll take them up myself."

Things ceased being sweet when she announced to me, in the presence of my two distinguished guests, "Mr. Ehrlichman's orders are that no one, *absolutely* no one, is permitted up there who doesn't have the pin."

"Gentlemen, please wait here for a minute. I'll be right back!"

I entered Ehrlichman's office with a little frustration, but nevertheless confident that the problem would be solved quickly. Not so. My nonpolitical associate firmly informed me that there would be no exceptions.

"John, old boy," I responded with some acerbity, "I'm going downstairs and I'm going to bring Bliss and Bellmon up to my floor. If you try to stop me, one or the other of us is going to be on the plane for either Arizona or Washington this afternoon."

They came up with me. Perhaps, for the country's sake, one of us should have gone home that day.

John Ehrlichman was, in fact, one of the few persons in either politics or government that I just couldn't quite communicate with, no matter how hard I tried. Circumstances made it necessary for us to come into contact with each other many times in the ensuing five years. Although there was not outright animosity between us, I cannot remember a time when we had a completely friendly meeting of minds over a problem. As I look back, I attribute some of the difficulty to differences in personality and background. I am, I know, a rather blunt, outgoing person. Some call me abrasive—I don't mean to be. I swear too much, a bad habit I acquired as a boy from the railroaders in Winslow, Arizona.

Ehrlichman, on the other hand, at that time in his life at least, was very precise, well organized, rather opinionated, and somewhat humorless. He was both intelligent and articulate. He professed to being a devout Christian Scientist. He did not drink, smoke, or swear. I did all three, sometimes all at once. It turned out to be unfortunate for both of us that we would butt heads over so many critical matters.

There was another ingredient in this relationship. Not only did Ehrlichman not care particularly for John Mitchell or me (I remember now some cruel and demeaning statements Ehrlichman made to the president about Mitchell in the days immediately after John left the Committee to Reelect the President), but Ehrlichman, so I was informed, decided, as the Nixon presidency went on, that he wanted most of all to be attorney general. During my confirmation hearings for attorney general in 1972, when prospects were not too sanguine, my old friend Bob Mardian, then head of the Internal Security Division of the Department of Justice, was asked one day to step out of my office to take a call from the White House. The caller was Ehrlichman, who asked Bob if he would consent to be deputy when Ehrlichman was nominated as attorney general!

For four and a half presidential years, John Ehrlichman began almost every day seated across the desk in the Oval Office from Nixon, summarizing recent events and offering position papers for decision. He had great ability in eloquent summation. He also had a penchant for enhancing his own stature by subtly cutting down those he deemed competitors. I believe that over weeks and months, like water wearing away stone, he cultivated suspicion in the president's mind about the ability and loyalty of his officers in the Justice Department. His gradual isolating of the president was to bear tragic fruit, as we shall see—an intemperate and untimely call to me about antitrust policy, and the hiring of men like Liddy and Hunt to conduct, from the basement of the Executive Office Building, enterprises in which the president knew or suspected the Justice Department would not participate.

The early months of 1968 brought several changes in the ranks of competitors about whom we, of the central staff in the Bible Society Building, had to worry. George Romney still was in the race at the end of 1967, widely respected as an innovative former governor of Michigan and a Republican party moderate. Then came his remarks on being "brainwashed" during the tour of the Vietnam battlefields—something which apparently the press and the country at large did not perceive as reflecting presidential quality, and his campaign folded in early 1968.

Reagan in California was issuing constant denials that he was considering running for the office. But Spiro Agnew, Maryland's governor, was actively recruiting a citizens' support group for Nelson Rockefeller, and we thought it was very likely Rockefeller would, in fact, be our principal competitor. Rockefeller was reported to be in the process of making up his mind. Came the day that he would hold a press conference to reveal his intentions. Governor Agnew, confident that his horse was ready to leave the starting gate, assembled a large number of his distinguished draft committee in his Annapolis office; the press and TV crews waited outside. He was surprised and outraged to hear, not having been notified in any way, that Rockefeller was regretfully taking himself out of the presidential race. The next Monday John Mitchell appeared in Governor Agnew's office in Annapolis and recruited Agnew for the campaign. Governor Hickel of Alaska and Senator Hiram Fong of Hawaii were also approached and became converts to Nixon's cause.

With Romney back in Michigan for keeps, and Rockefeller doing whatever a Rockefeller does, Nixon's nomination, in my opinion, was ensured by the end of May. I expressed the opinion to Nixon and the entire campaign staff at a meeting in Key Biscayne: "Even if Rockefeller tried to back in again we have enough of an edge to permit you to spend most of your time and energy organizing for the general election campaign." Everybody seemed to agree and a pleasant social hour ensued. The candidate played a few tunes on the piano, had a couple of cocktails, and was relaxed and optimistic. I think I was never with him again when he was so obviously happy.

In June Rockefeller changed his mind and reentered the race. At the same time, Governor Reagan of California started poking around, sensing that a confrontation between Rockefeller and Nixon in Miami Beach just might yield rewards for him.

Rockefeller's last-minute, almost frantic effort to get the 1968 nomination was unbelievable in its form and thrust. Having lost the opportunity to gather delegates in the usual and conventional way—in primaries and at state conventions—he sought them through a massive nationwide newspaper and television campaign. How much it cost is anybody's guess, but it had to be in the millions. What profoundly troubled and surprised us was that this campaign cast a variety of aspersions on Nixon's character, especially that Nixon would be hostile to minorities—that, in a word, he was a racist.

On a hot Sunday afternoon in New York City the telephone in our apartment rang. Nixon was on the line, wondering what to do about Rockefeller and whether to counter specifically his unjustified personal attacks. I lay on the bed with the receiver propped on my shoulder and talked to him casually but very directly. I told him I was still confident that we had collected so many delegates early in the campaign that we could still retain the lead despite some attrition by the Rockefeller forces and even a potential late move by Reagan. I sympathized with his concern about unfair and slanderous tactics—and they *were* in large measure slanderous. But I noted that retaliation only breeds retaliation, that we had deliberately built our campaign on goodwill and potential cooperation among the whole Republican party, and that those qualities would be precious to us in the general election—so precious that we should decide to lie low and absorb Rockefeller's verbal blows without comment. When the conversation finished, I walked into the next room and asked Marnie, who had been listening to my side of the dialogue, whether she thought I had been too blunt. She thought otherwise.

In any event, Nixon took my advice, and our campaign that summer ended as it had begun, on a positive note.

As far as I was concerned, Rockefeller's drive was not only a failure, but irrelevant to the objective of persuading delegates to switch to him at the convention. The content of his blitz seemed aimed at every segment of America except the typical Republican convention delegate. Indeed, it was similar to Robert Kennedy's public appeal for the Democratic nomination before his tragic death on the eve of the California primary. As long as I live, I'll never understand why Rockefeller did what he did in the way he did it.

As the summer wore on toward the Miami Beach rendezvous, the desperately hard-working field men in our office were consumed with preoccupation about delegates—how to hold ours and how to attract the increasingly few uncommitted. The projected delegate count of a candidate can be used as a tactical weapon throughout the campaign. As the hour approaches for the roll call, it can become a strategic as well as a tactical tool. To be used effectively, the candidate's spokesman refers only to the total number of sure delegates claimed by the candidate, rather than the state-by-state number claimed by him. The exception is the state whose delegates have publicly announced their support. The reason for this rule of conduct can readily be seen. A political reporter would attempt to interview the delegates of a state to determine the accuracy of the candidate's claim. Many delegates prefer not to make their choice known and frequently mislead the press. Thus, that reporter may come up with a story challenging the accuracy of the claimed delegates; and negative publicity can have a harmful effect on the delegates. As a consequence, the precise number of delegates in the committed or sure category is a carefully guarded secret.

As far as we were concerned, only Nixon, Mitchell, and I had that information in writing. During the drive for the nomination, Nixon, from time to time, would call me on the phone—at odd hours—and ask me to run down the list. I think he was always amused that from memory I could quickly go down the states in alphabetical order and give the number of our delegates for each state. (That memory trick I learned as a fry cook in my high school days when I had to remember the verbal orders of several waitresses over a period of several hours.) Such a memory trick could occasionally be used for a good purpose. On the evening before the roll call at the convention, Nixon asked me to give to Clement Stone, one of Nixon's most active financial supporters from Chicago, a list of our delegate support. I persuaded him to let me run down the list verbally instead. Having done so, I gave Mr. Stone the rather categorical opinion that we would have 696 delegates on the first ballot if Senator Fong was nominated by Hawaii as a favorite son; if he wasn't, we would receive 704. Fong was nominated and Nixon received 696 votes on the first ballot. The point of the story is, Stone was satisfied that he had been given the inside delegate count even though he did not have it in writing.

That projected vote was really not that concrete, however. The real drama of the '68 convention was being acted out in Ronald Reagan's trailer, adjacent to

the convention hall, on the night of the roll call. Several states followed the so-
called unit rule for delegates at the Republican convention. If a candidate has
a majority support among the delegates, he receives the vote of all the delegates.
If the majority support is slim, the switch of a few delegates can change the
numbers. Florida, Alabama, and Mississippi were unit-rule states. Florida and
Alabama, however, were susceptible to a switch from Nixon to Reagan. Now
president, but then aspirant, Reagan was using his most persuasive talents to
convince a few delegates from each of these three delegations to switch to him.
These efforts continued right up to and through the first part of the balloting.

Needed to nominate were 670 delegates. Alabama, first on the roll call, had
26; Florida, tenth, had 34; and Mississippi had 20. If the delegate switch Reagan
hoped for occurred, the claim of 696 for Nixon would evaporate in thin air. We
would have had only 596 on the first ballot. The Reagan effort almost succeeded.
Nixon, however, received 14 from Alabama, 32 from Florida, and the entire 20
from Mississippi. Wisconsin, the next to the last state, with its 30 votes, put
Nixon over the top and produced the "predicted" 696.

Whether Nixon would have been nominated after the first ballot is open to
question. Even though he received 696 votes on the first ballot, he received
either none or a handful from all the large stages—New York (4 of 92), Pennsylvania (22 of 64), Michigan (4 of 63), Ohio (2 of 58), and California (0).
With a break in the South by the defection from Nixon of Alabama, Florida,
and Mississippi, and before a second roll call could take place, feverish caucuses
and smoke-filled back-room negotiations would have taken place among the
powerbrokers of the larger delegations. Milliken and Romney of Michigan,
Rhodes of Ohio, Rockefeller of New York, and Scranton of Pennsylvania would
have been one bloc; Reagan of California (and Alabama, Florida, and Mississippi) would have been another; Nixon would have been in the middle. My own
opinion is that we would have eventually won. Rockefeller would not have gone
for Reagan, and vice versa. Eliminate them and whom did they have to challenge
Nixon? Perhaps Scranton, but he had destroyed his chance with the conservatives
(who found themselves yearning for Ronald Reagan in San Francisco in '64).
Although Richard Nixon wasn't loved by the liberal or the conservative, he at
least was not completely objectionable to either. His lifelong position in the
great middle of the Republican party would, in my opinion, have eventually
rewarded him with the nomination. Nevertheless, it was a tense group of managers sitting in the Nixon trailer as the roll call began.

Just before the roll call Nixon called our trailer and directed that I get Governor
Rhodes of Ohio off in a corner and, by going through our list of delegates,
persuade him to release the Nixon delegates in his delegation; we estimated them
to be about thirty-six, of fifty-eight. Ohio, however, had taken the firm position
that its delegation would vote for Rhodes as a favorite son on the first ballot.

I found Rhodes and went down my list. I even showed him the written
document. "Governor," I pleaded, "why not let the Nixon delegates register
their vote since we are going to win on the first ballot?" With expletives and

anger, he would have no part of it. At the time I couldn't understand his adamant posture. Later, I learned the answer. It seems that in January 1968 Rhodes and John Anderson, the state chairman, had met separately and personally with Nixon, Romney, and Rockefeller. In those meetings it was understood that Ohio would go for a favorite son on the first ballot; thereafter the delegates would be up for grabs. I think Governor Rhodes must have believed I was aware of this arrangement—which I was not—and therefore felt justified in chewing me out so grandly.

At last the introductory speeches were over, hours came down to minutes, and the roll call was imminent. The definitive judgment on our calculations was about to be recorded. Suddenly there was a call for me on one of the lines. It was Nixon. "All right, Kleindienst, it's your ass now."

"F—— you, Nixon." The phone clicked off.

Moments later the phone rang again. "You're right," Nixon said.

The result is history: 696 votes on the first ballot. The nomination was ours.

After the nomination, Nixon proceeded to spend all night meeting with person after person and delegation after delegation discussing the selection of the vice president. He invited opinions and suggestions about four possible candidates: Agnew, Senator Baker of Tennessee, George Bush, and Governor Volpe of Massachusetts. Any one of them, in my opinion, would have been an excellent running mate. Based upon his reputation at the time, each would have been a credible president if required by circumstances to serve as such.

The inside track was apparently held by Spiro Agnew, John Mitchell's recruit when Rockefeller withdrew his name early the previous spring. Why Agnew? Conjecture in retrospect might place his qualities of stubbornness and outspokenness as prime considerations. Nixon and the rest of us admired his steadfast allegiance to our campaign during weeks of incredible pressure from the Rockefeller forces up to and including the convention. But at the time other reasons were more frequently discussed, particularly those aspects of Agnew that seemed to make him a centrist candidate in the Republican party. The very location of Maryland, the state he then governed, pointed to him as middle ground between North and South. Too, he had begun the year as a strong advocate for Rockefeller and his northeastern Republican supporters.

Agnew was selected by Nixon to make his nominating speech. Mitchell met with him before the delivery of that speech and indicated to him that if he and the nominating speech were well received, he would be given top consideration by Nixon for the second spot. This was more than enough of an incentive to Spiro Agnew. He gave a superb performance and his nominating speech was well received by the delegates and, most important, by Richard M. Nixon.

For some reason, I seemed always to be around when a Republican presidential nominee picked a running mate. In 1960 I was present for the anointing ceremony of Lodge. I was with Goldwater when he asked me to get Bill Miller on the phone so he could ask him to join his ticket. And midmorning the day after Nixon's nomination I was walking through the lobby of our headquarters hotel when Nixon spotted me.

"Come on up with me."

I followed him into his suite and, except for an advance man at the door, found myself alone with him.

"Ted Agnew will be here in a minute. I thought you might like to be present when I ask him to be my running mate."

In the conversation with Agnew, I thought Dick Nixon was at his best, with a sensitivity and understanding acquired through long experience. He outlined to Agnew the challenge and the tribulations that go with running for vice president. He was especially eloquent as to what it meant to be a vice president. Agnew responded with a sincere humility and quiet confidence that I found to be refreshing. (As I left the room, I heard the advance man mutter under his breath, "I wonder how many [expletive deleted] Greeks there are in the U.S.?")

Mitchell assigned me to Washington, D.C., for the general election campaign to act as the liaison between Nixon's campaign organization and Ray Bliss's Republican National Committee. Several practical reasons justified his decision. First, an identification with the party isn't all that desirable in a general election and my public image was that of a Goldwater conservative. Second, friction and misunderstanding can develop between the national committee and the candidate. The party people usually feel ignored by a candidate and his manager after the nomination. Since I was regarded as being close to Mitchell, my presence at the national committee could help allay such attitudes. Third, Bliss and I were close friends. Fourth, Nixon did not particularly care for Bliss, personally. I was told Bliss had refused to make a private airplane available to him in 1966 when Nixon so effectively campaigned for Republican congressional candidates. Nixon never quite forgave Bliss that slight.

I immediately moved from New York into Barry Goldwater's Washington, D.C., apartment. "Holding Bliss's hand" for the next three months, with the temporary title of general counsel to the Republican National Committee, was a rewarding experience; Ray and I became even faster friends, and it provided me with a much needed recuperation from the arduous preceding six months of travel. Haldeman and Ehrlichman "invited" me to travel one day with Nixon in North Carolina in the middle of the campaign. My scheduled "two minutes" with the candidate conformed to Ehrlichman's usual standard of perfection.

Election night 1968 was an uneasy one. Senator Humphrey had been shown in the polls to be coming uncomfortably close. We were closeted with friends and two or three television sets on one of the lower floors of the Waldorf-Astoria. But by morning the worst was over and Richard Nixon was president-elect of the United States. And that morning Marnie and I congratulated the next president, shook hands with Pat, and jumped into a car for LaGuardia airport and home. I was eager to get back to my family in Phoenix and to my law firm.

The most valuable player of the campaign was, in my opinion, John Mitchell. From the beginning his quiet good humor, understanding, prodigious efforts, ability to relate to and motivate everyone from the candidate to the cleaning lady, and comprehensive grasp of the whole business made for an enviable performance. Regardless of the pressures or crises—presidential campaigns are replete with both—he never panicked, nor did he ever yield to an expedient or dishonorable solution. There were no "dirty tricks" in the 1968 campaign. There were no animosities. His rapport with his counterparts in the opposite party and among the Humphrey organization was excellent and on the highest level.

Is this the same John Mitchell who admittedly involved himself in the "cover-up" of Watergate? I believe so. Mitchell did what he did out of loyalty to the president and to his presidency. To him that also meant a responsibility to his country. In 1972 the choice was either Nixon or McGovern, and Mitchell sincerely believed the choice of the latter was untenable. I don't condone what Mitchell did. No election justifies the obstruction of justice. But he was tried and convicted, and served his sentence of imprisonment. He has paid a heavy and lasting price for a course of conduct which, if the choice were the same, he would probably repeat. To this day he has uttered no complaint.

I think my feeling of loyalty to Barry Goldwater is similar to that of Mitchell for Richard Nixon. Goldwater, of course, did not become president. If he had been elected, and if a Watergate crisis had been his lot, I think he would not have handled it the way Nixon did. I am confident that Barry's first loyalty would have been to his country, his second to his friends and lieutenants, and his third to himself. Barry Goldwater has, in fact, through all the years of tumult and change since 1964, kept in touch with his principal campaign staff members and concerned himself with their welfare. And based upon my years of intimate association with John Mitchell, I know that he likewise puts his country first and himself last. I admire him, and think of him as a friend.

PART II

People here fail in politics and
the press when they begin to think
they *are* what they, for a short
while, merely represent.

James Reston
New York Times
July 2, 1982

4
Christopher
Learning About Justice

Within a few days after Marnie and I had returned home to Phoenix following Richard Nixon's election as president, John Mitchell called me.

"Dick, the president-elect wants me to be the attorney general."

"Super, John, and congratulations," I responded with enthusiasm.

"Wait a minute. I really don't want the job. I'd much rather stay in New York and practice law. However, he is adamant. To come to the point, I've just informed him I would do it if I could have you as my deputy. How about it?"

"John, you should be the attorney general. You are a fine lawyer and an able administrator. Besides, by being a member of the president's cabinet, you would be available to him daily as a counselor and adviser. He really needs you. However, you don't need me for the same reasons he needs you. There are scores of lawyers better qualified than I who would jump at the opportunity. In addition, as you know, we have four children to educate and I'd better go back to making some money again."

There the matter lay, for a day or so. Then came another of those telephone calls from Richard Nixon which have had such an impact on me and my family.

"Dick, I need John as the attorney general. He's agreed to do it if you come back and help him."

"All right, sir, I'll do it."

I arrived in New York City the day after Thanksgiving to become a member of the transition team of the president-elect.

It is difficult, almost impossible, for a stranger to the federal government to comprehend the enormousness of the task, facing a newly elected president, of staffing the executive branch. The first priority is, of course, the selection of the members of the cabinet, and their deputies and assistant secretaries. Notwithstanding the prestige accorded those high positions, it is, more often than not, difficult to persuade qualified people to undertake such responsibilities. Personal financial sacrifice is usually involved. That such persons must be confirmed by the Senate is often enough to occasion a negative response.

However, hundreds of other positions on federal boards and commissions must also be filled. It is these positions that have come to mean the bureaucracy. They serve at the pleasure of the president and are customarily replaced by a newly elected president. And not without justification. They will be called upon to effect the policies of the new administration. Since many of these policies were the subject matter of political debate of the presidential campaign, it is only fair that the new president have in his administration persons who believe in those policies.

John Mitchell was engrossed in assisting Nixon in selecting persons for the cabinet when I arrived at my office in the Pierre Hotel, headquarters of the transition team. As a consequence, he delegated to me the responsibility of screening the large number of applications in the Department of Justice. Although more than anxious to get on with the assignment, I had no conception of the dimensions of the assignment.

My concept of the Department of Justice in late November 1968 was, to say the least, sophomoric. Like most lawyers around the country, I knew about the FBI and J. Edgar Hoover, was aware of the existence of U.S. attorneys and U.S. marshals, and, to be honest, that was about the extent of it. One hour after I had been handed the transition book pertaining to the Department of Justice, a book prepared by the outgoing administration, I knew I needed help, quickly.

Warren Christopher was the deputy attorney general then serving under Attorney General Ramsey Clark. In addition to having been a distinguished lawyer in Los Angeles, he had by everyone's account done an outstanding job at Justice. He was also a gentleman. Notwithstanding the obvious political differences between us, he made himself personally available to me as I endeavored to wade through the excellent summary of the department prepared under his supervision for the new administration. Without his selfless help, it would have been impossible for Mitchell and me to accomplish what we did before inauguration day.

Wisely it is said that a little bit of knowledge is a dangerous thing. Nevertheless, if there was to be a new administration at the Department of Justice, it was imperative that we, in the short span of six weeks, glimpse the many functions of the department. My eyes nearly popped out of my head at what I saw.

Eight assistant attorneys general were appointed by the president with the advice and consent of the Senate, and familiarization with the function of each was the first priority. The office of Legal Counsel is headed by an assistant attorney general, who is, in effect, the "lawyer's lawyer" for the president and the government. The other assistants headed these divisions of responsibilities: antitrust, civil, civil rights, criminal, internal security, land and natural resources, and tax. This was also my first introduction to the dedicated career lawyers at Justice. My respect for them would grow in the years ahead.

My first acquaintance with the bureaus of the department opened my eyes to the scope of Justice. J. Edgar Hoover and the FBI theretofore had been only a

TV series to me. The initial briefing given to me by the second in command, Cartha (Deke) DeLoach, convinced me that much intensive learning lay ahead. Jack Ingersoll outlined the staggering challenge faced by the Bureau of Narcotics and Dangerous Drugs in its attempt to deal with the burgeoning problem of marijuana, heroin, and other dangerous drugs; I resolved that this would be an area of deep concern to me. I had heard of the Border Patrol, but I little realized the problems presented by the millions of illegal aliens in the country. Immigration and Naturalization Service had an impossible task. Even though I was informed that the federal prison system was far superior to that of most of the states, it was made quite clear that the enormous problems of overcrowding and repeat offenders existed. The Community Relations Service impressed me as a thoughtful response to government's need for a listening post in our major cities, not only to anticipate violence, but, more important, to eradicate the roots of it. When I learned of the mission of the Law Enforcement Assistance Administration, however, I was relieved that Congress had finally devised a means by which the states and cities could come to grips with the growing problems of crime in America.

Perhaps the real eye-opener was the realization that there were ninety-three U.S. attorneys and the same number of U.S. marshals who were presidential appointees with the advice and consent of the Senate. Since they served at the pleasure of the president, they would be replaced, with few exceptions, in the coming months by the new president. Some thirty vacancies in the federal judiciary also had to be filled by presidential appointment, also with the advice and consent of the Senate. Filling all of these positions would acquaint me with the arcane ways of U.S. senators and provide lessons in the separation of powers of our federal government that I will never forget.

Amid this introduction to the Department of Justice, I inquired of Deputy Attorney General Christopher: "Just what is the deputy attorney general supposed to do about all of this?"

He smiled in a knowing way. "Pretty much what the attorney general decides." As usual, Christopher was right.

The deputy attorney general is just that—the attorney general's deputy. By law, the deputy attorney general becomes the acting attorney general in the absence of the attorney general or if the office of attorney general becomes vacant. Otherwise, the deputy does what the attorney general determines.

John Mitchell probably delegated more responsibility to me than most attorneys general had delegated to their deputies. For at least two reasons, I suppose. Since I had been one of his deputies in the recent presidential campaign, we knew each other better than most new attorneys general and their deputies did. Indeed, it is not uncommon for a new president to appoint a deputy attorney general who is a relative stranger to the attorney general. More important, Mitchell not only was the attorney general but would also function as a top policy adviser to the president in many other areas of responsibility. Consequently, he had less time for the administrative details of the department.

Mitchell and I worked well as a team. The president and Mitchell set the policy and I did my best to effect it. To do just that, I traumatized the bureaucracy by scheduling a meeting at 7:30 each morning on a rotating basis with each assistant attorney general and bureau head. (Hoover sent DeLoach in his stead.) The agenda of these meetings had been delivered to my office at least two days before. After these meetings I would meet at 9:00 A.M. with Mitchell and give him a rundown of the earlier briefing and receive from him any policy decision that had to be made. At 5:00 P.M. of each day I would again meet with Mitchell and rehearse the day's business. I can't remember a single day without a crisis of sorts. Depending on circumstances, these daily meetings could be over in minutes or consume hours. Otherwise, unless something unusual occurred, I rarely saw or talked to Mitchell during the day.

I had the highest opinion of John Mitchell as the sixty-seventh attorney general. Nothing that happened to him after he left that office on March 1, 1972, has changed that opinion. That opinion, I believe, is shared by most of the career lawyers and bureau personnel who served with him. He is an intelligent man and a great lawyer. A good listener, he never makes an impulsive or impromptu decision on anything of importance. He has no hangups and therefore is able to work effectively with all kinds of people.

The most important feature of his tenure, however, was the shield he erected between Justice and the White House staff. Not every attorney general has such a relationship with his president that permits that beneficial condition.

One of the most difficult situations an assistant attorney general or a bureau head can be confronted with is an end run around the attorney general by a member of the White House staff. The circumvention is more often than not born of a momentary crisis, poorly thought out, and inconsistent with the policy of the attorney general himself. Such interference, if permitted, can not only lead to mistakes with varying degrees of consequences, but also be detrimental to the morale of the department. Nevertheless, in the initial period of a new administration, confrontation is inevitable between a presidential aide and the attorney general. If the attorney general has the full confidence and respect of the president, he wins; if he does not, the White House staff wins. As the solicitor general Erwin Griswold and that old pro Henry Petersen of the criminal division can attest, Mitchell won the contest early on. Thereafter, and throughout his tenure as attorney general, requests from the White House came directly to him, as they should. Thus, Mitchell could get a report quickly from the proper source in the department, make his policy decision, and report back to the White House.

Mitchell thereby created an environment at Justice that made it an exhilarating place to work. The three and a half years I served as his deputy were the most rewarding years of my life. Others may judge whether I was effective or competent. I do know, however, that I never willingly worked so hard, never learned more, and never again will have the opportunity to gain such a knowledge of our government, of our fellow citizens, and the challenges we must face if we are to remain free.

Organizational politics is fun. It is heady business to motivate, then organize people in behalf of a candidate or party. At the same time, the politician doesn't have to assume the responsibility to govern.

It was readily apparent to me that discharging the duties of deputy attorney general might be challenging and exciting, but not fun. Indeed, it would be a deadly serious business, touching the whole social fabric of the country. I was awestruck—I would be involved in decisionmaking affecting dissent and protest, antitrust enforcement, organized crime, civil-rights enforcement, drug abuse, prisons, illegal aliens, and the FBI.

By the time I completed my six-week indoctrination course of the Department of Justice I had come to realize that my life as a politician had ended and that my life as an officer of the Department of Justice was beginning. Indeed, when in January 1969 I stood before Justice White in the Hall of Justice to take my oath of office, I concluded that so long as I held that office, I would have no further involvement in organizational politics.

5
Woody
Demonstration and Dissent in a Free Society

When I arrived in New York after Thanksgiving Day 1968, I was shocked to learn that one of the responsibilities of the attorney general was to help maintain law and order in the nation's capital in the event of mass demonstrations.

I was advised by Mitchell that one of my first assignments was to be his liaison with Attorney General Ramsey Clark and other officials of the outgoing administration who were involved in the security planning for Nixon's inauguration. "What are you talking about? What security planning?" I responded. It didn't take me long to find out.

Counterinaugural demonstrations had been planned—to my surprise—by the National Mobilization Committee to End the War in Vietnam, an organization that came to be known as MOBE. It had been formed in Washington, D.C., during the weekend of May 20–21, 1967. Deputy Attorney General Warren Christopher informed me that several hundred persons had registered at the conference. The registrants included over three hundred members of the Communist party, the W. B. DuBois Clubs of America, the Socialist Workers party, and the Young Socialist Alliance (also known as Youth Against War and Fascism). Christopher said that according to an extensive study by the House of Representatives Committee on Internal Security, MOBE was the successor to the November 8 Mobilization Committee, established in Cleveland on September 10–11, 1966, and the Spring Mobilization Committee to End the War in Vietnam, established on November 26–27, 1966, also in Cleveland.

The key leaders of MOBE had been identified by the House Internal Security Committee as members of the Communist party or of Communist youth groups:

- David Dellinger—cochairman and self-professed communist.
- Sidney M. Peck—cochairman and member of the Communist party.
- Helen Gurewit—New Mobe Staff and member of the Communist party.
- Sylvia Kushner—National Committee and member of the Communist party.

* Irving Sarnoff—National Committee and member of the Communist party.
* Douglas Dowd—Washington Action Committee cochairman and self-professed communist.
* Carleton Goodlett—National Committee and self-professed communist.

Coordinator for the counterinaugural was Rennie Davis, an open supporter of the Vietcong. Tom Hayden, a founder of the Students for a Democratic Society, and Dave Dellinger, then editor of *Liberation* and New MOBE chairman, were among those who assisted Davis.

At the conclusion of the initial briefing Christopher, moderately but forcefully, described the problem. How do you ensure the right of MOBE to exercise its constitutional right of free speech and assembly and at the same time discharge the duty of the government to regulate the exercise of that right in a manner calculated to protect the persons and property of others? The difficult problem for the government is to exercise its regulatory presence in such a way that it does not create an atmosphere that would tend to "inhibit the exercise of lawful speech and dissent." With that the briefing ended.

Having been raised in a small Arizona community composed mainly of a mixture of ethnic groups predominantly Roman Catholic and Democratic, and having been taught the Constitution by the like of Verla Oare, I was a devout believer in the First Amendment. Perhaps, like most Americans who have resided all their lives in smaller communities, far from the politics of their capital, free speech to me meant the right of an individual to stand before a gathering and say what he wanted. Most of us also have believed that the right of workers lawfully to picket their employer is a protected form of free speech. Martin Luther King gained national stature because he spoke in a peaceful manner about the injustice of racism in America. Whether we have agreed or not, we have espoused the right of citizens to speak as they wish, provided they do so lawfully.

But what do we do about those who seek to speak for causes that are not so inherently American? What about the communist who speaks to convince us that we should abolish our form of government—by force, if necessary—and substitute a socialist structure? What about those who publicly urge our young people to oppose our wars by refusing to serve when called? What do we do when such folk exhort massive demonstrations consisting of hundreds of thousands of protesters in our nation's capital and thereby potentially threaten the persons and property of others?

The easy answer for many without responsibility to act is usually, "Lock 'em up. If they don't love America, let 'em leave it." If, however, you have the responsibility to respond to mass dissent accompanied by unlawful conduct, you soon learn that there are no easy answers.

As a result of being directly involved in dissent commencing with the counterdemonstration to Nixon's inauguration in January 1969 and ending with the incident at Wounded Knee, South Dakota, in March 1973, I became convinced of two things. First, no matter how unpopular a cause, the federal government is obliged to provide an environment in which the dissenter can freely speak and function. Second, the federal government is obligated to do everything it lawfully can to prevent that dissent from deteriorating into anarchy and lawlessness. The difficulty is to discharge both obligations at the same time. It can be done, however, if the first obligation is approached with a deep commitment to the First Amendment and if the second obligation is met by careful planning in advance.

Two circumstances may necessitate a federal response to mass dissent that might lead to civil disorder: when it takes place in a state, and when it takes place in the District of Columbia.

A federal presence in a state comes about only when the governor or the state legislature certifies to the president that the regular police and the National Guard cannot maintain order. Thereupon, the president *may*, at his discretion, declare a state of emergency and employ federal resources to restore order. The phrase "federal resources" usually means the United States Army. If, however, a president really wants to chill the atmosphere of a civil demonstration, he may position a soldier with a gun at each intersection of a city, but such should be done very judiciously. Presidential discretion should also be exercised with caution for political purposes. Governors and state legislatures are creatures of the political process. Civil disorders can appear to have got out of hand and politicians may panic. When this happens, a governor or a legislature may be inclined to avoid political responsibility for an impending disaster by transferring the responsibility to the president. If the disaster does materialize, that governor or legislature may be quick to blame the man in the White House. Since the president got there through the same political process, he should be wary of a panic call for help. Still, the president has to be prepared to act in a proper situation.

The District of Columbia is a federal city and, therefore, presents a different problem. The president is the commander in chief of the District National Guard. The buildings that house the federal government—courts, Congress, and executive departments—are the most valuable property in the District. Federal employees constitute the largest work force in the city and have a right to protection of their persons in the event of civil disorder. The president must not rely only on the District police force to protect federal interests. Although he should act in cooperation with the police, he must be prepared to act on his own. In acting, he might have to call on regular federal troops if the National Guard proves inadequate. If he does call out the army, the National Guard is usually "federalized" as well.

Since the army is under the direction of the secretary of defense, one might logically assume that the secretary would be in charge of the federal response to civil disorders in the nation's capital. That is not the case. In modern times, presidents wisely have turned to the civil side of the federal government to advise them in this delicate area. The tactics taught to the professional soldier are usually incompatible with the broader dimension of internal civil dissent. Besides, the mere public presence of the secretary of defense could send a chill through the bones not only of the dissenter, but of the general public as well.

Before Nixon, our presidents delegated to the attorney general the responsibility to recommend whether a state of emergency should be proclaimed and the military should be used. Once such a decision was made, however, those presidents left it largely to the secretary of defense to decide what to do, how much to do, and how long to do it.

Perhaps because President Nixon took the oath of office in January 1969 amidst the disorder of a counterinaugural demonstration, or perhaps because John Mitchell was not only the attorney general but an intimate counselor of the president, or perhaps because of the combination of the two, the role of the attorney general was greatly expanded.

One of the first things that John Ehrlichman did after the president took office was prepare a memorandum for the president. Dated May 19, 1969, the memo was titled "Federal Response to Civil Disturbances." On April 1, Mel Laird, the secretary of defense, and John Mitchell, the attorney general, had submitted a memorandum to the president. Its subject was "Interdepartmental Action Plan for Civil Disturbances." To the great credit of both Laird and Mitchell, they advised the president that the attorney general—that is, the civil side of government—should recommend not only whether, but when, what, and how long federal troops should be employed.

Mitchell designated me his chief of staff with respect to this function, and I in turn looked to Harlington Wood, Jr., as my top sidekick. I never made a wiser decision in my years at Justice.

Wood is presently a federal judge on the U.S. Court of Appeals for the Seventh Circuit in Chicago. He was born in Springfield, Illinois, and is the most Lincolnesque man, in personal habits and public life, I have ever known. His public life started by his appointment as the United States attorney for the Southern District of Illinois in 1959 by President Eisenhower. In 1969 I recruited him for the Department of Justice and designated him as associate deputy attorney general for United States attorneys. In November 1970 he was named associate deputy attorney general in the capacity of the first assistant to the deputy attorney general. In 1972 President Nixon nominated and the Senate confirmed him as the assistant attorney general for the civil division. The next year President Nixon nominated him to be a federal district judge in the same district where he had been U.S. attorney. In 1976 President Ford appointed him to the prestigious court where he now sits.

Several principles guided us in the discharge of our security responsibilities from 1969 to 1973.

The first, and most important, was preparation. Preparation to deal with a demonstration that might not be or remain lawful is critical. Not being prepared to respond immediately to unlawful conduct means that it will inevitably escalate. And if it escalates, the fat is in the fire. The only response left is massive force and martial law. And the result is a failure for freedom.

How, then, should one prepare? At the outset, in 1969, we instinctively felt that preparation entailed, in essence, information, communication, and decision.

Information is vital. The best way to be prepared is to know—what is likely to happen, who or what will cause it to happen, how many, in what way, to what effect. In an open society like ours this information is easily obtained. When we came to Justice we were materially assisted by the existence of the Interdepartment Information Unit (IDIU), which Ramsey Clark had established in 1967. It was a single intelligence unit and had been created in the department to "determine the available facilities for keeping abreast of information received about organizations and individuals who may or may not be a force to be taken into account in evaluating the causes of civil disorders." The IDIU was also directed to "make full use of, and constantly endeavor to increase and refine the intelligence available, both from internal and external sources, concerning organizations and individuals throughout the country who may play a role either in instituting or spreading disorders or in preventing or checking them."

We needed a team of experts to analyze the facts and come up with judgments. We refined the IDIU by creating such a team. Cartha (Deke) DeLoach (then the number two officer of the FBI and one of the coolest men I have ever known) and, later, my close friend Bob Mardian, as the assistant attorney general of the Internal Security Division, headed the team. Their work was exemplary. By providing a measured analysis, they enabled us time and again to avoid decisions of hysteria on the one hand and ill preparation on the other. "Mayday" was our ultimate success.

Communication is also critical. The lack of it between human beings is responsible for many ills of mankind. If civil disorder threatens, many persons must become involved. In Washington, D.C., to name but a few in addition to the Department of Justice, they are: the mayor, chief of police, attorney for the District, commanding general of the National Guard, chief of the Capitol police, chief of the Park Service Police, head of the General Services Administration, White House, secretary or undersecretary of the army, U.S. attorney, Secret Service, FBI, U.S. marshals, Bureau of Prisons, and press.

Now, if your information tells you that civil disorder might occur and, if so, all these people might be involved, what is the best course to pursue? I'm convinced that the best course is to bring them all together at the beginning, share whatever information is available, and have each acknowledge his own particular responsibility—if the worst comes to the worst. For this approach to succeed, however, everyone involved must know everything. Secrecy is no aid. The labor of endless meetings is no undue expense. The endless planning and communication are the principal reasons why, in the nation's capital, not one person died or was seriously injured in a period of more active demonstrations than any other period in our country's history.

Information and its communication mean nothing, however, if decisions are not made. And that responsibility usually falls on one person—the president. Assembling the information, communicating it to all concerned, relating it to the attorney general, and presenting it to the president are for naught if the chief executive wavers or equivocates. I cannot recall of a single time when President

Nixon erred in his decision after having been presented all the facts. His uncanny ability to distinguish between the interests of free speech and dissent on the one hand, and the preservation of order on the other has always commanded my respect.

But, you may ask, what is the deputy attorney general or the attorney general doing coordinating these preparatory activities if his only function is to advise the president in an emergency? If he is to be involved at the end, he should be involved at the beginning. Perhaps by doing so, he may not have to be involved at the end. Having functioned as the information-communication coordinator for some four years, I think that procedure is correct.

The antecedents of the counterinaugural, Mayday, and other demonstrations trace to Vietnam. Our involvement there was one of the most tragic chapters of our history. Not because we were there, but because of the political bungling of the matter. I am an anticommunist. I oppose a political ideology that reduces mankind to nothing more than an economic being and a pawn of the state. I oppose a system of government that suppresses liberty—in religion, speech, art, philosophy, travel, science, work, and business.

Beginning with President Eisenhower, our reason for being in Vietnam was to prevent the spread of communism by other than democratic means. We learned from Hitler that acquiescence to imperialistic aggression thousands of miles from home will sooner or later bring it to our shores. A Chamberlainesque posture will eventually bring the enemy to the beaches of Hawaii or Southern California.

But in our free society we *cannot* send our sons thousands of miles away to fight a war and not tell them why. We do not fight wars for the sake of fighting wars. We fight them for freedom—to preserve the soul and dignity of man. The irredeemable misjudgment of President Johnson, in my opinion, is that he escalated our involvement in Vietnam without telling us why. No matter the 1964 campaign and LBJ's attack on Goldwater as a warmonger, and, while making the attack, his doing that which he criticized. What did matter was that the youth of America discovered that it was being bloodied eight thousand miles from home for reasons theretofore fuzzy. The result was predictable—dissent.

I know this feeling firsthand. My wonderful son Alfred was at Harvard College in 1969, when I became the deputy attorney general. It was hard for him to be the son of the deputy attorney general; it was hard for me to have him at Harvard at that time. It was my practice to call Kleinie (my nickname for him, which he has always hated) at school to get a reading on the temper of things there. I could rely upon his absolute candor and judgment. One morning our conversation went like this:

"How's everything going, Kleinie?"

He told me he had a tough decision to make that day.

"A tough decision about what?"

"I have to decide whether to strike against Harvard over the war."

"Kleinie, before you strike against the school you voluntarily have become a part of, you better get all the facts—you'd better know what I'm going to do if you in fact strike.''

"What are you doing—trying to repress me?"

"Kleinie, if you are big enough to strike, you're big enough to be on your own from here on out!"

Click went the phone. The next day he called to advise me that he and the rest of the "jocks" had decided not to strike. (Kleinie became a world champion in crew.) I'm glad he didn't strike. At the same time, as a result of knowing his character, I felt keenly the impact of the Vietnam War on our young people.

As could be expected, the antipathy of so many well-meaning Americans toward the war attracted some sordid folk. Among them were communists and their sympathizers, who sincerely desired our failure in Vietnam and the success of Hanoi. It is a measure of their political skill that they perceived and then seized upon the war as an opportunity worthy of exploitation. This, in my opinion, was the real antecedent of Mayday. For, as I will endeavor to demonstrate, that war protest by hundreds of thousands of decent, patriotic American citizens was used by a handful of dedicated communist revolutionaries in an attempt first to disrupt and then to destroy the institutions of freedom in America.

On January 19, 1969, some four thousand people staged demonstrations. Objects were thrown in front of the Smithsonian where there was a reception for Vice President and Mrs. Agnew. On inauguration day, several hundred demonstrators appeared along Pennsylvania Avenue, the parade route. Many threw rocks and smoke bombs at the parade in an attempt to halt and disrupt—and almost succeeded at Fifteenth Street—as I observed from my vantage point on a balcony at the Department of Justice. After the inaugural parade, they staged their own parade. Then many spread out, disrupting traffic and breaking windows. During the three-day period 119 people were arrested. Six were charged with the mutilation, burning, or desecration of the American flag.

In summer 1969, a group of antiwar leaders met again in Cleveland on July 4–5 to broaden and unify, as their call stated, the antiwar forces in the United States and to plan coordinated national antiwar actions for the fall. Sidney Peck, a leading MOBE official and a self-professed communist, was the primary organizer of the movement. From this meeting came the New Mobilization Committee to End the War in Vietnam (New MOBE). In addition to Peck, Dave Dellinger and Rennie Davis emerged as top leaders. They and New MOBE began preparations for what resulted in the mass demonstration of nearly three hundred thousand in Washington, D.C., November 15, 1969.

The same year, before November 15, several people connected with New MOBE attended two significant conferences organized by an international communist front, the World Peace Council. The first was in Stockholm on May 16–18, and the second was in East Berlin, June 21–24. The basic purpose of both meetings was to bring about the end of the war. Dr. Carleton Goodlett, a top MOBE official, attended both conferences and Irving Sarnoff, a member of the New MOBE Steering Committee and an identified member of the Communist party, USA, addressed the East Berlin assembly at length. He denounced the United States, supported the Vietcong and Hanoi, and urged the need to broaden and unify the antiwar movement in America.

New MOBE leaders then began the preparations for November 15, 1969, holding several planning meetings in various cities in the country. Their planning had become so successful that by October 24, 1969, the North Vietnamese prime minister Pham Van Dong cabled a long message from Hanoi to New MOBE. It ended by saying: "I wish your 'fall offensive' a brilliant success."

The demonstration on November 15 in Washington, D.C., drew people nationwide. The overwhelming majority of the three hundred thousand were peaceful, law-abiding citizens who wanted to demonstrate their opposition to the war. Others were not. Dave Dellinger, the last speaker, addressed the large crowd on the Washington Monument grounds. What took place afterward convinces me beyond a doubt that the New MOBE leaders deliberately planned mob violence. Dellinger delivered one of the most fiery revolutionary speeches ever given to such a large gathering in our history. It was a call to arms against America and its institutions of government. The object of attack was the Department of Justice and its lovely building five blocks away at Tenth and Constitution Avenue. As long as I live, I will never forget watching from John Mitchell's office as some ten thousand revolutionaries began their march down Constitution Avenue toward us. They marched in tight formation, thirty to forty abreast. Nearly all carried flags, banners, and signs—the hammer and sickle of communism, the flag of North Vietnam, and antiwar and anti-Nixon slogans—and all chanted: "One, two, three, four, we don't want your fucking war."

Soon the formation had completely filled Constitution Avenue in front of our building from Ninth Street to Tenth Street, spilling over into the Smithsonian across the street. Then came the assault: rocks, paint, noise bombs, stink bombs, and gas. The American flag was hauled down and destroyed; in its place was hoisted the flag of North Vietnam. When several policemen attempted to bring it down, they were stoned, beaten, and kicked.

Here one of the most able police chiefs in America, Jerry Wilson, took over. Leading his fellow officers without weapon or other protection except a helmet, he began a tear-gas assault on the mob that eventually led to its dispersal. For three days Wilson, as the tactical field commander, had acted with restraint. His well trained officers stoically endured every indignity—even having human waste thrown upon them. But enough was enough, and in but a few minutes the mob was dispersed. The demonstration was over.

The results of the mob: property damage, more than $1 million; injuries, 606; arrests, 338.

November 15 taught us much. Principally, we learned that our government could do two things at the same time: permit massive dissent by peaceful citizens and control the violence of a revolutionary mob. So far as I was concerned, no real basis existed for fearing that in America a violent mob could ever overthrow our government by force.

Little did we realize that November 15 would be our training ground for Mayday. But that training produced an experienced group of government officials who shared common experiences and, most important, common goals. Their mettle would be tried by many demonstrations in Washington and throughout the country before April 1971. Spring 1970, for instance, saw numerous demonstrations on college campuses. Kent State turned out to be the peak. There some two thousand students engaged in lawlessness, which included the destruction by fire of an ROTC building. Five hundred National Guardsmen were called out. On May 4, 1970, four students were killed and seven wounded by rifle fire. Although that tragic event merits its own treatise, suffice it to say that it seemed to shock students, administrators, police, and National Guard units around the country into the realization that unrestrained violence leads inevitably to tragedy.

On April 24, 1971, the National Peace Action Coalition, composed of nonviolent and lawful persons and groups, staged perhaps the largest demonstration ever held in Washington, D.C. The antiwar theme attracted over four hundred thousand, who marched from the Washington Monument area to the Capitol. It was nonviolent and only twenty-five persons were arrested.

During the latter part of 1970 an organization known as the Peoples Coalition for Peace and Justice (PCPJ) began to make noise. It was an offshoot of New MOBE. Its principal spokesman at the outset was Sidney Peck. Besides Peck, some thirty-five present or former members of the Communist party were active in the formation of PCPJ. At least seven members of its coordinating committee were influential members of the Communist party. As early as June 1970 these PCPJ leaders had met at a strategy action conference in Milwaukee and begun to plan Mayday. Thereafter, they traversed the country, speaking to students and inviting them to Washington to shut down the government by blocking the streets and bridges of the capital. The PCPJ chiefs also met repeatedly with representatives of the Vietcong in conference at Stockholm. A PCPJ leader met twice with the North Vietnam delegation at the Paris Peace Talks. Later, in 1970, movement heads went to Hanoi and negotiated a so-called Peoples Peace Treaty with North Vietnamese students. On February 7, 1971, at Ann Arbor, Michigan, a meeting styled a student and youth conference on a "people's peace" approved final plans for the Mayday disruption and sent out a call for support. A Washington headquarters was established. Participants were recruited all over the country. Orientation sessions for regional leaders were held in Washington in early April. A twenty-four-page Mayday Tactical Manual was printed and distributed through the coalition's regional offices; and PCPJ's tabloid, "Quicksilver Times," printed a special Mayday issue. They gave detailed descriptions of the key bridges and traffic circles leading into the central city, explicit instructions on how to block them, and assignments to specific groups.

Washington, D.C., is a compact area, separated from Virginia by the Potomac River. Encircling it is U.S. 495, the Beltway, an expressway. Some three hundred thousand commuters use it to enter the capital from the suburbs. Most of the commuters are employed by the government. Bridges cross the Potomac into the District; morning and evening traffic is slow and tedious. If an accident occurs on one of the Beltway exits or on one of the bridges, traffic backs up for miles and can be delayed several hours. We resided in McLean, Virginia, fifteen miles from my office. It could take from thirty minutes to two hours to get to work in the morning. To the PCPJ, "stopping the government" simply meant stopping the government worker from getting to and from work. The Mayday issue of the "Quicksilver Times" demonstrates the mentality we were dealing with:

Washington, D.C. is a colony. It is ruled by a committee of Congress made up of racist white southerners. The overwhelming number of people living in Washington are black. Virtually the only industry in Washington is the Federal Government with the overwhelming majority of the employees being white and with a few exceptions, all upper echelon employees being white. This means that most employees of the Federal Government commute to work each day from the suburbs of Virginia and Maryland.

Because of the racist nature of the Federal Government, closing down the apparatus that controls the War against Indochina and America's oppressed is a relatively easy operation if it is coordinated.

Our disruption of Washington must be seen as an attack on the Federal Government, specifically those sections dealing with the war against the people of Indochina and America. It must not be seen as an attack on the employees of the Federal Government. We wish to win them as allies and so we need to minimize their antagonism towards us.

By May every government employee will know that to attempt to get to work he or she will have to brave a six-hour traffic jam. We are attempting to create a "four-day weekend" consciousness among government employees. If this is successful any employees caught in traffic jams will blame themselves for attempting to get to work and therefore, not us.

The main defect of PCPJ's audacious plan to stop the government was that, to attract the thousands of bodies it required to succeed, PCPJ had to go public. Consequently, we were informed from the outset what the plan was. The only thing we didn't know was how many. The answer to that vital question would determine how many of us. The police force of the District was then in excess of 5,000; the National Guard, 2,000; the Park Service Police, 500; the Capitol police, 400. The surrounding cities of Maryland and Virginia could contribute up to 800 police officers. If we were to be met by two or three thousand, no problem; if, on the other hand, by ten to twenty thousand, that would be another story.

Ten days before Mayday our best estimates of the force out to stop the government did not exceed four thousand. Good planning dictated contingencies for more, but our judgment argued to the contrary. We were to be rudely shocked.

I felt government should presume that our citizens would act lawfully; therefore, we recommended that a demonstration-site permit be negotiated with the PCPJ. Woody was the negotiator for the government. It was issued for West Potomac Park, a large area bounded on the south by the Potomac River and on the north by Independence Avenue, and away from business and residential areas. Its eastern end narrowed to meet at a small bridge. The western end was open and near the Lincoln Memorial.

On Friday evening, April 30, there was only a handful of persons in West Potomac Park. Then things began to happen. By midnight, a thousand; by 6:00 A.M., Saturday, May 1, four thousand; and by midmorning the same day, nearly eight thousand.

One technique of leaders of a mass demonstration was to plan, schedule, and announce a rock festival. Given the right entertainers, such a festival can attract many thousands. The PCPJ had a "rock festival," beginning late Saturday afternoon in West Potomac Park. At midnight a hundred thousand populated the park and environs.

This presented our most difficult problems. How many would remain and participate in Mayday? Even if they did not participate, how many would remain for the show? Both questions were critical. By now we all were agreed that we had to meet a force of over five thousand and that the army would be necessary to secure the bridges and their entrances. But where could we secure personnel to manage some eighty thousand onlookers and simultaneously deal with the anticipated violence of those determined to stop the government?

A permit for a group to use a park in Washington carries with it the obligation to do and not do certain things. The PCPJ, by Saturday evening, May 1, had violated every term of its permit—use of drugs, indecent exposure, fires, etc. Accordingly, by Saturday evening the planning committee had decided to cancel the permit and declare the assembly unlawful. The primary basis of this decision was to determine how many would remain for Mayday. Accordingly, at daybreak on Sunday, May 2, Chief Wilson aroused the mass of people at the park with a bullhorn and intoned: "This is an unlawful assembly. You are requested to leave. You have an hour to do so. Those remaining thereafter will be subject to arrest."

They left, nearly a hundred thousand of them.

This accomplished our first objective. But now the perplexing question, Where did the Mayday force disappear and how many were there? We were soon to get our answers.

By Sunday afternoon, we all agreed that we had to contend with about ten thousand the next morning. That figure was double our estimate of just a few days before. Consequently, to free the civilian police forces for maintaining order, the decision was made to situate army personnel on and near the bridges during the night. Near the soldiers would be civilian officers to make arrests, if needed. Fire trucks, tow trucks, buses, cranes, and other equipment were moved to strategic locations. Medical teams were prepositioned to come to the aid of victims stranded on the parkways in the anticipated traffic jam.

If stopping the government meant preventing the government workers from getting to work, we would implement a plan to catch the PCPJ with its pants down. One telephone call from me on Sunday evening set in motion a series of telephone calls in the government. By 5:00 A.M. Monday, some fifty thousand key government employees were in their offices. The plan worked without a slip. My hat will ever be off to those fellow citizens who worked for their government in Washington; they showed that ideological hoods could not keep them from discharging their responsibilities.

At midnight Chief Wilson, Roland Gleszer, commanding general of the Military District of Washington, and I made our last round of the city. Wilson and I agreed to meet again at 4:30 the next morning. As we toured the city, what we saw made our eyes pop out. From everywhere—alleys, streets, buildings—thousands of young people began walking to their predetermined destinations. We soon realized that our estimate of ten thousand was low by at least half. We also were soon to discover that we had grossly misjudged their plans.

Approximately twenty thousand disrupters tried their best to fulfill their announced intention of paralyzing Washington and stopping the government. They did this by widespread and unremitting acts of violence. The minute-by-minute police log of May 3 and numerous on-the-spot photographs of the incidents show conclusively that the disrupters endangered people and property.

They rolled boulders into streets, laid metal pipes across roadbeds, strung barbed wire and ropes across streets, set fire to trash cans, spread nails on roads, threw rocks and bottles at passing motorists, removed manhole covers, slashed at motorists with wooden poles, smashed windows, slashed tires, overturned cars, pushed parked vehicles into traffic lanes, ripped down signs and traffic markers. They stopped a fire truck trying to get to a fire and took away its ladders to use in blocking traffic. They pushed an automobile trailer down a steep hill, completely destroying the trailer and spilling its contents over the street. They cleared a path through the underbrush on a steep hill overlooking a boulevard, held a truck in place at the top with steel cables, then cut the cables; the truck plummeted into the street. They blocked police emergency vehicles, turned on fire hydrants, disabled city buses and commuters' autos, abandoned old cars on bridge approaches and in tunnels, and dumped all manner of trash into the streets. They stoned and beat policemen and tried to prevent them from making arrests. The number of policemen injured by the end of Mayday week was thirty-nine.

At 6:30 A.M. on Monday, Chief Wilson suspended normal field arrest processes, thus enabling the rapid arrest of thousands of persons engaging in unlawful conduct.

Chief Wilson addressed the Philadelphia Bar Association on June 7, 1971. With his permission, I quote a portion of that address:

Before the morning of May 3 broke, we estimated that the demonstrators might have developed the capacity to produce upwards of ten thousand or more demonstrators, we believed, in illegally blocking traffic. Given the lower figure, we established our details for that date, prepared to use standard field arrest procedures, which require contemporaneous report writing and photographing, a process which consumes ideally about one minute for each individual arrest. However, by 6:30 that morning, it was obvious to me that if normal field arrest procedures were continued, all traffic in the downtown area could be stopped by the demonstrators, the government might be prevented from opening, and the city would be exposed to the great potential hazards which are presented by any traffic blockage preventing movement of fire, ambulance, and police emergency vehicles. Consequently, I ordered that normal field arrest processes be suspended so that the thousands of persons engaging in disorderly conduct and traffic stoppage could be rapidly arrested.

Let me read to you a few excerpts from a log of radio transmissions broadcast during the critical moments before the decision to suspend the field arrest processes was made.

0603	North Capitol Street—group heading south.
0604	Connecticut and R. Blocking street—about 50.
0604	50 1700 Massachusetts blocking. 2 cars overturned Connecticut and Calvert.
0604	14th & Independence—SOD bus responding.
0605	Injured officer at Wisconson & M.
0606	Cr. 6—all units hold transmissions to emergency only.
0606	Prisoner control bus needed at Potomac Avenue, S.E.
0606	14th & Jefferson need more police—large crowd.
0606	34th & Prospect N.W.—large group.
0607	Large group Dupont Circle—trash on Massachusetts—large group in roadway 1600 block of New York.
0608	Mount Vernon Park—large group about 1,000.
0608	17th and Q being now blocked.
0608	3100 M needs a bus—bus 51 going in.
0609	New Hampshire Ave. north of Dupont—barricades in road.
0609	East side Dupont 500 in roadway—send help and bus.
0610	Gas is being used on Prospect Street.
0612	100 at 9th and New York.
0613	P Street blocked north of Dupont—cars and trash in road.
0613	Connecticut and N laying pipes in road.

These excerpts demonstrate the nature of the situation which confronted us during those early hours on May 3, and the problems depicted in the log increased in intensity until I made the decision at approximately 6:30, to discontinue the use of field arrest forms. That decision, as you well know, has been severely damned by a few and greatly praised by many. The mail my department has received from across the country has been better than 90 percent supportive of the action we took, and a poll by the Opinion Research Corporation indicated 76 percent of Americans thought that the large-scale arrests were justified.

You, as lawyers, know, however, that police work must meet a standard different than public sentiment. An all-important question is whether or not the police action in any given instance is reasonable and justified for preservation of order and domestic tranquility.

Now, some say that the police acted illegally—that they suspended the Constitution on May 3, 1971. At the president's press conference on June 1, 1971, a reporter stated that the defendants "are not being released on the grounds that guilt isn't proven. They are being released on the grounds that they weren't properly arrested."

The validity of the arrests was *not* challenged by the court, which dismissed cases not for lack of evidence, but for inability to relate the evidence to a particular defendant. There is no requirement in the Constitution or in D.C. law for using field arrest forms. Those forms had been previously adopted as an administrative procedure, and their use can be suspended during an emergency situation at the discretion of the chief of police.

The reason for the suspension of forms for seven hours and twenty-five minutes on May 3, was that the offenses of thousands bent on destroying government were coming so fast that there was no opportunity for officers to fill out the forms. To do so at the time would have kept the officers from preventing the disruption of the nation's capital. This is not an excuse for violating lawful processes. The arrests made without the forms were perfectly legal. But according to the critics, the policemen should have turned their backs on the rampaging mob to busy themselves with clerical duties.

The sheer volume of unlawful acts necessitating arrests made it very difficult for arresting officers later to link up defendants with specific offenses. Some innocent bystanders who ignored warnings to leave certain areas unfortunately were arrested in the confusion. But this was part of the calculated scheme of the lawbreakers to disrupt all the processes of government, including those of the police.

That the courts did not consider these arrests illegal is shown by the statement of the chief judge of the Superior Court of the District of Columbia: "The fact is that thousands of persons were arrested under circumstances which in many instances would not permit the gathering of evidence. This court has no criticism of that procedure."

Again, some urged that those arrested were detained for a long period of time to keep them from going back on the streets and creating more disturbances. A spokesman of the ACLU wrote: "There is not a shred of evidence that there was any intention of releasing them until after the crisis had passed. . . ."

The record, however, shows that the police processed the defendants as fast as physically possible in the face of the massive enforcement problem forced upon them, and that undue delays were caused mainly by the defendants themselves—including the hundreds who refused to identify themselves.

Of about 7,500 arrested on May 3, most were given the opportunity, beginning the same day, to be released by posting collateral of $10 each. By noon of the next day about 4,700, or more than 60 percent, were released. The same Monday 400 persons were presented by the police in court and released on bail. Of the remaining 2,400, approximately 1,000 were released after submitting to court-ordered photographing and fingerprinting. About 600 were released without even that requirement, so that by Tuesday night only about 500 persons who refused to be processed were in custody. They were released the next day, May 5. The remaining 300 or so either were charged with more serious offenses or were juveniles and processed in a separate manner.

Those are the facts. Under the conditions deliberately imposed by the organized disrupters, the police did a remarkably fast job of processing those arrested—faster than the law itself required under the circumstances. The real cause of any delay was the determination of the disrupters to shut down the services of the city, including the processes of justice. As their Mayday Tactical Manual said, "It greatly enhances our tactical position if the jails and detention facilities are filled with demonstrators." And the "Quicksilver Times" reported: "Many people are choosing to post no bail in Washington, since it is expected that tens of thousands of arrests will take place and the judicial system can be effectively paralyzed if people stay in jail."

The critics who charged that due process of law was inadequate said little about the masses of people whose express purpose was overwhelming the legal processes. That is like a skyjacker forcing a pilot to fly to Cuba and then complaining because the plane runs out of gas on the way.

Moreover, those eager to return to the streets for more "free speech" were certainly accommodated. Over a two-week period some 630 persons were arrested two and even three times.

Mayday marked the end of deliberately planned violence in the nation's capital as a mean of demonstrating against the Vietnam War. Distinguished from prior demonstrations, Mayday was no umbrella operation; it was an open attempt by a mob to disrupt and paralyze our federal government. It failed. And not one gun was fired by the police, the National Guard, or the army. Not one person died. Chief Wilson, General Gleszer of the Military District of Washington, Major General Southward of the D.C. National Guard, their officers and men, and all others who assisted deserve much praise.

Mayday should tell us that violence as a means of articulating our beliefs in America is self-defeating. Senator Kennedy was too quick to say, immediately after Mayday, that its activities were "civil disobedience in the American tradition of Thoreau and Martin Luther King." This was not correct and I doubt that the senator now believes it is correct.

I think the principal reason Mayday failed was that the protesters had no basis of complaint; they had been deprived of no constitutional right to articulate their lawful protests. Woody saw to that. He placed the presumption of lawful conduct in their favor, devoting days to patient dialogue with the PCPJ leaders. Every reasonable request for demonstration permits was granted. Sanitation facilities were provided and the city even made public address equipment available for their use.

When Jane Fonda insisted upon a permit to address a crowd of a hundred thousand persons in the Elipse, just south of and in full view of the White House, it was granted. Woody was of the opinion—and I agreed—that if Jane Fonda were denied the right to be heard in such a significant location, she would have the basis for a new political action organization. One can easily imagine what it might have been called, what the new slogans might have been. She and her cause were defeated, however, for the simple reason that she was given the opportunity to speak. Woody and I were part of the throng that had gathered to hear her. By the time her harangue had finished, we both were certain the day was ours. Hers was not a reasoned protest against an unpopular war, but an unreasoned indictment of the institutions of our government, one being the First Amendment right of free speech and assembly. Her remarks turned off the large majority of her audience. If all Americans could have heard her on that day, their faith in this unique system of government would have been reaffirmed. Miss Fonda confirmed my belief that free speech can stand on its own.

Mayday prepared us to meet the problems that were forecast for the national political conventions of both parties in Miami Beach the following year. The memory of the shocking violence at the Democratic convention in Chicago in 1968 was still vivid in the minds of many Americans, especially Reubin Askew, the governor of Florida. The Vietnam War invited trouble.

The Democratic convention was to open on July 10 and the Republican convention on August 21. In early 1972 our Interdepartmental Intelligence Unit predicted the high probability of huge demonstrations, with violence, at both conventions, particularly the Democratic. The prediction created a difficult situation for us in the Republican Department of Justice. If our response proved to be inadequate and the convention process of the Democrats was interfered with, we could be accused that the inadequacy was politically motivated. If our response was excessive, we would be open to the accusation that we deliberately interfered with legitimate speech and dissent.

Neither accusation was made, thanks to Governor Askew and Harlington Wood, Jr.

Reubin Askew is one of the outstanding men in public life I have met. He is proof that one can be a statesman while a politician. He and Woody were made for each other. Together they ensured that the two conventions would function as they should have.

Our intelligence forecast prompted me to ask Woody, on May 1, 1972, to assume the direct responsibility, as the senior civilian representative of the federal government, for the Miami conventions. Although he was then the assistant attorney general in charge of the department's civil division, practically all of his time was devoted to this responsibility until August 25, when he returned to Washington after the Republican convention.

On May 8 I called Governor Askew and briefly outlined what our intelligence was and what the function of the federal government was in such situations. His response was thoughtful and polite. He advised that he would be in Washington on May 12 and suggested a meeting. Woody and I met him at 2:00 P.M. in his suite at the Washington Hilton Hotel. The governor was accompanied by William Reed, commissioner of the Florida Department of Law Enforcement, and Edward Dunn, his general counsel and now a Florida state senator. The meeting set the tone for the next four months. Not before or since have so many governmental agencies functioned so harmoniously in such a delicate political environment. Each agency did what it was supposed to do—not more and no less.

By June 7 Woody attended the first general meeting in Miami Beach of all the federal, state, county, and local officials that would be involved. The role of the federal government was fully explained. Those from the Florida agencies were relieved to know that theirs was the first responsibility and that the federal presence would be felt only if their resources proved inadequate. They were able to understand, however, that if the federal response, if needed, was to be effective, the representatives of the federal agencies must be involved in all phases of planning from the very beginning.

By June 20, preparations had progressed sufficiently to justify briefing the Congress and the chairmen of the two parties. Woody and I met Governor Askew and his party at National Airport at 2:30 P.M. We proceeded to the office of Senator Mansfield, the distinguished majority leader of the Senate and now our ambassador to Japan. The presence of the Democratic governor of Florida made this meeting productive. He described in detail the cooperative planning between the federal government and the state of Florida. The presentation cleared the air politically. Larry O'Brien, chairman of the Democratic party, and the Democratic congressional delegation left Mansfield's office generally satisfied. When one considers the charged atmosphere of a presidential election year and the probability of nasty demonstrations at the conventions, the meeting was no mean achievement. Especially so in light of the facts that I had been sworn in as the attorney general only a week before (after a long and politically charged confirmation hearing) and that on the preceding Friday, three days before, burglars had broken into O'Brien's Watergate office.

The conventions were relatively noneventful. To be sure, there were demonstrations. At 5:00 P.M., July 11, the second day of the Democratic convention, a large demonstration by Cubans, gays, Students for a Democratic Society, and the like took place. It was soon dispersed by state and local authorities. On July 12 another demonstration tried to get off the ground, without success. A small demonstration took place the next day and that was the end of it. Without advance planning, complete coordination, and hour-by-hour communication among all concerned, the results probably would have been different.

The convention of the Republicans in August was characterized by smaller demonstrations but more violence and arrests. On August 20 the VVAW (Vietnam Veterans Against War) and the Attica Brigade staged a march, and at eight o'clock that evening some three hundred SDSers roughed up older citizens and beat on cans in front of the Fontainbleu Hotel, convention headquarters. The last event took place the next day when the VVAW marched to a nearby high school. Some marchers gained access to the roof and were taken into custody by the National Guard, without incident.

On August 24, the day after the convention adjourned, there was a general meeting of all participants at the Dade County Command Post. All were unanimous in their opinion that potential troubles had been avoided and that the two major political parties had had successful conventions. As it turned out, the problems that developed were carefully handled by local authorities, without any call for federal help.

In spring 1973 Senator Ervin requested the executive branch to submit to his committee a report on the federal response at the two conventions. Governor Askew wrote me a letter on May 23, 1973, for inclusion in our report. It read, in part:

> Prior to the conventions, we—the officers of the local, state and federal governments charged with the responsibility of assuring public safety—pledged to do everything within our power to insure that both conventions were held in an atmosphere of respect for the constitutional rights and safety of all persons, delegates and non-delegates, residents and non-residents.
>
> Our pledge was well kept. . . . It was, in the final analysis, a great "team effort."
>
> The intelligence information furnished to our law enforcement community by the Department of Justice was, in our opinion, invaluable in planning for all contingencies to insure public safety and the right of free expression for all those who were to attend the conventions. . . .
> Credit for the success of the public safety responsibility is due to the combined efforts of many persons and agencies. But I want to take this opportunity to reiterate my particular appreciation to you and Mr. Harlington Wood, Jr., the Senior Civilian Representative of the Department of Justice, for the tremendous non-partisan cooperation and assistance which you gave us in the planning, funding and execution of our state's responsibilities in the area of public safety . . . at no time since becoming Governor have I received greater cooperation from federal agencies.
>
> Congrats, Woody!

Wounded Knee was the last time Woody and I were together in responding to dissent. He was soon to leave the department to become the federal district judge in his hometown of Springfield, Illinois. I was soon to exit out the back door of the department by resigning out of sheer frustration with the idiocies that surfaced in the carnival atmosphere of Watergate.

On the night of February 27, 1973, a caravan of armed Indians occupied Wounded Knee, South Dakota, on the Pine Ridge Reservation of the Oglala Sioux. Thereupon, one of the saddest and potentially most explosive incidents of modern dissent unfolded. If the talents and personality of Woody were needed, Wounded Knee was the place.

I was born and raised on the southernmost tip of the Navajo Indian Reservation. When our mother died in the 1930s, Marion Chisinez, a young Navajo woman, came to live with us. She kept the house and tried her hand at cooking. My father didn't think much of either, but here "depression compensation" made amends. Marion also began teaching me the Navajo language. To this day I can count and speak enough words to buy and sell. On weekends her relatives often came to town in their wagons. Usually they parked in our back yard and visited Marion in her room. There they chanted and sang the ballads of the Navajo to the accompaniment of my clapping and humming. Several times she and her family invited me to witness tribal dances on the reservation. They have a long and proud history. But they bore then, as today, the sadness acquired when white men from far away began to come west and settle on lands used by the Navajo for hunting, fishing, herding, and growing.

All American Indians have grown up hearing of the atrocities of the white man, of his broken promises, and of the many broken treaties by his government in Washington. Placed on "reservations," on the least desirable lands, the Indians have endured as wards of Uncle Sam; that is, as third-class citizens subject to governmental policies. The object of those policies has been to degrade the Indians' culture and to make them a part of the white man's culture. I say "a part of" advisedly. Even though our government has made some attempts at education, it has failed miserably in equipping the American Indian for the white man's way of life.

The modern story of Wounded Knee began in December 1890, after U.S. Indian Service police killed the Sioux leader Sitting Bull at Standing Rock. Chief Big Foot, then old and sick, wanted to surrender rather than become a target of the police himself. But first he decided to lead his band of Minneconjau Sioux to Pine Ridge. Once there, he intended to surrender under the hoped-for protection of the great Oglala chief, Red Cloud. This movement was determined to be aggressive by the U.S. Cavalry and the War Department issued orders for the immediate arrest of Chief Big Foot. Big Foot, of course, was not aware of such an order. Accordingly, when on December 28 he and his people approached Porcupine Creek, he ran up a white flag when four troops of cavalry appeared. When the cavalry major informed Big Foot that his orders required him to take the Sioux to the cavalry camp on Wounded Knee Creek, Big Foot willingly consented since Pine Ridge was in that direction.

When they arrived at Wounded Knee Creek, the Indians were counted and assigned a camp area. There were 120 men and over 200 women and children. The next morning the soldiers surrounded the Indian camp and ordered that all arms be surrendered. This order was complied with by all except one young Sioux named Black Coyote. He raised his Winchester above his head and shouted that he had paid a lot for it and that it was his. The soldiers grabbed him and spun him around. The gun went off, harming no one. The massacre of Wounded Knee began. Four men and forty-seven women and children survived.[1]

The leaders of the modern Indians who occupied two churches, a trading post, a museum, and two private homes at Wounded Knee that night in February 1973 are different from the likes of Chief Big Foot. They are part of the American Indian Movement (AIM). They are young, educated, articulate, and militant. They are fighting against the despair that has settled upon their communities. Eschewing the resignation that long has characterized the American Indian, they are doing what other minority groups have done for three decades—engaging in political action. Sometimes their political action has been deliberately unlawful. They fully understand the probable consequences of unlawful conduct, however; they are willing to pay the price. If nothing else, incidents like Wounded Knee dramatize the plight of the Indian in modern America. Consequently, if law-enforcement authorities deal with them in a manner that ignores the basic forces that motivate their conduct, if the authorities deal with them as if they were hoodlums and criminals, the end result may be tragedy and martyrdom. This could have been the result at Wounded Knee in 1973, had it not been for the arrival of Woody on the scene on March 13.

AIM took over Wounded Knee to protest its longstanding objection to the general policies of the Bureau of Indian Affairs, an agency of the Department of the Interior. It also believed that the tribal council chairman, Richard Wilson, was guilty of maladministration of tribal affairs and, most important, was dominated by white ranchers who leased reservation lands for cattle grazing.

Whether you sympathize with the motives of AIM or not, the seizure of property and the holding of persons hostage cannot be condoned. The response came from the federal government, not South Dakota, because of unlawful conduct on an Indian reservation. The response was immediate and, in my opinion, overpowering.

At the outset FBI agents and Bureau of Indian Affairs police blocked all roads leading out of the seized village. Unfortunately, shots were fired by the occupying Indians, leading to a state of siege that lasted seventy-one days.

The United States Marshal's Service is an arm of the Department of Justice and was then headed by Wayne Colburn, one of my closest friends and a trusted fellow officer. He had created a special operations group, comparable to an elite strike force, for a situation like this. I asked Colburn to take his group to the scene and remain there as long as necessary. Wayne had been up and down the

1. Dee Brown, *Bury My Heart at Wounded Knee*, gives a full account of this tragic event.

hill with Woody and me many times in the past and shared our basic philosophy. He understood his mission—avoid bloodshed and hold the fort until lines of communication could be established with the Indian leaders. His mission was not easy to fulfill. The Bureau of Indian Affairs transferred additional police and also requested that the Department of Defense make available armored personnel carriers for placement at the roadblocks. The government forces operated under strict fire-control procedures and were to return fire only when necessary to protect their own lives. Hundreds of shots were fired each night by the offending Indians. The weather was bitter cold.

Wilson, the tribal council chairman, regarded the seizure as an act of insurrection against him and the government, and had no patience for a standoff until negotiations could begin. He opted for a frontal assault and said that he could muster several hundred armed white ranchers to back his own forces. It was Colburn's job to inform him, in no uncertain terms, that that was precisely what he would not do.

Opening a dialogue with armed political activists is extremely difficult. At first it seemed impossible. Providentially, however, the Reverend John P. Adams, a minister of the United Methodist church, had been dispatched to the area by his bishop, Rt. Rev. James Armstrong, and directed to remain there as his personal representative. Bishop Armstrong had been asked to intercede in the confrontation by Dr. W. Sterling Corey, president of the National Council of Churches. That organization had affirmed in a telegram to the president, to me as attorney general, and to others, that "as Christians, we are compelled to express our deep concern that this current conflict be resolved through sympathetic negotiation with those who are aggrieved."

John Adams arrived in Pine Ridge on Friday afternoon, March 2, 1973. He has written of his experiences at Wounded Knee, Resurrection City, and Kent State in his thought-provoking *At the Heart of the Whirlwind* (New York: Harper & Row, 1976). The book is his firsthand report on a new Christian ministry—healing mediation in special conflict.

Even though it was late afternoon when he arrived, Adams immediately made arrangements to go through the federal roadblock. When he informed the three young Indians at the Indian roadblock of his mission, he was allowed to pass. He met with officers of the Oglala Sioux Civil Rights Organization as well as with the national leaders of AIM—Dennis Banks, Russell Means, Clyde Bellecourt, and Carter Camp. Of that first meeting Adams wrote: "Local leaders and AIM representatives declared that they stood ready to die and that the occupation would continue until some high-level official in Washington came to Wounded Knee to engage in good-faith discussions about treaty rights and take action on problems endemic to the Pine Ridge Reservation specifically." In addition, they discussed the problems confronted by the residents trapped inside. Food was running short and the bitter cold had caused a number of persons to become sick. The AIM leaders also wanted one phone so that they could talk to their lawyers.

How does one begin a good-faith dialogue with persons willing to die on the one hand, and, on the other, wanting to renegotiate treaties that were negotiated decades ago? Only a person of the caliber of John Adams could even hope to find a beginning place.

When Adams arrived on March 2, the chief negotiator for the federal government was Ralph Erickson, the former deputy attorney general. He and Colburn had advised me that he had just about run out his string and that if the impasse was to be broken, a new face with a new approach was needed. We all agreed that the time for Woody had arrived.

Woody made some inquiries with friends close to the peace movement to see if there was anybody at Wounded Knee he had met during the D.C. demonstrations. He was informed of the presence of John Adams. As he hurriedly departed Washington for Pine Ridge he asked that word be sent to Adams that he wanted to talk to him as soon as he arrived.

The next morning, March 13, Woody and Adams got together at reservation headquarters and Woody advised him that he wanted to talk to the AIM leaders as soon as he could. Adams departed for Wounded Knee. The AIM leaders informed Adams that they were willing to open negotiations again, but only on the condition that Woody come inside the blockade. Adams drove back to Pine Ridge fearful that Woody would refuse to meet the condition. (Adams believed that an assistant attorney general would run no risk of being taken hostage.) He didn't know Woody. By 12:30 P.M. they both were in Adams' car on the way to Wounded Knee. Before they left, both Colburn and the FBI special agent in charge urged Woody not to go. Colburn knew Woody well enough to know that he would not follow their advice.

Woody is six feet four inches tall. He appears even taller because of his ramrod manner of walking. He is mild-mannered and soft-spoken. He is also a great horseman and prefers to wear western garb and cowboy boots, but no hat. He looked nothing like a top Washington official that day—luckily for him probably. It's difficult to tell what Woody is thinking when you look into his eyes. When he speaks, however, you are taken by his sincerity and thoughtfulness. His face seldom shows emotion. If he was frightened while with the Indians, he would not have shown it. In short, Woody was a man with whom the Indians could communicate and whom they could trust, if they only realized it. He was also part Indian but did not reveal this to them.

The Indian leaders, surrounded by some of their armed followers, met Adams and Woody at the barricade, and having taken one look at Woody, relaxed and extended him every courtesy. His opening session lasted for two and a half hours. As Adams put it, ''Wood's going into Wounded Knee was a turning point. It sealed the government's commitment to a negotiated settlement. Woody's warmth and the Indians' openness illustrated that an agreement was possible.''

Woody rushed back to Washington for discussions with us at Justice and with top officials at Interior. He returned quickly with specific proposals for a settlement. The Indians rejected them. Rather than throw his hands up in frustration and walk away, Woody insisted that negotiations be continued.

The white ranchers and Wilson were becoming increasingly impatient with not only the slow pace of the negotiations but also the continuation of the unlawful occupation. Their attitude was exhibited when a vigilante force was organized and roadblocks established outside the federal roadblocks. The vigilantes even went so far as to prevent agents of the Community Relations Service, the conciliation arm of the Department of Justice, from entering Wounded Knee. Wayne Colburn and four deputy marshals, with pointed guns, escorted them past the unauthorized roadblocks.

On May 5, over three months after the occupation of Wounded Knee, a final agreement was signed. A costly price had been paid for it: two Indians were killed, a United States marshal was paralyzed from the waist down, eleven other persons were injured, several buildings were destroyed, and thousands of rounds of ammunition had been fired, most by the Indians.

The militant Indians also paid the price they were willing to pay from the outset. For two years the federal government prosecuted some one hundred fifty persons for crimes arising from the seizure of Wounded Knee.

Woody and John Adams emerged as the heroes of Wounded Knee, if such a tragedy can have heroes. Others would disagree. For many, the easy way to deal with a Wounded Knee is by the immediate use of force. Suppose, however, that method had been permitted. Suppose fifty or a hundred Indians had been killed along with a dozen law officers. I think I know what would have followed. Thousands of law-abiding but disenchanted young American Indians would have turned to violence and martyrdom. Thousands of other Americans would have been turned against the sad plight of the Indians.

There is only one way by which social grievances can be addressed in our country—by the tedious process of political action. Russell Means and his fellow officers of AIM deliberately flouted the laws of the United States. That cannot be condoned. They made their political statement and paid the price.

But perhaps they have aroused other young Indians to seek by political means solutions to the near tragic conditions under which they live on their reservations. In 1970 their unemployment rates ranged from 40 percent to 80 percent; 80 percent of their incomes fell below the poverty line; their average education under federal supervision was six years; their health lagged twenty to twenty-five years behind that of the general population; their average life span was forty-four years; their infant mortality was 50 percent higher than the national average and their tuberculosis rate was eight times higher; not unexpectedly, their suicide rate was twice as high.

Russell Means and his AIM cohorts did have something to demonstrate against. They fully agreed with the statement of President Nixon on July 18, 1970: "The first Americans—the Indians—are the most deprived and most isolated minority group in our nation."

General conclusions can be drawn from these incidents of dissent.

First, each incident involved an issue of great importance to the dissenters. Vietnam, for example, meant life and death to thousands of turned-off young Americans.

Second, agreement with the objectives of dissenters is not the question. The First Amendment is. I wanted to win the war in Vietnam and was appalled by LBJ's political mishandling of it. Our acceptance of defeat brought about brutal communist oppression in most of Indochina. Many of our children didn't see it that way. Had we not had the escape valve of the First Amendment—had we been like repressive Russia—our institutions of government might have been torn apart.

Third, government—federal, state, local—has a duty to perform when dissent occurs. The duty is twofold: to provide an environment for the dissent, and to protect against illegal violence and destruction. The fulfillment of the latter duty presents the difficulties. Underreaction to and lack of understanding of the social grievance will lead to the rule of the mob; overreaction and the creation of an atmosphere of restraint will lead to the same end.

Mass demonstration and dissent will continue in America—so long as we are free. I hope that every new attorney general will familiarize himself, upon assuming his great office, with the literature of modern dissent. I also hope that somewhere in the halls of Justice he will find another Woody.

6

McLaren and Griswold

The "Scandal" Known as ITT

On Monday afternoon, April 19, 1971, I was working in my office when I received the most fateful telephone call of my life. It was also the most unexpected. No communication whatever about the subject matter had preceded it.

"Dick, the president has instructed me to order you to drop the appeal before the Supreme Court in the *Grinnell* case," said John Ehrlichman.

I almost fell out of my chair. Struggling to maintain my composure—something I usually found myself doing with Ehrlichman—I informed him that a decision had already been made to proceed with the case, and that I had approved of that decision. Since the time to file the appeal on the case expired the next day, I asked him to convey my regrets to the president. I also asked him to inform the president that I would welcome the opportunity to discuss the matter with him and the reasons why I felt that, for his sake and that of the department, his "order" was inadvisable.

Ehrlichman made no effort to ascertain what those reasons were or why I felt so deeply about the matter that I would disobey a direct order from the president of the United States. "Oh, we'll see about that!" He hung up.

Ehrlichman never made a more truthful statement. Within a minute or two an irate president was on the telephone. In the presence of Ehrlichman and George Schultz, the secretary of labor, the president conveyed his displeasure. I have since learned that a partial transcript of a presidential tape reveals:

> PRESIDENT: I don't want to know anything about the case. Don't tell me a—
>
> EHRLICHMAN: Yeah, I won't—
>
> PRESIDENT: Thing about it. I don't want to know about Geneen. I've

met him and I don't know—I don't know whether ITT is bad or good, or indifferent. But there is not going to be any more antitrust actions as long as I am in this chair.

EHRLICHMAN: Well, there's one—

PRESIDENT: Goddamn it, we're going to stop it.

PRESIDENT: (Picks up telephone.) Yeah. Hi, Dick, how are you?

Fine, fine, I'm going to talk to John tomorrow about my general attitude on antitrust, and in the meantime, I know that he has left with you, uh, the ITT thing because apparently he says he had something to do with them once.

Well, I have, I have nothing to do with them, and I want something clearly understood, McLaren's ass is to be out within one hour. The ITT thing—stay the hell out of it. Is that clear? That's an order.

The order is to leave the goddamned thing alone. Now, I've said this, Dick, a number of times, and you fellows don't get the me—, the message over there.

I did not want McLaren to run around prosecuting people, raising hell about conglomerates, stirring things up at this point. Now, you keep him the hell out of that. Is that clear?

Or either he resigns. I'd rather have him out anyway. I don't like the son-of-a-bitch.

The question is, I know, that the jurisdiction—I know all the legal things, Dick, you don't have to spell out the legal—

That's right.

That's right. Don't file the brief.

Your—my order is to drop the goddamn thing. Is that clear? [The phone slammed in my ear. Tapes show the conversation continued as follows.]

SCHULTZ: From the standpoint of the economics of it, uh, I would be the last to say we should not continue, uh, to, uh, pursue the antitrust laws in the proper way, but, the, uh—I think the conglomerates have taken a bum rap.

PRESIDENT: This is the problem. The problem is McLaren's a nice little fellow who's a good little antitrust lawyer out in Chicago. Now he comes in and all these bright little bastards that worked for the antitrust department for years and years and years and who hate business with a passion—any business—have taken him over. They haven't taken him over.

Then of course McLaren is the man. They go into—Kleindienst is busy appointing judges, Mitchell is busy doing other things, so they're afraid to overrule him. By God they're not going to do it. . . . They've gone off on a kick that'll make them big goddamn trustbusters. That was all right fifty years ago. Fifty years ago maybe it was a good thing for the country. It's not a good thing for the country today.

EHRLICHMAN: McLaren has a very strong sense of mission here.

PRESIDENT: Good—Jesus, he's—Get him out. In one hour.

EHRLICHMAN: He's got a—

PRESIDENT: One hour.

EHRLICHMAN: Very strong—

PRESIDENT: And he's not going to be a judge either. He is out of the goddamn government. . . . Today. Anybody that didn't follow what we've done per the latest'd have his ass out. Unless he is a— What is he, is he a Republican hack or something?

EHRLICHMAN: No, I don't even know who he is.

When President Nixon had hung up I sat in a state of shock. I finally pulled myself together, picked up the phone, and dialed Mitchell on the intercom. His secretary answered.

"Susie," I blurted, "I have to see Mr. Mitchell immediately."

"I'm sorry, Dick, but he is in a meeting in his office."

"I don't care what he is doing or who he is meeting with, Susie. I'll either come up there and interrupt his meeting or, if he chooses, he can come down to my office. I have to talk to him immediately."

The office of the attorney general is on the southwest corner of the fifth floor of the Department of Justice building. The office of the deputy attorney general is directly below on the fourth floor. The attorney general's private elevator connects the two offices. Within minutes after my conversation with his secretary, Mitchell walked into my office. I think that was the first and only time he was ever in my office.

I related to him what had just happened. Instantly amazed, he said only, "You've got to be kidding."

"John, if I have to comply with that order I'll have to resign; McLaren and Griswold will also resign. This will cause the biggest rhubarb of his administration. The president doesn't understand the facts of the matter. He doesn't need this kind of a problem."

Mitchell agreed. After a short discussion we decided that I should ask McLaren and Griswold to petition the Supreme Court for an extension of time within which to file the *Grinnell* appeal, thereby enabling Mitchell to try to do something about the situation.

When he left, I asked Trixie, my secretary, to call McLaren personally and inform him that it was urgent that he come to my office immediately. McLaren's office was directly below mine on the third floor and was likewise connected by the private elevator. In less than three minutes he was in my office.

"Dick," I began, "as a personal favor to me, will you consent to a motion before the Supreme Court for an extension of time to file the appeal in the *Grinnell* case as requested by Judge Walsh?"

McLaren was visibly surprised by the request, as expected. When I assured him that my request was not for the purpose of changing his basic theory of the ITT cases, he reluctantly agreed.

I then requested Trixie to ask the solicitor general, Erwin Griswold, to come to my office for the same reason of urgency. Although he had to walk from his office on the southeast corner of the fifth floor, he arrived in a few minutes.

I asked him what the time situation was in the ITT cases before the Supreme Court. He replied that the next day, April 20, was the last day for filing an appeal. Either I or McLaren referred his attention to the Walsh letter and the request contained in it.

"Is it possible to get an extension of time, Dean?" I asked.

He thought it was, even though such requests are usually made ten days in advance. He then departed. The motion was filed and granted.

A few days later, just as I was leaving Mitchell's office at the conclusion of our daily 9 A.M. meeting, Mitchell stopped me and said, in his typical understated manner, "By the way, your friend at the White House says that you can handle your [expletive deleted] antitrust cases any way you want."

I smiled, said nothing, and took the elevator to McLaren's office on the third floor. Walking into his office unannounced, I blurted out: "Don't ask me any questions, Dick, but feel free to go forward with the *Grinnell* and other ITT cases as originally planned."

"Swell."

I returned to my office and sat down at my desk with a sigh of relief. At least for the time being, Marnie and I would put aside thoughts of returning to Phoenix and the private practice of law.

Why all the fuss over *Grinnell*? Why would the deputy attorney general disobey a direct order of the president of the United States? Why would the solicitor general and an assistant attorney general probably resign if the ITT cases were dismissed?

After the president's election, Richard McLaren, an attorney from Chicago, was one of several persons under consideration by Mitchell for appointment as assistant attorney general for the antitrust division. I was in Mitchell's office in New York's Pierre Hotel on a cold December afternoon when Mitchell asked McLaren to take the job. The latter accepted.

As the meeting broke up McLaren stated, "I want you both to realize that I believe in the vigorous enforcement of the antitrust laws." He departed.

I turned to Mitchell. "You know something, John, I think he really means it."

"I know it."

McLaren was recognized as one of the leading antitrust lawyers in the country. At the time he was appointed to head the antitrust division of Justice, he was the immediate past president of the antitrust section of the American Bar Association. Although he represented large American corporations that were charged with antitrust violations by the government, he was nonetheless committed to the Sherman Antitrust Acts. To him, the productive miracle of the American economy depended upon free competition in the marketplace. He had become deeply concerned that this free competition was being threatened by the conglomerate mergers that had been taking place on an ever increasing scale in the 1960s. As he often pointed out to me, "If this trend is permitted to continue, it won't be long before 90 percent of the productive capacity of the United States will reside in fewer than a hundred corporations." Even though the Kennedy and Johnson administrations had been unsuccessful in coming up with a legal theory to combat this trend, McLaren believed that anticompetitive conglomerate mergers could be attacked in the Supreme Court through the existing Sherman and Clayton Antitrust acts.

In 1969, therefore, McLaren decided to make the recent massive acquisitions by ITT the occasion for testing his theory that existing law could be applied to correct certain kinds of conglomerate mergers. ITT had recently acquired the Sheraton Hotel chain, Canteen Catering Corporation, Avis Rent-a-Car, Grinnell Fire Extinguisher Company, and the massive Hartford Insurance Company. One could see how each company could subtly dovetail with the other. ITT had become the world's biggest conglomerate. Consequently, under McLaren's direction, the antitrust division of the Department of Jusice moved in court to seek divestiture by ITT of its acquisition of Hartford, Canteen, and Grinnell. This was done with Mitchell's approval. However, since his former law firm had represented an ITT subsidiary, he disqualified himself in these actions and I became, in effect, the attorney general for the ITT litigation. In that capacity, I gave my ongoing approval to McLaren's recommendations.

By spring 1971 McLaren had lost all three divestiture cases in the lower courts. He forged on, despite mounting criticism and skepticism. I supported his efforts. The Canteen and Hartford divestitures were already on appeal before the Supreme Court and McLaren was preparing a similar appeal in the matter of Grinnell Company. That appeal occasioned the president's call to me.

ITT, on the other hand, was doing everything it could to pressure McLaren and the Department of Justice to drop these cases. It was especially concerned about the Hartford divestiture. Hartford supplied the liquidity which this mammoth conglomerate so desperately needed in the slumping economy of 1970 and 1971. With Mitchell disqualified, I was the top officer of Justice who was approached from time to time to do something about that "crazy" McLaren. The argument was always the same. "McLaren is wrong—as a matter of law."

My stock reply was, "I don't know that much about antitrust law. If he is wrong, then why worry, the Supreme Court will tell him so. If you can persuade McLaren he is wrong, fine with me."

On the morning of Friday, April 16, 1971, Edward Walsh, a former federal judge and a deputy attorney general under President Johnson, phoned me. Judge Walsh and I had become well acquainted as a result of his being the chairman of the Standing Committee on the Judiciary of the American Bar Association. He said his law firm had represented ITT for many years and that he wanted to deliver to me a legal memorandum as to why the Department of Justice should delay its filing of the Supreme Court appeal in *Grinnell*. This was the first and only time an attorney for ITT had contacted me instead of going directly to McLaren. I was surprised and a little put out that Judge Walsh would presume on our friendship by contacting me directly. Nevertheless, because of that friendship, I agreed to receive it. The memorandum arrived in my office in a few hours by messenger from New York. Since McLaren was absent, I handed the unopened envelope to Brock Comegys, McLaren's deputy.

Next Monday morning, April 19, 1971, around eight-forty-five, McLaren came to my office. He brought with him a formal written memorandum in which he set forth his strong conviction that the Walsh request should not be granted. When McLaren explained the contents of his memorandum, I agreed with his views and instructed him to proceed with the filing of the *Grinnell* appeal to the Supreme Court. Immediately after he left my office I called Judge Walsh and informed him that his request would not be granted.

My call to Judge Walsh was on the morning of the same day that I received the calls from John Ehrlichman and President Nixon. On what happened at the White House after I declined to accede to Walsh's request, I can only speculate. ITT probably—and correctly—concluded that if Walsh couldn't persuade me to overrule McLaren, no one else could, except the one at 1600 Pennsylvania Avenue.

Thus someone from ITT probably called someone at the White House that day. Whatever advice Nixon received, he responded to it in an impulsive manner. A few days later, in a calmer setting, Mitchell was able to turn his head around and put our antitrust policy back on the track.

Why I would have resigned had the president let his order stand is an entirely different matter. The decision would not have been for personal reasons. Simply put, I could not have functioned effectively as deputy attorney general or as the person responsible for the ITT cases. Granted, the president heads the Department of Justice, and we are to effect *his* policies. But how these policies are arrived at in the first place, and how they are thereafter changed are essential matters. Mitchell generally supported McLaren, as did I. If the attorney general's approach to antitrust enforcement was to be altered, that change should be the result only of thoughtful policy discussions at the highest level, not of impulse.

It was never necessary for me to discuss with McLaren whether he would, in fact, have resigned if the president's order had stood. I've always regretted that we never talked about it before his untimely death in 1972. I'm sure, however, of his resignation also. The ITT appeals were too important to him. Judicial decision was his way of coping with the threat to competition by conglomerate acquisitions. It wasn't a question of bigness. General Motors and Exxon were big but not unfairly competitive. If, however, ITT should own the Sheraton Hotels and Avis Rent-a-Car, perhaps Avis would have a favored location in the hotel lobby over Hertz. Grinnell was the largest manufacturer of firefighting equipment and Hartford was the largest underwriter of fire insurance. Would the Hartford rate be lower if a firm met a safety specification by using only Grinnell equipment? These are simplistic examples, of course. But they do illustrate in part what McLaren was seeking to prevent.

The solicitor general, Griswold, was similarly interested. He made the decisions as to whether the government should appeal adverse lower-court decisions to the Supreme Court. He and McLaren were in agreement on the theory behind the need for the ITT appeals. That decisionmaking process had been set in motion. Reverse that by peremptory means and you order the solicitor general back to teaching or practicing law.

I was concerned about another dimension of Nixon's order, however. The alleged favoritism of big business by Republican administrations is a political fable seized upon with alacrity by liberal Democrats and their media supporters. If the ITT matter, as developed in my confirmation hearings in 1972, was an attempt to make it the scandal of the Nixon administration in an election year, the resignation of the deputy attorney general in 1971 under these circumstances would have created a real scandal about favoritism to "bigness in business" a year in advance. The fact, of course, is that because of McLaren, the Nixon tenure in the White House was marked by the most vigorous antitrust enforcement ever.

In any event, I was relieved that an unnecessary episode had been successfully closed. Or so I thought.

On April 20, 1971, the day after the president's call, I received a phone call from a person who identified himself as Felix Rohatyn from New York City. Who was he and what did he want? He identified himself as a financier and a member of the board of ITT. He wanted an appointment to see me; he was quick to mention that he did not want to talk about the ITT matter from a legal standpoint. I agreed to see him.

Rohatyn called me, I later learned, as a result of a conversation I had had some two weeks earlier with John Ryan, an officer of ITT. The Ryans were neighbors of ours in McLean. Rene Ryan attended St. John's Episcopal Church, as did my family. We had come to know the Ryans socially at neighborhood cocktail parties. In early April the Ryans were hosting a similar affair. As Marnie and I were leaving, Ryan, in an almost belligerent manner, demanded to know why McLaren and I were so determined in our position on the ITT cases. He also asserted that if we persisted in requiring the divestiture of Hartford, the company could suffer severe economic consequences.

"John," I replied, "this is the first time that contention has ever been put forth. I'm certain McLaren would be willing to listen to any facts that would support such a proposition."

Ryan stated that he would have a qualified representative of ITT contact me. Hence Rohatyn's call.

Rohatyn came in either the next day or soon thereafter. In addition to his acknowledged expertise in finance, he was exceedingly pleasant. He disarmed me at the outset when he admitted that he had no "political" clout with the Nixon administration because of his public support for Senator Muskie and his candidacy for the presidency. He further disarmed me by prefacing his remarks with the statement that anything he would say to me would be predicated on the assumption that, as a matter of law, McLaren was right and ITT was wrong. As he surely intended, that statement captured my attention.

What he came to say also got my attention. As a financier on the ITT board of directors, he had been concerned for some time that if at any point the Department of Justice won its appeal and the divestiture of Hartford by ITT was subsequently ordered, a financial disaster not only to ITT but perhaps to the stock market and the economy would follow. His reasons, briefly, were that ITT had paid a premium price for the purchase of Hartford and would suffer a very substantial loss if it was forced to sell it. That loss, combined with its current overextended debt posture and its financial difficulties with some major foreign ventures, could lead to the collapse of ITT. He requested the opportunity for conveying this information in detail to McLaren.

I told him I would relay his request to Mr. McLaren. McLaren, after I related my conversation, stated that this was a serious contention, that it was the first time it had been urged by ITT, that a similar problem was involved in the LTV conglomerate case, and that he would be willing to hear what ITT had to say. He also said that the objective of antitrust enforcement was not to eliminate companies but to maintain competition. On April 29, 1971, a team of ITT financial experts met with McLaren. I attended the meeting but made no comment; I entrusted the ensuing negotiations to McLaren.

On or about July 31, 1971, after obtaining an independent evaluation of ITT's financial representations, McLaren came to me and said he had worked out a settlement with the ITT attorneys. (The overwhelming majority of antitrust cases are resolved by settlement.) The agreement, however, represented the most extensive divestiture proceeding in the history of the Department of Justice. ITT would keep Hartford Insurance Company, but would have to divest itself of many other acquisitions, among them Avis Rent-a-Car, Canteen, Levitt Corporation, and half of Grinnell Fire Extinguisher Company. All together, the total of divested assets exceeded one billion dollars. Moreover, for all practical purposes, ITT could not make major future acquisitions without the prior approval of the Department of Justice.

The ITT problem for Justice was now a thing of the past, or so I thought.

In December 1971 Mitchell informed me that the president wanted him to manage his reelection campaign and that he would be resigning as attorney general. He also informed me that the president would probably nominate me to succeed him.

I was flattered by the suggestion. As Mitchell's deputy for three years, I felt I had some qualifications for the job. The transition from him to me would be uneventful and relatively smooth within the department.

Nevertheless, it seemed not to be a wise decision by the president. Mitchell was his closest adviser and confidant. He could continue to be such as a cabinet officer. But could he be that and run a political campaign? Others were available and qualified to run the campaign—even myself.

When I expressed these feelings to Mitchell his only response was, "That's what the president has decided and that's what I'm going to do!"

If the decision had been implemented in December 1971 or in early January, Watergate would not, in my opinion, have taken place. But delays ensued.

My nomination to succeed Mitchell was not made until mid-February because of Mitchell's involvement in problems of the administration. In the interim, however, the campaign committee to reelect Nixon, which had already been announced, with offices on Pennsylvania Avenue within sight of the White House, functioned without responsible direction. Jeb Magruder, with a few other younger and inexperienced enthusiasts, occupied the committee offices. By the time Mitchell had arrived in March the damage had been done. The "plumbers" were in full operation. The Watergate break-in had been approved. This I sadly learned later.

I had another reason for feeling apprehensive about my nomination to succeed Mitchell. That year, 1972, was a presidential election year. For three and a half years the Department of Justice had been an arena of many controversial battles. The liberal Democrats on the Senate Judiciary Committee could be expected to exploit the confirmation hearing of the new attorney general by dredging up those controversies. They would do that no matter who the nominee might be, but more intensely if the nominee was the deputy attorney general. Mitchell's deputy would be obliged to adopt as his own and then defend every major policy position of the preceding three and a half years. This presented no philosophical problem for me but it should have served notice on the administration that my nomination hearing would not be a mere formality.

Mitchell summarily dismissed my concerns. "The Senate will let the president have the attorney general he wants."

"Maybe so, John, but if I'm going to be it, I'm going to be ready for a real knockdown-dragout."

James O. Eastland, chairman of the Senate Judiciary Committee, placed a notice in the *Congressional Record* of February 15, 1972, that the nominations of myself as attorney general and Louis Patrick Gray III as deputy attorney general would be heard by the committee commencing at 10:40 A.M., Tuesday, February 22.

Pat Gray's nomination was heard first. He was introduced to the committee by Senator Lowell Weicker "with a great deal of pride." Abraham Ribicoff, the Democratic senator from Connecticut, endorsed the nomination "with great enthusiasm."

I was also enthusiastic about Pat. He had graduated from the Naval Academy in 1940, served in the navy for twenty years, and studied law at the George Washington University, in the navy's postgraduate education program. In 1960 he retired from the navy and joined the personal staff of the vice president—Richard M. Nixon. In 1969 he served as the executive assistant to Robert Finch, the secretary of the Department of Health, Education, and Welfare. President Nixon then asked him to work with Bob Mardian to develop a plan to assist southern states to make the transition from the dual to the unitary school system. Their efforts were outstanding. By reaching out to black and white leaders in a low-key, nonpolitical manner, they made it possible for communities to accept the reality of school desegregation. Gray then came to the Department of Justice with an appointment by the president as the assistant attorney general in charge of the civil division. From working with Pat for the year and a half at Justice before our nominations, I had nothing but the highest respect for him.

His nomination hearing was short. Senator Hart of Michigan brought out his accomplishments in the southern school situation. Senator Thurmond of South Carolina inserted in the record a statement of high praise. Observing this proceeding, I had to admit to myself that Mitchell was right and I was wrong. The confirmation business would be a cakewalk.

When it came my turn, Barry Goldwater and Paul Fannin, my two senators, flanked me and made flattering statements by way of introduction. Goldwater concluded his remarks by saying: "So, Mr. Chairman, it is with real pride that I introduce a lifelong friend to this committee once again and urge his favorable consideration as attorney general." Fannin concluded by commending me to the committee "with confidence and personal pride." The pleased smile on my face was erased in a matter of seconds; the cakewalk became political confrontation.

Birch Bayh of Indiana led off on the subject whether or not there should be a federal law prohibiting handguns. From there he went to juvenile delinquency, penal reform, corrections, wiretapping, bugging, the right to privacy, demonstrations like Mayday, arrest procedures, preventive detention, national security wiretapping, and appointments by the president to the Supreme Court. These subjects were, of course, appropriate. The interrogation, however, was conducted, in my opinion, for the primary purpose of affording Senator Bayh the opportunity to make a political speech to his constituents in the Democratic party.

Senator Hart of Michigan was next. Our dialogue concerned itself primarily with the use of marijuana, capital punishment, and the voting-rights law. I had pretty fixed views in these areas, as did the senator. We were at odds on the question of marijuana, were somewhat at odds on the issue of capital punishment, and clashed over voting rights. It seemed to me he was using my hearing for the political purpose of demonstrating that Nixon's Department of Justice had not enforced the Voting Rights Act and other civil-rights statutes. I emphatically pointed out that "with respect to all the civil-rights laws, Attorney General Mitchell and this administration have given them more vigorous enforcement than any administration since they have been enacted." On that note Hart's interrogation ended.

Senator Tunney of California began by congratulating me on my nomination and then proceeded to inquire whether I was going to be able to exercise control over J. Edgar Hoover and the FBI. That was a good question inasmuch as previous attorneys general—including Robert Kennedy and Ramsey Clark—had had difficulty with the problem. I allowed as how I would do my best. Senator Tunney, however, did his best to exploit the politics of a live issue in the U.S.

Senator Kennedy of Massachusetts was the last batter up. He had been absent during my dialogue with Bayh, Hart, and Tunney, and apologized. He then proceeded to read a prepared statement. The gist of it was that because of the conduct of the Nixon administration during the past three years "the people of America are crying for justice," and "for all Americans, these three years have been disappointing and disillusioning." He then read the litany of the liberal political grievances against Nixon and his administration. The concluding paragraph of the "speech" indicates its tone:[1]

> And so it is our obligation to take this opportunity to see how the man who will hold the stewardship of the Justice for the next eleven months views these past disappointments and what his vision of the future is. We want to get an idea of what kind of Attorney General he will make—whether he will use the tools that Congress has already given him or allow them to decay and atrophy while he seeks to fight the war on crime with speeches and press releases; whether he will use his Harvard-trained mind to come up with ideas for progress in such vital areas as gun control, or to promote new gimmicks that teeter at the edge of constitutionality; and most important, whether he views "justice" as a mission and a goal for his department.

The senator's interrogation that followed centered upon those subjects about which the liberals faulted Nixon and Mitchell. Why hadn't the Department of Justice convened a federal grand jury in the Kent State "massacre"? What about Mayday and the mass arrests? What about gun legislation? What about wiretapping?

Questions like these do not lend themselves to easy answers. Being asked in the manner in which they were by Senator Kennedy made it clear to me that they were mere political rhetoric for a certain segment of the body politic and not a sincere effort to determine my fitness to be the attorney general. But I had anticipated this.

---

1. Kennedy seemed subdued as he read his speech. Later that day an aide of Kennedy came to me and apologized on behalf of the senator. Apparently, he hadn't read it in advance and was embarrassed by its stridency—the product of an overzealous staff member.

What I had not expected took place at the end of the hearing on Wednesday, February 23.

Clarence Mitchell, director of the Washington Bureau of the National Association for the Advancement of Colored People, appeared as a witness. His purpose, by a prepared written statement, was to oppose my nomination because the president had refused to appoint Clarence Clyde Ferguson, Jr., a distinguished black, to the U.S. Court of Appeals for the Third Circuit. The charge was that his appointment was not made because he was black. When he finished, I vehemently denied the charge and vigorously defended our previous record of appointing more blacks to the judiciary than any other administration. Clarence and I, in the presence of the committee, had a little personal chat that ended so congenially that Senator Mathias of Maryland remarked: "There is a rather extraordinary scene before us here." At that point the formal hearing ended.

What Kennedy then stated—off the record—came so unexpectedly that I couldn't believe my ears: "Mr. Chairman [Senator Eastland], I move that the committee unanimously support the nomination of Mr. Kleindienst to be the attorney general."

Senators Bayh and Tunney immediately seconded the motion. Senator Eastland then stated that the nomination would be sent to the Senate the next day.

"Mr. Chairman," Kennedy interrupted, "may I have seven days within which to prepare my reasons for supporting the nomination?"

Eastland agreed and the hearing finally ended. So I thought.

I returned to the department and immediately went to Mitchell's office. "John, something funny is going on here. Why would Kennedy make such a motion after having kicked the hell out of the president, you, and me for two days?"

"That was just politics, ol' boy. I told you the Senate will always let a president have his own attorney general."

"Okay, Mr. A.G., but I have a funny feeling about it."

Seven days after Wednesday, February 23, ran to Wednesday, March 1. Kennedy requested those seven days to prepare his supporting remarks—the rules of the committee would have given him an automatic period of ten days. Why seven?

I will believe until the day I die that Kennedy requested only seven days to coincide with the first of three newspaper columns by Jack Anderson that appeared in the *Washington Post*. The first was on Tuesday, February 29; the second on Wednesday, March 1; the third on Friday, March 3.

The heading of the Anderson column that Tuesday announced: "Secret Memo Bares Mitchell-ITT Move." I received an advance copy of the column during the latter part of Monday afternoon, February 28. It revealed the infamous "Dita Beard" memorandum that the ITT settlement "was privately arranged between Attorney General John Mitchell and the top lobbyist for the company." The fix was reported to have been a "payoff for ITT's pledge of up to $400,000 for the upcoming Republican convention in San Diego." According to the column, the arrangements were made between Mitchell and Beard "at the governor's mansion in Kentucky during a dinner reception given by Republican Governor Louis Nunn last May after the Kentucky Derby.''

When I read the whole article, I turned to Jack Hushen, the department's public affairs officer who brought me the advance copy, and burst out: "What the ———— is this all about? Mitchell had nothing, absolutely nothing, to do with that settlement! I never heard of $400,000 or any other sum for the convention in San Diego in my life! I've got to see Mitchell right now!''

Up the private elevator to Mitchell's office I went and burst into his office shaking with disbelief and anger. "Didn't I say there was something funny the way my hearing was concluded last week by Kennedy? He knew this column by that muckraker Anderson was going to appear and he wanted my nomination to be out of committee and on the floor of the Senate by the time this article appeared!''

Mitchell looked up in his usual quiet way and asked: "What are you talking about? Have you lost your marbles?''

"Read it, damn it.''

Mitchell read it and started to laugh. "Nobody is going to believe a bunch of trash like that from Anderson. Forget it.''

As I left his office, in a state of agitation still, I shot back, "Instead of no one paying attention to this thing, it's going to develop into the biggest headline scandal you ever heard of—mark my words!''

The next day the second Anderson column appeared. Its headline read: "Kleindienst Accused in ITT Case.'' The article then quoted from a letter I had written on December 13, 1971, to the Democratic national chairman Larry O'Brien, in which I stated that the ITT settlement "was handled and negotiated exclusively by Assistant Attorney General Richard W. McLaren.'' On the basis of that, Anderson charged that I "told an outright lie about the Justice Department's *sudden* out-of-court settlement of the Nixon administration's biggest antitrust case'' (emphasis supplied). I had, according to the report in the article, "held roughly a half-dozen secret meetings on the ITT case with a director of the company before the settlement was reached.'' That director, of course, was named as Felix Rohatyn.

Now, no such "secret'' meetings were ever held. Every meeting I had with Rohatyn was by appointment and scheduled on my calendar. As noted above, the first meeting took place shortly after his phone call to me on April 20. As a result of our meeting, I put him in contact with McLaren. The next time I saw Rohatyn was on April 29 in McLaren's office. There were at least a dozen persons present to hear the financial presentation of ITT to the antitrust division. I took no part in the discussion. On May 10, Rohatyn visited my office to inquire as to what McLaren was doing about that presentation. I informed him that McLaren had not reached a decision. My next contact with him was on June 17 by telephone; McLaren, also on the line, read to Rohatyn the proposed basis for a settlement, a proposal Rohatyn thought onerous and unfair. Thereafter, Rohatyn visited my office on June 29 and July 15 to complain about McLaren's rigid attitude in the settlement negotiations. Each time I informed him that I would not inject myself into the negotiations and that the problem had to be worked out with the ITT lawyers and McLaren. The matter was finally settled between ITT and McLaren on Saturday, July 31, the night before McLaren called me to inform me of the fact of the settlement.

Knowing these to be the facts, I also knew that something had to be done immediately to clear the record. The floor of the Senate was no place to do that. By the time Anderson wrote additional false and accusatory columns, not only I, but also McLaren, the Department of Justice, and the White House would be portrayed in the public's mind as participants in a bribery scheme and as liars. Whether or not I could be confirmed as the attorney general by the Senate in such an environment was less important to me than getting the facts into the daylight. I did not want to live the rest of my life under a cloud of suspicion, mistrust, and breach of public trust. Without consulting anyone, I decided that the only thing I could do was request that my confirmation hearing be reopened by the Judiciary Committee immediately.

Having decided upon that course of action, I located Mitchell at the White House. In a few minutes I was there and, in a private room, showed him the second Anderson column and informed him of my decision. He counseled against it.

I was adamant. "John, if the record isn't made straight at once, this matter will make the Tea Pot Dome scandal look like a tea party by comparison!"

I left him and proceeded to the Senate office of Chairman Eastland.

When I got to his office I asked him if he would ask Senator Hugh Scott from Pennsylvania and the ranking Republican member of the committee to join us at once. When Senator Scott arrived I reviewed the two Anderson columns with them, together with my vehement denial of their contents.

"Gentlemen, I respectfully and urgently request that my confirmation hearing be reopened without delay."

They too raised some questions about the prudence of this course of action. However, they finally agreed to honor my request. Senator Eastland advised that I should contact Senators Hart, Kennedy, Bayh, and Tunney and inform them of my reasons for asking that my hearing be reopened. I concurred and left Eastland's office to visit first with Senator Hart.

Senator Hart of Michigan was more versed in antitrust law than any other member of the committee. He was obviously disturbed about the Anderson columns and readily agreed that the matter should be fully aired before the committee. Senator Hart was a man of the highest integrity and universally admired as a man of decency and compassion. He was generous in his understanding of my position.

I next met with Senators Bayh and Tunney and members of their staff, together with staff members of Senator Kennedy. Kennedy was unable to be present. This meeting was slightly different in tone. It was my impression that some staff members seemed interested more in having another crack at me than in sympathizing with my problem. That impression was later borne out.

Chairman Eastland convened the committee at 10:40 A.M., the next day, on Thursday, March 2, the day before the last Anderson rehash column appeared.

My unilateral—to some, impulsive—decision has been criticized by many persons, both in and out of government. President Nixon and various members of his staff, including Ehrlichman, Haldeman, and Colson, thought my action unwise. But even knowing what would later occur, I would make the same decision again. I admit, however, that I naively believed that if the persons involved in the whole matter appeared before the Judiciary Committee and, under oath, testified to the actual facts, the matter would be laid to rest in no more than one day.

Instead of one day, what ensued was, at the time, the longest confirmation hearing in the history of the Senate. Thirty-two witnesses appeared before the committee. Testimony was taken on March 2, 3, 6–10, 14–16, 26, and 29, and on April 10, 11, 13, 14, 17–20, and 27. It consists of 1,791 pages. And 193 separate exhibits were made part of the record. It turned out to be a free-for-all.

I (joined by McLaren and Rohatyn who came at my request) appeared before the committee at 10:40 A.M., March 2. Having no time for the preparation of a formal statement, I led off by making a general statement from my recollection as to how the ITT settlement came about, including the date and nature of every meeting I had with Rohatyn. McLaren followed me and, assisted only by hastily prepared notes, made his statement. Mr. Rohatyn had a prepared statement from which he read. His testimony was corroborative of ours. My participation in the settlement negotiations was limited to that described above; McLaren handled the negotiation and worked out the settlement without interference from or participation by me; Rohatyn confirmed the nature of his meetings with me and, contrary to the Anderson column, the fact that they were not "secret." The three of us testified that San Diego as a site for the Republican convention and that the sum of $400,000—or any other sum—were fantasies of someone's imagination as far as we were concerned. That should have ended the matter.

On the first day of the resumed hearing, Senator Bayh asked me: "In the course of the whole business, did you ever talk to anybody at the White House staff, any advisers to the president, on the ITT matter?"

I replied: "For me to say that no one in the White House with whom I might have talked would not have raised the ITT question, I would not be prepared to say that. So far as discussing with anybody on the staff of the White House what I was doing, what do you think I ought to do, what do you feel about it, what are your recommendations—no."

Bayh: "No suggestions coming from the White House as to what action should be taken by Justice Department?"

I replied, "No, sir."

The next day, Senator Bayh asked me if I had had "a chance to reflect, overnight, on whether I had ever talked to anybody down at the White House about the ITT case." I gave the same answer that I had given the day before.

I was deeply conscious of that fateful telephone call I had received from the president in April of 1971, when these exchanges took place. I was also deeply disturbed that one of the senators might ask whether I had even talked to the president at any time and for any reason about the ITT case. Marnie, the only other person other than Mitchell who knew of the president's call, and I had determined what I would do if such a direct question were ever asked. I had decided to determine a method to avoid answering the question, to figure out a way either to ask for a recess or to excuse myself and then seek an immediate meeting with the president. If he would not object to my revealing his call, I would return to the committee and do so—with appropriate and satisfactory explanations, I hoped. If he should object—as I think he would have—I would be left with no other alternative than to withdraw my name as the nominee.

I testified before the committee on two other days, the last time being the last day of the hearings, April 27. On several occasions, a senator would refer to possible contacts by White House staff or I would volunteer that I had not been interfered with by the White House in the settlement of the ITT cases. The $64 question, I'm thankful, was never put. In the charged political environment that mesmerized my confirmation hearing, if that impulsive call from the president had been revealed, certain segments of the press would have exploded it into a "scandal" that never in fact existed.

Mitchell testified that the allegations in the Beard memorandum concerning his conversations with Mrs. Beard about ITT were false. Governor Nunn of Kentucky testified that he had to admonish Mrs. Beard to refrain from attempting to discuss the matter with Mitchell.

The appearance of Jack Anderson and his reporter, Bret Hume, before the committee as *witnesses* for two full days—Thursday and Friday, March 8 and 9—was both unusual and revealing. Their "testimony" consists of 147 pages of questions emanating primarily from Senators Kennedy and Bayh. Each was afforded the opportunity to restate over and over again the opinions and conclusions that were contained in the three Anderson columns. "How did Kleindienst lie, Mr. Anderson?" he was asked over and over. Anderson repeatedly answered that the lie came about in Kleindienst's letter to O'Brien when he asserted that McLaren alone negotiated the "settlement." When confronted with McLaren's testimony, Anderson would reply that because of the "secret" meetings I had with Rohatyn, I was involved in the settlement negotiations. Yet, Rohatyn and I both testified that I was not so involved. "Why were the meetings secret, Mr. Anderson?" "Because they were not made a public record and no press release was made of them," he rejoined. And on it went, ad infinitum.

Even though Anderson and Hume appeared at the insistence of Senator Kennedy, if there was any doubt as to their political motive, it was dispelled by a telling incident. Hume, in his testimony, referred to notes he made after his last interview of Mrs. Beard commencing at 10:00 P.M. in her home on Thursday, February 24. One of the senators asked to have his notes put in the record. Citing the First Amendment privilege of a reporter, Hume refused. It later developed that Hume had given a copy of the notes to the staff of Senator Kennedy. When?

Hume guesses "it would have been the Wednesday night before the Thursday morning hearing—one or two weeks ago." With this admission, Hume then offered to make his notes available to the entire committee. The interesting revelation, however, is that, as I always suspected, Kennedy and his staff were aware of the "ITT scandal" at the time of my original hearing. In my mind, that explains the reversal of Kennedy's posture from aggressiveness to support. Senator Kennedy and his staff wanted the nomination out of the committee and on the floor of the Senate before the first Anderson column would appear the next week, on February 29.

Hume's testimony was, as characterized by Senator Hruska, "totally hearsay." It was also contradicted by Mrs. Beard herself.

I don't know Dita Beard, and am sure I never will. I don't know what she is doing now. I do feel certain that her life and career were damaged beyond repair by this lamentable episode. Following the turmoil of the three Anderson columns and the daily publicity given to the reopened confirmation hearing, she found herself in the Rocky Mountain Osteopathic Hospital in Denver. It was there on Sunday, March 26, 1972, commencing at 9:30 A.M., that she was interrogated under oath in the matter. The senators present were: Hart (presiding), Kennedy, Burdick, Tunney, Cook, and Gurney. To ensure that the action of the committee would not disadvantage Mrs. Beard publicly, telegrams had been exchanged with her doctors.

A prepared statement from the doctors was read into the record. The diagnosis was "angina pectoris with arteriosclerotic heart disease, and also a possible prediabetic status." Their opinion was that she could not travel to Washington and that if her testimony was to be taken, it should be done at her bedside with her physician attending.

In this setting, Mrs. Beard made her statement before she was interrogated. By way of summary she stated: she had not written or dictated any part of the memorandum shown to her by Hume on February 23, 1972; the last paragraphs set forth allegations about which she had no knowledge; although she remembered commenting to Hume that the D looked like hers, she categorically stated to the committee that she did not write the "Anderson" memorandum; on the night of February 24, at her home, she was using Valium and was in a state of total despair; she told Hume "again and again the memo wasn't mine"; when she asked Hume where he got the memo, his only response was: "Who did you give it to?" Again and again she asked Hume: "Why are you trying to destroy me?" She corroborated the testimony of Mitchell and Nunn with respect to the alleged incident at the governor's mansion following the Kentucky Derby; Mitchell kept telling her he couldn't discuss the ITT matter with her and her persistence was rewarded by an admonishment from Governor Nunn. Concluding, she stated: "The Anderson memorandum is not my memorandum . . . I shall spend the rest of my life, for however long that might be, in an unceasing effort to find out who did this to me and why."

Dita Beard had been, until this incident, a successful Washington lobbyist for many years. ITT was her sole source of support. She raised five children from her compensation as a lobbyist for ITT. Her employment was gone. She was very ill and bedridden in a hospital. Was her testimony under oath false? Did she have a motive to lie that Sunday, March 26? Only Mrs. Beard can provide the answers. Her testimony, however, did serve to defuse the Anderson charges as the month of March came to a close.

Testimony on other matters was taken for ten days in April. I reappeared on the last day of the hearing—April 27. Senator Fong of Hawaii best expressed what I felt knowing it was finally over: "I'm glad that the hearing is coming to a close at five o'clock today. Some, however, would like to see it go on forever or at least until the November election."

The adverse political consequences of my prolonged hearing did not escape the attention of the White House. The president and his top staff became convinced that their first reaction to the reopened hearing was absolutely correct—Kleindienst was a damn fool to have done it.

Clark MacGregor, a former congressman from Minnesota, was the White House liaison officer with the Congress and was continually in contact with Senator Eastland and other senators of the Judiciary Committee during March and April 1972. From time to time Senator Eastland would remark to me when I was in his office: "Dick, that MacGregor fellow is no friend of yours." When I would inquire as to his reason for saying that, the senator would only say, "Mark my words, he is no friend of yours."

At the time I dismissed the matter from my mind. Clark had a tough job and I assumed he reflected the general attitude of the White House on the adverse publicity my hearing was generating. Not until I left the government, however, did I learn that one of MacGregor's duties was to inform Chairman Eastland that the president was considering withdrawing my nomination in favor of another nominee. I was told that Senator Eastland allowed as how the president had the right to do whatever he wanted, but that he, Senator Eastland, the chairman of the Judiciary Committee, had a similar right. Apparently, MacGregor left that meeting with the senator convinced that if the president did withdraw my name, I would be the acting attorney general for a long time. I speculate that Senator Eastland intimated that he would be in no hurry to schedule another confirmation hearing. Both Ehrlichman and MacGregor wanted to be the attorney general. MacGregor had written a White House memo suggesting that he become the new deputy attorney general upon my confirmation and then, at an appropriate early time, succeed me as the attorney general. Ehrlichman went so far as to call my best friend, Bob Mardian, and ask him if he would like to be his deputy attorney general. Chairman Eastland's reported attitude must have discouraged those aspirations.

In any event, the Senate, by a vote of 64 to 19, confirmed the nomination. What was purported to be the great election scandal took its rightful place in the dustbin of political history. Once again, McLaren, Griswold, and I believed that ITT had been consigned to the past.

Dick McLaren and Dean Griswold were public servants of the highest quality. To them, the opportunity to serve as top officers of the Department of Justice was just a means of fulfilling their commitment to law and the administration of justice. McLaren really meant it when he informed Mitchell and me that cold dreary afternoon in December 1968 that he believed in the vigorous enforcement of the antitrust laws.

It takes a person of courage and character to enforce the antitrust laws. In a sense, they are to our economic environment what the civil-rights laws are to our social environment. The enforcement of both bodies of law is fraught with controversy; fixed interests are necessarily disturbed. McLaren knew that if the 1960s trend of conglomerate acquisitions was to continue, before long nearly 90 percent of the productive capacity of America would be in the hands of less than a hundred corporations. That would effectively eliminate competition in the marketplace.

My nomination was seized upon by some Democratic senators to exploit the political myth that big business is the handmaiden of the Republican party. The real issue, however, was the antitrust policy of Richard McLaren. Even though he was sitting as a federal district judge in Chicago in March 1972, he left the bench to defend those policies. The vote of the U.S. Senate in May 1972 really signified that the senators, even if some disagreed with the antitrust policies, had no doubt in their minds about McLaren's integrity and commitment. Men and women are often called upon to defend their beliefs and conduct in the political docks of America. Dick McLaren defended his even though an unusual disease was at work within him. He died from it on June 8, 1972. He served his country well, and left a legacy dear to his heart—a marketplace still relatively competitive.

Erwin Griswold has to rank with the great lawyers, scholars, and public servants of our country. A great teacher, he is affectionately referred to by thousands of Harvard-trained lawyers as "the Dean." His scholarship has been recognized in the form of thirty-three honorary doctor-of-law degrees. Five presidents have benefited from his service to our government. It embarrasses me to think that for a short time I was technically his superior in the bureaucracy.

It is the human side of Erwin Griswold that, in my opinion, establishes him on his pedestal. Dean (I always called him Decanus, Latin for "dean"; his name appears on my law diploma in that form) is a humanist and a person of humble spirit. His scholarship has a dimension beyond the law itself. He believes warmly in the uniqueness of our political institutions; those institutions survive, he holds, not in spite of the participation of ordinary persons such as myself, but because of them. He believes that if our politics are free, then each of us will be a free American.

He was always available to me, and generously gave of himself and his counsel. Because he insisted upon coming to my office when I wanted to talk to him, I would go to his office unannounced. Many of the problems of a deputy attorney general or an attorney general are problems of policy and priorities.

Policy and *priority* are often synonyms for something political. Decanus was as adept in discussing the process by which a policy was evolved or a priority established as he was in advising what the law was or perhaps could be.

Griswold understood McLaren's theory in the ITT cases. He also agreed that even though they had been lost in the lower courts, the Supreme Court was the forum in which that theory should receive its verdict. As a practical matter, however, he supported McLaren's decision to settle the ITT cases. He also supported McLaren in those charged confirmation hearings and thereby demonstrated that, in addition to scholarship, he had great courage. The Senate's vote of 64 to 19 was as much for Erwin Griswold as for Richard McLaren. I trust I'm a better person because the Decanus has been my teacher, counselor, and friend.

Oh, yes—my thanks to ITT and Senator Kennedy, for proving the mettle and professionalism of two great men.

7
Eastland
Supreme Court and Federal Judges

From early childhood we Americans are fed this simple explanation of our constitutional government: Its magic and strength derive from its separation of powers. The executive branch, the judicial branch, and the legislative branch are separate; each thereby functions as a check and a balance with respect to the two others. With such a system of checks and balances, we are further assured, no branch of our government is able to abuse its power; our liberties are thus preserved.

By the time I had entered the eighth grade, my imagination saw those three centers of power as combatants. But subsequent years of schooling, politics and government revealed that this is not exactly the way the system works. True, occasionally a combatant takes a swing at one or both of the others. But over the years each has learned the hard way that such fisticuffs are counterproductive, because each depends upon the two others for its functional existence. So ordained the Founding Fathers, who were either geniuses or magicians when they prescribed a government based on the separation of powers.

The Congress enacts our laws, but it must look to the president for their enforcement. The Congress must also act with cautious respect for those eight old men and one lovely woman of the Supreme Court. They have the power to void a congressional enactment on the ground that it offends the Constitution. What protection does the Congress have, then? The power of the purse, and its power to repeal laws as well as pass them. The Constitution decrees that "the judicial power of the United States shall be vested in one Supreme Court, and in such inferior courts as the Congress may from time to time ordain and establish," but it is silent as to the number of justices to serve on the Court. The Congress thus has the power to eliminate most of the members of an unruly Court and deprive it of staff support and facilities. We say it would never do such a thing because, with a free press around, the people would exercise their power and vote such a Congress out of office. Nevertheless, the Congress has the power, and of that the Supreme Court is mindful.

The executive branch is likewise dependent upon the Congress. The salary of the president is set by Congress as well as the moneys needed to staff and support the divisions of the executive branch. Many a secretary of state or other cabinet officer has come to know full well what it can mean to offend the chairman of the Appropriations Committee of either the Senate or the House. The president has his own powers, which must be respected by the courts. The Supreme Court can pontificate all it wants, but it must look to the executive branch to enforce its judicial decrees. The "enforcer" is the U.S. marshal, who is appointed by the president, with the advice and consent of the Senate, and serves at his pleasure. What happens, many have wondered, when the chief justice hands an order directed against a president to the U.S. marshal, and halfway between the Court building and the White House the president fires the U.S. marshal?

The president has two other powers that he can exercise. He can refuse to nominate persons to fill vacancies in the federal courts and thereby deplete their numbers. He is also the commander in chief of the armed forces. Endless speculation arises as to what use a president would make of the military in a confrontation with the Congress or the judiciary. I am reminded of Stalin's response when informed of the power of the pope: "How many divisions does he have?"

The process by which Supreme Court justices and other federal judges are selected for their lifetime positions provides a dramatic illustration of the successful interplay between the power forces of our government.

There are 93 federal judicial districts in the U.S.; they are composed of 515 federal district judges when all vacancies are filled. Those judicial districts are divided into 13 circuits, composed of 132 courts-of-appeals judges. Then, of course, there are 9 justices of the Supreme Court.

Technically, the president nominates all federal judges. Practically, however, he is usually involved directly in only the selection of nominees to the Supreme Court. Occasionally he will involve himself in the selection of nominees to the various courts of appeals for the thirteen circuits. Very seldom does the president find himself originating nominees to the federal district courts. The reasons for this apparent departure from the Constitution make an interesting story, to be set forth later in this chapter. But first, a look at how justices are appointed to the Supreme Court.

The most important political appointment a president makes, I believe, is that of a person to the Supreme Court. Not infrequently the appointee represents a political-interest group. Justice Thurgood Marshall was the first black to serve when he was appointed by President Kennedy. Kennedy also appointed Arthur Goldberg, who had a distinguished legal career culminating as the general counsel for the AFL-CIO. President Reagan appointed Justice O'Connor, the first woman to serve on the Supreme Court. Presidents like to believe that their Court appointees generally share their political philosophy, but not seldom an appointee will surprise.

Because of the advice-and-consent function of the Senate, a president must take into account its political makeup. As President Nixon learned from a Senate consisting of a majority of Democrats, a nominee can be turned down. Occasionally the best political course for a president to follow is a nonpolitical one, especially if he has been turned down by the Senate and wishes to avoid further controversy. It is, of course, never bad politics for a president to nominate a distinguished lawyer, scholar, or jurist who has no particular political identity.

President Nixon experienced nearly everything a president can in his relationship to the Supreme Court. When he took office on January 20, 1969, the composition of the Court was: Chief Justice Earl Warren and Associate Justices Hugo Lafayette Black, William O. Douglas, John M. Harlan, William J. Brennan, Potter Stewart, Byron R. White, Abe Fortas, and Thurgood Marshall. Between January 20, 1969, and August 8, 1974, when Nixon left office, a new chief justice was appointed, one justice, Abe Fortas, was compelled to resign, Justice Black died, and Justice Harlan retired. As each of these vacancies arose, the president knew exactly what his objective was in selecting his nominees. A Democratic Senate did not always consent to those objectives. As a result, the separate roles of the president and the Senate as envisaged by the Constitution were amply tested.

Earl Warren was the Republican governor of California in 1953, when President Eisenhower appointed him to be chief justice of the Supreme Court. One option available to lifetime members of the federal judiciary is the timing of their retirement. Not infrequently a federal judge will time his retirement to permit a president of his choosing to appoint his successor, usually when a president of his own party is in office. Not so with Warren, who reputedly intensely disliked Richard Nixon. In early June 1968 Nixon seemed certain to be the nominee of the Republican party, and so must the chief justice have concluded. Warren was seventy-seven and had labored for fifteen years on the Court. Rather than run the risk that the next chief justice would be selected by Nixon, he submitted his resignation to President Johnson, to become effective upon the appointment and qualification of his successor.

The retiring chief justice had forgotten the rules of practical politics, which he must have known from his ten years as governor of California. He apparently did not have a prior understanding with President Johnson who his successor would be or, at the very least, who he would not be. The chief justice was reportedly shocked when Johnson, on June 26, announced the appointment of his crony Justice Fortas to be the next chief justice.

Many in the Senate were likewise shocked, including Strom Thurmond of South Carolina. Senator Thurmond and several other senators mounted such an intense public attack against Abe Fortas that President Johnson was forced to withdraw the nomination without a vote of the full Senate. That occurred on October 4, a mere month before the general election. The unforeseen turn of events left the chief justice in his high position and, presumably, with more than a casual interest in the outcome of the contest between Hubert Humphrey and Richard Nixon. His resignation, however, was on the desk of the president. Nixon won the election and would appoint the new chief justice.

Presidents usually turn to the attorney general for recommendations of potential nominees to the Supreme Court. Few attorneys general have had the intimate relationship with a president that Mitchell had with Nixon. Mitchell, better than anybody else, knew what kind of a person to recommend to the president to be the next chief justice. In his usual thorough manner, Mitchell immediately went to work formulating a list of persons for consideration by the president. The process had been going on for some time when Mitchell informed me one morning that Judge Burger of the U.S. Court of Appeals for the District of Columbia had agreed to meet with him that afternoon. Mitchell wanted to have the benefit of Burger's opinion about the names on his list, as well as any suggestions the judge might have himself. I was invited to be present.

I had never met Warren Burger, but I had argued an appeal before him two or three years before. When I walked into Mitchell's office I easily recognized his distinguished features and warm manner. He laughed when I reminded him of the case that I had argued before him. He also complimented me for my friendship with one of his best friends in Washington, D.C.—Roger Robb.

Mitchell and Burger then spent the next hour or two going over a long list of judges, lawyers, and professors. Burger was familiar with almost every person on the list. He knew most personally and commented specifically about the judicial philosophy of nearly all. What impressed me even more, however, was the absence of negative remarks about the persons he discussed. He sought only to point out the positive qualities of each. Not once did he so much as hint that he should be included on the list under consideration. His conversation with Mitchell was impressive and objective.

When Judge Burger departed, Mitchell turned to me and asked, "What did you think of that?"

"Unbelievable."

"I'm glad you think so. He's going to be the next chief justice."

On Monday next, May 20, 1969, Mitchell indicated to me that the appointment of Burger as chief justice was almost a certainty. He asked me, however, to run the thought by Robb without indicating that a decision had been made. Robb, a recent appointee of Nixon on the same court as Burger, the U.S. Court of Appeals for the District of Columbia, was in his chambers when I called.

"What do you think of Burger for the Supreme Court?"

"I think he ought to be chief justice," he replied.

"Why?"

Judge Burger, he stated, was an able lawyer, whose judicial philosophy and viewpoints were sound, and who was a leader.

I reported the conversation to Mitchell later that day. He then directed me to call Judge Robb in the morning to determine if he knew Judge Burger well enough to get his income-tax returns.

Unlike the nominations of judges to the lower federal courts, a Supreme Court nominee is not, according to the practice of presidents, subject to a full field investigation by the FBI, nor does the Standing Committee on the Judiciary of the American Bar Association conduct its investigation. By the time the FBI and the bar have completed their investigations, a nominee can be shot full of holes by earnest advocates of other candidates for the coveted position. Income-tax returns, on the other hand, can tell much about a person; and besides, they are in the possession of the Internal Revenue Service, an arm of the executive branch.

I called Robb early Tuesday morning and asked him if he knew Burger well enough to get his returns. He certainly did, he said, and added that he had known Burger since the latter had come to Washington in 1953 to serve in the Department of Justice as an assistant attorney general. Later that day I called Robb again and asked if it would be possible to get the tax returns by noon the next day, Wednesday, May 22. "I'll find out," Robb said. Shortly he called back to report that the returns were in the possession of Judge Burger's brother-in-law, who was his accountant and who also was on a fishing trip in a remote part of Minnesota. "Tell him to take a canoe back to civilization immediately," I replied and hung up. While not known to Robb, the situation had become urgent. Mitchell had just informed me that the president had decided to announce Burger's nomination the next evening, Wednesday, May 22.

The brother-in-law returned to civilization Tuesday evening and dictated the relevant information over the phone on Wednesday morning. Robb and I agreed to meet for lunch at the Georgetown Club on Wisconsin Avenue near M Street. When Robb arrived he confided to me that Burger had just informed him that he was invited to have lunch with Mitchell. I still couldn't tell Robb that Burger was the one; however, my sense of urgency as we scrutinized the returns must have transmitted a message to Judge Robb. The returns were in order and by 1:30 P.M. we had both departed. I immediately reported to Mitchell.

"That's a relief. Burger just looked a little dazed. I told him his nomination would be announced tonight."

"What would you have done if he hadn't been paying his taxes?" I asked, half seriously and half jokingly.

Mitchell resorted to an expression he often used when a crisis loomed: "Go back to the drawing boards, I guess."

I learned several years later from Judge Robb that after our meeting he returned to his chambers and Burger called and asked him to come to his chambers. According to Robb, Mitchell's impression was accurate. "Burger looked rather dazed." Burger then informed Robb that his nomination as chief justice was to be announced that night. Noting that it was then after two o'clock, Robb asked him where he had been to delay his return to his chambers. Burger confessed that after leaving Mitchell's dining room he decided to walk back to the courthouse, a distance of a few blocks. Instead of going east on Pennsylvania Avenue, he mistakenly turned left and, after walking many blocks, found himself in front of St. John's Episcopal Church at Sixteenth and H Streets. He went in, knelt down, and prayed.

Burger and Robb left for Robb's home to avoid being available for comment in the event the nomination had been leaked to the press. Robb recalls that it wasn't until four that Burger was able to find his wife, Elvira, to inform her that they both must be at the White House at 7:00 P.M. Robb also recalls that Judge Burger called his office that afternoon to inquire if there had been any news. The law clerk who answered the phone proudly conveyed the latest inside dope to his boss—Justice Potter Stewart was certain to be the new chief justice. The White House, it seems, was leaking its own news to the press.

Burger's nomination was sent to the Senate the next day, May 23. He was confirmed on June 9. The vote was 74 to 3. On June 23 he took his place on the Supreme Court as its chief justice.

In the nomination, confirmation, and appointment of Warren Earl Burger, the constitutional processes contemplated by the Founding Fathers functioned at their best. The president had acted wisely and promptly. He wisely nominated a person of proven stature, experience, and ability. By acting promptly he fulfilled his constitutional responsibility to provide the country with a new chief justice in a setting devoid of political controversy. The Senate advised and consented, without delay. The judicial philosophy of Warren Burger might not have coincided with that of many of the senators who voted to confirm his nomination. However, no senator in good conscience could have turned him down on the grounds of character, learning, and experience. Those ingredients were supplied by the nominee and they made their own contribution to the success of the constitutional system.

Burger graduated from his law school with high academic honors, and successfully engaged in the private practice of law for twenty-two years. He then became an assistant attorney general in the Department of Justice and served in that capacity for three years until his appointment in 1956 to the U.S. Court of Appeals for the District of Columbia. I believe he has been a great chief justice.

On May 14, 1969, Justice Fortas, for reasons not relevant to this discussion, was compelled to resign. This created a new vacancy on the Court at the very time the president and Mitchell were engrossed in the difficult process of selecting a new chief justice. From that standpoint, the Fortas resignation was an irritant. From the standpoint of the Supreme Court, however, it was providential that this sad affair was administered by the retiring chief justice. Mitchell maintained the strictest confidence regarding the information he had received about Justice Fortas, placed the documentary materials in a sealed envelope, and delivered them personally to Warren. Soon after, Fortas voluntarily resigned. Being absorbed with the selection of Warren's successor also meant that the Fortas vacancy was placed on the back burner, and that eventually benefited the Court.

That vacancy gave Nixon the opportunity to make a political statement. Although the Supreme Court had a black justice in Thurgood Marshall, it did not have a justice who was clearly identified as a modern southerner. I mean no disrespect to the memory of Hugo Black of Alabama. He was appointed to the Court in 1937 by President Roosevelt and resided in the Washington, D.C., area while serving as an associate justice until his death in 1971. In those thirty-four years Justice Black had become a national justice. Many in the South felt that they had no voice on the Court of the 1960s and '70s. Whether this attitude was justified—whether, indeed, regional considerations should have any part in the selection of Supreme Court justices—was not the point. President Nixon thought so, and that was that.

"Back to the drawing boards, boys," Mitchell announced. "Let's find the best qualified Republican from the southern states to recommend to the president to fill the Fortas vacancy."

It was as important to the president that the nominee be a Republican as that he be a southerner. The 1960s witnessed many changes in the social and economic structure of the South. The Republican party had begun to emerge in state after state as a genuine alternative to the Democratic party, which since Reconstruction had been virtually unopposed. There is no better way to encourage participation in a minority party than to recognize it with the reward of significant political appointments. Since Franklin Roosevelt, Democratic presidents, whose elections resulted from the vote of the "solid South," have looked to the interest groups of the northern states for appointments to the Supreme Court. Richard Nixon understood the political significance of this omission and seized the Fortas vacancy as a golden political opportunity.

Judge Haynsworth was nominated to fill the Fortas slot. Clement F. Haynsworth, Jr., who was born in Greenville, South Carolina, in 1912, had been serving since 1957 on the United States Court of Appeals for the Fourth Circuit. He was the best qualified person from the South to be an associate justice of the Supreme Court. I believed that then, and still do. When it was all over on November 21, 1969, the Senate rejected his nomination 55 to 45. In so doing, the Senate exhibited its lowest character.

The genesis of the Senate's rejection of Haynsworth was the rejection of Abe Fortas as chief justice of the United States the preceding year. Some seventeen liberal Democratic senators, led by Birch Bayh of Indiana, were determined to avenge the Fortas rejection.

Fortas had the well-deserved reputation as a liberal member of the Court. He was also its only Jewish member. As a private practitioner, Abe Fortas had fought hard and with great distinction in behalf of many black and liberal causes. That Strom Thurmond of South Carolina had spearheaded the forces opposed to Fortas made it easy for organizations like the National Association for the Advancement of Colored People to conclude that Fortas was turned down because he espoused causes of black America. Likewise, many national Jewish organizations were encouraged to believe that his Jewishness played a part in his rejection. Clement Haynsworth, an Anglo-Saxon Republican from South Carolina, too greatly symbolized past grievances. Unfortunately, however, in the politics of the United States, the symbol often becomes the issue, submerging the merits of the individual. Judge Haynsworth became painfully aware of this fact of life when, during his confirmation hearing, a senator leading the fight against him stopped him in a corridor and, half apologetically, said, "Judge Haynsworth, I hope you don't think any of this is directed to you."

Shortly after Haynsworth's confirmation hearings began, organized labor joined the forces opposed to Haynsworth. The media, generally, opposed the nomination. Day after day sensational charges filled the air. Spokesmen for the NAACP, labor, and some Jewish organizations found they had daily access to the Washington press and television. Opposing senators were routinely interviewed and quoted.

When the fourth estate becomes a participant instead of a reporter in a contest, the fight ceases to be fair. To begin with, if one is chief justice of the U.S. Court of Appeals for the Fourth Circuit, he cannot be an equal contestant. The dignity of the federal judiciary prevents him from being a nightly TV star. In the eyes of the public it would demean him. Even if that were not so, he would probably be denied equal access to the very media that had joined the forces against him. And when that one is Clement Haynsworth, his native reticence will constrain him to shun publicity, especially if he is the subject of a controversy.

The extent to which the media opposition degenerated is, in part, illustrated by the "Bobby Baker incident" and David Brinkley of NBC news. Haynsworth had disclosed all of his stockholdings. It thereafter came to light that Baker, for a short time, owned a few shares in a corporation in which Judge Haynsworth also owned a few shares. The judge was unaware of this. Baker, however, was a person of notoriety at the time, having been convicted and sent to prison. In an NBC news report observed by millions of Americans, Brinkley reported that Haynsworth had been involved in prior business dealings with Baker. After carefully enumerating all of the past errors and omissions of Bobby Baker, Brinkley ended his report with the suggestion that we now know what kind of a person Judge Haynsworth really is. When a retraction was demanded, it was refused because of the passage of time.

When it came time to vote, the outcome had been preordained. For many senators, a vote for Haynsworth would have been a vote against blacks, against labor, against Jews, and in favor of a person who had business dealings with Bobby Baker. The real Clement Haynsworth was lost in the shuffle, and the country lost a potentially great justice.

And the real Clement Haynsworth? The record tells us the following: He was born on October 30, 1912, in Greenville, South Carolina. He received his AB degree in 1933 from Furman University (summa cum laude) and his law degree from Harvard in 1936. He was appointed to the U.S. Court of Appeals for the Fourth Circuit by President Eisenhower in 1957, and served as its chief justice from December 1964 until April 1981, when he took senior judge status.

Judge Haynsworth, you will note, served as chief justice of his circuit until 1981. Rejected by the U.S. Senate after having been the object of unfounded and scurrilous attacks in the national media, Haynsworth, one might surmise, must have given serious thought to retiring from the federal branch. To his great credit, he did not. He returned to the circuit court and served as its chief justice for an additional twelve years.

Tributes are usually reserved for mortals after they have departed this earthly life. Not so with Judge Haynsworth. On the occasion of his retirement as an active judge in 1981, all of the judges of the fourth circuit honored him with a formal tribute. His successor as chief justice of the circuit, Judge Winter, lauded Clement Haynsworth as the "living embodiment of all that is the best of the Deep South," and said of Haynsworth's experience before the U.S. Senate:

> What occurred would have felled a lesser man, but it did not fell Judge Haynsworth. With unequaled courage, he continued to conduct himself with the dignity that he has always displayed, and went about his business of judging despite what must have been bitterness and disappointment in his heart. The result is and has been that not only has he emerged the greater man for what befell him, but there has developed a broad consensus that the Chief Justice together with the nation was unfairly denied a worthy and able colleague.

It is very rare for a member of the Supreme Court to publish writings that are not germane to the business of the Court. Associate Justice Lewis F. Powell, Jr., however, departed from custom and, in the spring 1982 edition of the *Washington and Lee Law Review,* wrote his own personal tribute to Haynsworth. He likewise noted his courage and referred to him as a "hero." Justice Powell then struck at the heart of the matter when he observed that the rejection of Haynsworth by the Senate was for reasons political, "in the least creditable sense of that word. In the case of Judge Haynsworth, certain senators sought an opportunity to strike politically against the president who had nominated him."

The Senate stooped low in the Haynsworth nomination. It doesn't often do so. On the whole, it has been faithful to its constitutional obligation to advise and consent with fairness. In its own way, the Senate has apologized to Clement Haynsworth. On Friday, October 1, 1982, that body, together with the House of Representatives, passed a law that designated a federal building in Greenville, South Carolina, the Clement F. Haynsworth, Jr., Federal Building. The vote in the Senate was unanimous.

President Nixon was still determined to appoint a Republican from the South to the Supreme Court. Was there someone else who might embody the best of the Deep South? Other pressing matters were put aside and we pursued Mitchell's directions to come up with another Haynsworth, if possible.

On paper, Harold Carswell of the U.S. Court of Appeals for the Fifth Circuit appeared to be the answer. He was, first of all, a Republican. President Eisenhower had appointed him as a U.S. attorney and as a federal district judge in northern Florida. Later, President Nixon appointed him to the court of appeals. Senator Gurney, the Republican senator from Florida, recommended Carswell. That virtually meant his nomination. The Standing Committee on the Judiciary of the American Bar Association did its job of evaluating his qualifications and reported to me that Judge Carswell was "exceptionally well qualified." Every written opinion of Carswell, both as a district judge and as a circuit judge, was read and reread by the task force at the Department of Justice. The FBI was directed to conduct the most complete investigation possible of the life and career of the prospective nominee. Everything checked out. Proceeding with abundant caution, Mitchell then instructed me to meet personally with Carswell. "Act as if you were a prosecutor and cross-examine him as if he were an adverse witness," Mitchell directed. I did just that. For several hours I attempted to pry into every aspect of Carswell's personal and public life. Among other things, I wanted to know about his attitudes and past practices on the issue of race. The judge gave the right answers with, so far as I was concerned, convincing sincerity. I so reported and soon thereafter Harold Carswell was announced as the nominee to the Supreme Court.

Senator Bayh, to the distress of the president and the rest of us, immediately promised another political fight over the nomination. In view of what had happened to Clement Haynsworth, we were concerned from the very outset, but nevertheless confident of ultimate success.

Harold Carswell, as a witness for himself before the Senate Judiciary Committee, was not as "exceptionally well qualified" as he appeared on paper. From his demeanor and personality traits, he just didn't come across as a person of judicial temperament. Senator Eastland was heard to remark that "that fellow Carswell is his own worst enemy." The Bayh group began to charge that he was, at best, mediocre. The dean of the Yale Law School publicly stated that he had the fewest credentials for the Court of any man put forward in this century. Roman Hruska, the ranking Republican of the Senate Judiciary Committee and a supporter of Carswell, was quoted as having inadvertently observed, "There are a lot of mediocre judges and people and lawyers and they are entitled to a little representation!"

The roof blew off, however, when an energetic reporter in Florida dug up the fact that Carswell, when he was running for a minor office in northern Florida in 1948, in a speech said, "Segregation of the races is proper and the only practical and correct way of life in our states. I have always so believed and I shall always so act." Despite the judge's vigorous renunciations, that became the beginning of the end for Harold Carswell. The Senate rejected his nomination by a vote of 51 to 45.

I believe the Senate was justified in its decision. In addition, unlike Clement Haynsworth's, Carswell's life unfortunately seemed to take a downhill course thereafter. He resigned from the fifth circuit to run in the Republican primary for the U.S. Senate and was badly defeated. Following that he became a bankruptcy referee. When he became involved in an unfortunate personal incident, he left that position and, I understand, took up farming near Tallahassee.

Had the FBI been more thorough, the Carswell nomination would not have been made. The Carswell nomination also tells us what can happen to persons who find themselves involved in the politics of high positions in our government.

Having been twice frustrated in his attempt to place a Republican from the South on the Court, Nixon did the prudent thing and made a tactical political retreat. The business of the Court demanded that the Fortas vacancy be filled. Another brawl with Birch Bayh would doubtless damage the prestige of the Court. The best politics argued for the nomination of a noncontroversial candidate, in addition to one well qualified, of course. Harry A. Blackmun of Minnesota, a judge of the U.S. Court of Appeals for the Eighth Circuit, was the ideal answer. He had been appointed to the eighth circuit by President Eisenhower in 1959 and had served with distinction on that court since. Unlike Carswell, Judge Blackmun was his own best friend. He was liked and respected by all. The Senate was no exception. On May 12, 1970, less than one month after his nomination, Blackmun was confirmed by a vote of 94 to 1.

The political scoreboard between the president and the Senate was about even. The Burger round was a draw. Both sides were at their best. The Senate clearly lost the Haynsworth round, however, and the president lost the Carswell round by the same margin. In the Blackmun round, the Senate had a slight edge only because the president had been forced to retreat from the legitimate political objective of appointing a southerner to the Court.

On September 23, 1971, Justice John M. Harlan retired for reasons of health. He had served for sixteen years. On September 25, 1971, Justice Hugo L. Black died. He had served since 1937. In less than forty-eight hours, two giants of the Court were no longer there.

One of the important services of the American Bar Association is the work of its Standing Committee on the Judiciary. For many years, the committee had sought to be consulted in advance by presidents as to its opinion whether a prospective nominee to the Supreme Court was qualified. Presidents, however, shied away from such assistance for rather obvious reasons. Lawyers, *per se,* were not politicians and therefore could not be expected to make a fair evaluation of a legitimate political objective of a president. The framers of the Constitution contemplated a Supreme Court having its origins in the political process; otherwise, the nominating function would not have been assigned to the most political office in the government—the presidency. A more realistic reason exists, however, for a president to say "thanks, but no thanks" to the organized bar. The leaders of the bar have their own ideas as to who should be placed upon the nation's highest court. If the prospective nominee of the president didn't happen to coincide with the characteristics deemed essential by the bar, the bar had the easy expedient of simply saying he wasn't qualified. A leak to the press that the president was considering the nomination of a person deemed unqualified by the prestigious American Bar Association would effectively kill the nomination. It is no small wonder, then, that presidents are reluctant to make lawyers silent partners in such a sensitive political matter.

The rejection by the Senate of Haynsworth and Carswell and the unexpected vacancies on the Court, created by the retirement of Justice Harlan and the death of Justice Black, caused Nixon and Mitchell to reexamine the question of the proffered services of the bar. Suppose, for instance, the bar was given not just two prospective nominees, but a list of several persons. If the bar's Standing Committee on the Judiciary would agree to keep confidential not only the list but also its conclusions, perhaps it might work. That was in September 1971, and the next year was a presidential election year. This was not the time to be making risky political statements about the Supreme Court. Nor the time for a return match with Senator Bayh.

Accordingly, but reluctantly, Mitchell put together a list of seven potential nominees and sent the list to the Standing Committee on the Judiciary of the American Bar Association. The accompanying letter set forth the understanding that the committee would inquire into the qualifications of each person and report its findings to the attorney general. Mitchell's letter made it implicit that he would not recommend to the president the name of any person whom the committee found to be unqualified. The very nature of the committee's procedures, however, immediately made public the identity of the persons being considered. And, as we had feared, for one reason or another each person was shot down in the press. Lawyers and law professors throughout the country made public their dissatisfaction with the list of potential nominees. When the chairman of the bar committee informed Mitchell that the two leading candidates—Herschel Friday of Arkansas and Mildred Lillie, a California court-of-appeals judge—would probably not be approved, the president and Mitchell decided to select two nominees without the prior assistance of the committee. Indeed, William Rehnquist, the assistant attorney general in the office of Legal Counsel, was instructed to draft a new letter to the bar committee by which the understandings enunciated in the first letter would be withdrawn.

Lewis F. Powell, Jr., of Richmond, Virginia, was a lawyer of such distinction and accomplishment that he would find himself on any president's list of potential nominees to the Court. He was one of the first names seriously considered by President Nixon when the Fortas vacancy had occurred. However, when inquiries were directed to him at that time, the response was negative. Then sixty-two, Lewis Powell preferred to look forward to something less strenuous than a Supreme Court career. Might he now reconsider the matter, even though two years had elapsed since the Fortas vacancy? A personal call from the president finally compelled his affirmative response. This was, indeed, a triumph not only for the president, but also for the Court, bar, and public. Even though he was a Democrat, the modern South would have its voice on the Court. His scholarship was undenied—Phi Beta Kappa and Harvard Law School. He had performed public service on so many levels of federal and state government that their recital would require a separate chapter. His service as president of the American Bar Association and the American College of Trial Lawyers made his acceptance by the press a certainty.

That William Hubbs Rehnquist of Arizona found himself on the nation's highest court, however, was the product of many seemingly unrelated factors. So many, in fact, that the likelihood of their coming together again to produce a similar result is beyond probability. In one sense, Rehnquist became a justice of the Court because I had known him for many years as a lawyer in Phoenix. My view of him as a lawyer of the highest intellect, ability, scholarship, and integrity was shared by the bar of Arizona. Upon my first briefing on the scope of the work of the Department of Justice in November 1968, I understood that the position of assistant attorney general for the office of Legal Counsel was extremely important. The person who held this position was the lawyer, not only for the attorney general, but for the president as well. He gave the legal opinion on a proposed course of conduct.

Whenever Mitchell asked me for my recommendations to fill that vital post, I came back with the same name—Rehnquist.

"Damn it, Kleindienst, there has to be at least one other person smart enough for the job. It's bad enough that the deputy attorney general will be a cowboy from Arizona; two cowboys at one time would be ridiculous."

"Listen to me, Mr. A.G. You are going to need the best person you can get. Why don't you get off your New York City high horse and at least talk to him?"

Mitchell reluctantly agreed, if only to get me off his back. When Rehnquist came to New York to visit Mitchell in his office in the Pierre Hotel, I introduced them to each other and departed. An hour later Rehnquist came down to my office and announced that Mitchell had persuaded him to take the job.

The basic reason why Rehnquist became an associate justice of the Court was Rehnquist himself. For over two and a half years he discharged the difficult requirements of his position with such distinction that he was indeed regarded by all as *the* lawyer for the Department of Justice, as well as for the executive branch. His performance set the stage for what was about to occur.

Howard Baker of Tennessee was one of the most able members of the Senate. He was of broad political persuasion, had a keen intellect, and was one of the staunchest supporters the president had among the Republicans in the Senate. In light of the disappointing experience with the bar committee and the practical necessity of coming up with a second nominee who would be accepted by the Senate, Nixon asked Senator Baker if he would accept the nomination. The senator said he would think about it overnight and call Mitchell with his answer.

Richard Moore, a close friend and counselor of both the president and the attorney general, happened to be in Nixon's office and was informed of the offer to Baker. Moore turned to the president and said, "If Baker doesn't accept, how about Rehnquist?"

According to Moore, the president at first dismissed him out of hand. Rehnquist was just an assistant attorney general.

"Not so," replied Moore. "He's a lot more than that. He's a brilliant scholar. He's a lawyer's lawyer. Having been a clerk to former Justice Robert Jackson, he knows the Court. He is real quality."

The president's mind apparently began to twirl.

At 9:00 A.M. on Wednesday, October 20, 1971, Baker, as promised, called Mitchell and informed him he would accept the nomination. Mitchell then called

Nixon to report Baker's decision. The president, however, had developed second thoughts about the Baker nomination. Was this a good time to take Baker out of the Senate? Didn't he need his talents and loyalty more than ever on the eve of a presidential election year? There would always be another opportunity to put Baker on the Court. As a result, the president directed Mitchell to persuade Senator Baker that his highest duty to his country at that time was to serve in the Senate and not on the Court. Mitchell complied. Being the loyal man that he is, Baker agreed. The next morning, in the presence of myself and Moore, Mitchell informed Rehnquist that the president would announce, at the White House, the nominations of himself and Lewis Powell to the Court. I was ecstatic not only because of my part in bringing Rehnquist to Washington, but also knowing that a man of his caliber would probably be sitting on the Supreme Court for many years.

Unlike Powell's, Rehnquist's nomination was no political bonanza. "Who is this Rehnquist?" was the question aired the minute after the nomination was made.

Chairman Eastland scheduled hearings on both nominations to commence on November 3. They were concluded in one week. If a separate hearing had been held for each nominee, Powell's would have been concluded in one day; Rehnquist's, perhaps never. From a political standpoint, scarcely a member of the U.S. Senate could challenge Powell's character and career, even if he might have disagreed with aspects of his personal philosophy. He was deservedly regarded as a "great man's great man."

Rehnquist was a different matter. Although his character, scholarship, and private and public legal practice were beyond question, his position in the Department of Justice as the lawyer's lawyer for the Nixon administration offered the opportunity of political controversy. And with a presidential election on the horizon, Rehnquist's hearing could have turned sour.

Senator Eastland understood this full well. He also realized that it was imperative for the Senate to do its part punctually in filling the Harlan and Black vacancies on the Court. The urgent requirements of the Court combined with the undisputed qualifications of both nominees persuaded Eastland that this was no time for a contest between the president and the Senate. By holding the confirmation of the popular Powell hostage to the confirmation of Rehnquist, Eastland could sidestep that contest. That is what he did.

The Senate confirmed Powell on December 6, 1971, by a vote of 84 to 1 and confirmed Rehnquist on December 10 by 68 to 26. Both were sworn in on January 7, 1972.

The modern presidential candidate might be inclined to suggest to the electorate that, if elected, he will appoint better persons to the lower federal courts. To his dismay, however, he will discover soon after his election that, contrary to what the framers of our Constitution intended, the U.S. Senate nominates the federal district judge and the federal court-of-appeals judge. That circumstance has arisen for reasons unforeseeable two centuries ago.

The Founding Fathers might have foreseen a time when the federal judiciary would be so large that a busy president must delegate the initial nominating process to one of his executive aides. I dare say, however, that the thought never occurred to them that the internal workings of the U.S. Senate would so evolve as to usurp that presidential power. But that is exactly the case.

To understand how this happened, one must become acquainted with James O. Eastland of Mississippi and the power he wielded for twenty years as chairman of the Judiciary Committee of the U.S. Senate.

During the transition period before I became deputy attorney general, Warren Christopher informed me that I would deal with Senator Eastland in connection with my responsibilities in the nomination of federal judges. I was uneasy. Eastland, I perceived, was an unreconstructed southerner who used his senatorial power to prevent the enactment of long-delayed civil-rights legislation. I was a conservative Republican in fiscal matters and foreign affairs, but a liberal in civil rights. Senator Eastland and I would very likely never have a satisfactory working relationship. As it turned out, not only was I wrong about Eastland, but we became intimate friends as well. I also came to have an understanding for the first time of the workings and essence of the U.S. Senate.

James Oliver Eastland was born at Doddsville, Mississippi, on November 28, 1904. The Eastlands originally came from Tennessee. His great-grandfather, Hiram Eastland, who was over the age limit to serve in the Confederate Army, moved the family to Scott County, Mississippi, and became its first sheriff. His grandfather, Oliver, and his father, Woods, were born and raised in Scott County. One year after Senator Eastland was born in Doddsville, his father took his family back to Scott County and Eastland attended the public schools of Forest, a small community in that county. He then attended the Universities of Mississippi and Alabama, and Vanderbilt University. In 1927 he was admitted to the Mississippi bar and was elected to the state legislature from Scott County. At the age of twenty-three, a more authentic product of the Deep South than James O. Eastland would be difficult to describe. In 1932 he married Elizabeth Coleman of Doddsville, whither they returned in 1934. There he practiced law and farmed. His father was a successful lawyer and farmer in the Doddsville area.

The Hederman and Eastland families were fast friends, and both families enjoyed the friendship of Paul Johnson, Sr., the governor of Mississippi. In 1941 a vacancy from Mississippi existed in the U.S. Senate. The governor offered the appointment to T. M. Hederman, Sr., publisher of the *Clarion Ledger,* the paper with the largest statewide circulation. Hederman was also a prominent figure in the Baptist church. He declined the appointment and recommended young Eastland instead. Eastland assumed the vacant Senate seat on June 30, 1941, and served until September 28, 1941. Those three months later determined that under the rules of the Senate, Eastland would be the chairman of the Judiciary Committee, and eventually president pro tem of the Senate and twice acting vice president of the United States.

A special election was held in September 1941 to fill the Senate vacancy to which Eastland had been appointed. Eastland did not run in that election and the seat was won by a protégé of Theodore Bilbo, William Doxey. Eastland, however, ran against Doxey in the Democratic primary in September 1942, for a full term of six years. By defeating Doxey, Eastland earned the enmity of Bilbo and, at the same time, a secure seat in the Senate until he voluntarily resigned in 1978.

James O. Eastland and John L. McClellan of Arkansas began their service in the Senate on January 3, 1943. They both became members of the Judiciary Committee that year. Because of the ninety days of service in 1941, however, Eastland outranked McClellan in seniority. Had it not been for that period, McClellan, because of his previous service in the House of Representatives, would have outranked Eastland and would have become the chairman of the Judiciary Committee. If that had been the case, perhaps the Senate might not have come to usurp the constitutional prerogative of the president in the nomination and appointment of federal judges.

From the day James Eastland took his seat in the Senate, none ever doubted that he was there to represent the interests of Mississippi. Two other dimensions made Eastland a bit more than a senator from Mississippi. He was loyal to the discipline of the Democratic party. He was also an astute politician; he recognized the real basis of power in the Senate and knew what to do with it when he had it.

When Eastland ran against Bilbo's man, Doxey, in the 1942 Mississippi Democratic primary, he campaigned more against Franklin Delano Roosevelt than against either Bilbo or Doxey. To most politicians of the Deep South, President Roosevelt was too liberal on race and labor. Nevertheless, Eastland went to the Senate as a Democrat.

Shortly after he arrived in Washington, Eastland was introduced to President Roosevelt by majority leader Alben Barkley of Kentucky at a White House Smoker—a customary means of introducing newly elected Democratic senators and congressmen to the president. When Eastland's turn in the line came up, Roosevelt, according to Eastland, looked up at him from his wheelchair, started to laugh, and said, "Jim, goddamn it, sit down over there in the corner. I want to talk to you when this line has gone through."

When the line passed by, the president wheeled over to the young upstart from Mississippi.

"Son, you think you played hell with me down there in that primary, don't you?"

"No, sir, Mr. President, not really!" the startled Eastland lamely replied.

Always the consummate politician, Roosevelt broke out in his famous jovial grin, and added: "You ran an anti–New Deal campaign just like a Mississippi farmer going to market with a load of corn and a few bales of hay on top to finish out the load. But, don't worry about that, son. We're both good Democrats and we're going to get along together."

Roosevelt then explained what he meant by "get along together": "If you want something for your state from me, come in that door over there and I'll give you two minutes to tell me what you want and I'll see to it that you get it. Then I'm going to spend fifteen minutes telling you what I want from you and you are going to do it. Understood?"

"Yes, sir, Mr. President. Yes, sir."

From everything I have come to know about Senator Eastland, the bargain was faithfully kept by each. That bargain Eastland would also have with every Democratic president as long as he remained in the Senate.

The lesson of his "understanding" with President Roosevelt was not lost on Eastland in his dealing with his Senate colleagues, Democrat or Republican. By the time he succeeded to the chairmanship of the Judiciary Committee he had earned their respect as a person whose word was his bond—no matter the political cost. Fourteen continuous years of observation as a member of the Judiciary Committee also taught him how, with a change or two in committee rules, a senator could dominate the judicial appointment process and yet be protected from political embarrassment back home.

For many years before March 1956, when the president sent to the Senate a nomination for a federal judgeship, the Judiciary Committee staff would send a "blue slip" to each senator from the state in which the nominee resided. On the blue slip the two senators were to indicate their approval or objection. Frequently, though, a senator did not wish to express his opinion in writing. So, Senator McCarran of Nevada, chairman of the committee for many years, informed the members of the Senate that if they didn't return their blue slips by a certain time, the president's nominee would be approved. That rule worked quite well during those many years when a Democratic president occupied the White House and when his party usually had a majority in the Senate. Politically, however, the situation was a little different during the Eisenhower years, in which, excepting 1953 and 1954, the Democrats controlled the Senate. From time to time a Democratic senator found it uncomfortable to write his objection to a judicial nominee of a popular Republican president.

Senator McCarran had another rule. If a senator objected to a presidential nominee, he had to state that objection on the floor of the Senate. That really put the political monkey on his back, and many senators grumbled that their senatorial prerogative was inhibited.

The first change Eastland made in the rules of the Judiciary Committee was the most significant. He informally advised the Senate that henceforth, if a senator objected to a judicial nominee from his state, all he had to do was hold onto his blue slip. He also assured each senator that no hearing on a judicial nomination would be scheduled unless the committee had received both blue slips indicating no objection to the nomination.

The second change he made was almost as significant. Thereafter a senator would not be required to state his reasons on the Senate floor for objecting to a nomination.

With those two innovations, the Senate, for all practical purposes, assumed the power granted to the president in the nomination of judges to the lower federal courts.

All options belonged to the senator. If the president, through the attorney general, submitted a nomination to the Senate Judiciary Committee, the two senators could either return their blue slips without objection or do nothing. If they did nothing, nothing happened. The vacancy went unfilled as long as a senator could withstand the political pressure back home created by the press.

Another option a senator had was to stay out of the process completely. This he exercised when the political situation back home dictated. Not infrequently, the selection of a federal judge becomes the subject of controversy arising from the intense competition between aspirants. A senator, to avoid a damaging political hassle—especially in an election year—can simply wash his hands of the matter by transferring the political problem to the White House: "I'll support any nominee of the president." Whereupon, the competitors descend upon the White House, which in turn ships the problem to the Department of Justice.

Senator Eastland knew by instinct and experience that his new rules would work only if they were applied without exception. There could be no deviation because of party or ideological differences. If a senator did not return his blue slip, that was it. No hearing would be scheduled.

When Chairman Eastland explained the rules of his committee to me the first time we met, which was immediately after I became deputy attorney general, he didn't volunteer the history of these rules. There was likewise no reason for him to point out to me the practical effect the rules had on the appointive power of the president. Although it was not until much later that I learned the history, it didn't take me long to realize the practical effect of the rules.

The problem faced by the attorney general and the Department of Justice was easy to see. If, under the rules of the Senate, the senator had the actual appointive power, how did one protect the president, who had the constitutional appointive power? If a senator insisted upon a relatively unqualified person to be appointed to the federal judiciary, the president would be blamed, not the senator.

A satisfactory solution to the problem, however, was less easy. President Nixon was faced with the prospect of having to appoint more federal judges than any of his predecessors. A solution thus had to be found, soon. As is usually the case in government and politics, solutions to problems result from compromise. In this case, the Standing Committee on the Judiciary of the American Bar Association provided the vehicle of compromise.

Since the early 1950s that committee of the American bar had endeavored to have the attorney general commit himself to a procedure whereby he would nominate no federal judge unless the committee had first determined that the prospective nominee was qualified. I first met with the committee shortly after my first meeting with Eastland. When the members of the committee outlined this concept to me, my first reaction was that it was rather presumptuous for the organized bar to seek such a prerogative. In one sense, it constituted a veto of the president's constitutional responsibility. Indeed, even though Eisenhower,

Kennedy, and Johnson had given some recognition to the opinions of the Standing Committee of the bar, none had gone so far as to agree to be bound by its evaluation in every instance. Nevertheless, because I became convinced that the sole objective of the committee was the selection of only qualified persons to be lifetime federal judges, I concluded that the concept could work if the bar committee would agree to two conditions: first, that it not concern itself with recommending prospective nominees (that function would be the exclusive prerogative of the president—or the Senate); second, that political affiliation or political activities of prospective nominees be disregarded. When the committee indicated its willingness to abide by the two conditions, I informed it that I would recommend the procedure to the attorney general.

Mitchell agreed to the proposal with the admonition, however, that the system would work only if it was made clear to all senators at the outset that there would be no exceptions.

As a general proposition, the Senate accepted the procedure, and with little difficulty when it was made clear that the senators would be directly involved from the beginning of the selection process. Thus, in the case of Republican senators, they would be given the option to recommend nominations. If there were two Republican senators from a state, they would have to work out the selection process between themselves before the Justice Department would proceed. In the case of a state with two Democratic senators, the name of a prospective nominee would not be submitted to the bar committee for evaluation if either senator indicated in advance that he would object to the nomination; that is, he would not return his blue slip. This difference in applying the ground rules to the parties derives from a longstanding custom in the Senate. When a Democratic president is in office, Republicans defer to the Democratic senators to originate judicial nominations and vice versa. When a state has no senator of the president's party, the opposition senators defer to the president's political sources but nevertheless retain the right of veto if the nominee is either politically or personally obnoxious to them.

So, there it was. Chairman Eastland had rules that he applied without exception. The Department of Justice had a rule that it applied without exception. It also had an agreement with the senators that would likewise be applied without exception.

Generally, the senators welcomed the role of the Standing Committee on the Judiciary of the American Bar Association. Knowing that the Justice Department would not process a prospective candidate who was not qualified, a senator could avoid political problems back home even if he were compelled to submit for consideration the name of a marginally qualified person. If such a person were turned down by the bar, the senator could truthfully say he was sorry, but don't blame him. Blame the bar and the deputy attorney general. If, on the other hand, a senator submitted three names for a vacancy, and one was deemed qualified, another well qualified, and the third exceptionally well qualified, he had an easy solution to the problem by selecting the best qualified.

On one or two occasions, however, a Republican senator just couldn't live with the system—or so he thought. In one instance, a large financial backer of a senator wanted his young son appointed a federal district judge. He did not have the requisite five years of active practice and would have been deemed unqualified by the bar. The senator insisted that I send his name to the bar anyway. It came back designated unqualified, as expected. The senator then insisted that I meet with him and the young man's father. The father had no interest in the bar. He did have a close relationship with the senator, however.

"Senator, you tell this deputy attorney general that he is going to send my son's name to the White House, do you understand?"

"Mr. ———," I interjected, "this deputy attorney general isn't going to do that. The best thing for the senator to do for you is to persuade the president to get another deputy attorney general. Good day."

Another time a Republican senator, a good friend of mine, insisted on nominating a good friend of his back home who obviously lacked the minimum qualifications prescribed by the bar committee. When the bar report came in, the senator refused to accept it. I visited him in his office and we almost came to fisticuffs as a result of my adamant position that there would be no exception to the rule.

"I'm going to see the president about this," he shouted.

"Be my guest."

Later I learned that he did see the president, who, as I understand it, assured the senator that he would nominate his candidate—"Just clear it first with Kleindienst." That ended that.

I suppose the most heated argument I had with anyone over the system was with President Ford when he was the minority leader of the House. He was trying to help a Republican colleague in the House who desired the nomination of a person from a midwestern state that had no Republican senator. Around and around we went. Ford couldn't accept the fact that a committee of the American Bar Association could be given such a veto. When he informed me in no uncertain terms that he was going to the president, I could only reply that if he was able to persuade the president to overrule me, I would have to resign. I tried to explain to him that if I yielded to one exception, my credibility with the senators would be at an end. He did see the president and I didn't have to resign. I fully understood Ford's position, however. He did what a minority leader should have done. That's why he was a great leader—both in the Congress and as president.

It had to be irritating to President Nixon to have Republican members of the Congress complain to him about the rigidity of our department on judicial nominations. To his great credit, he put a qualified federal judiciary ahead of temporary political pressure. By so doing, he was able to make a notable contribution to our federal courts.

In the first two years of his presidency, Nixon appointed 115 persons to the lower federal courts and two to the Supreme Court. In 1970 eighty-three vacancies in the federal district courts were filled. That was the largest number of federal trial judges appointed in one year in the history of the United States, exceeding by thirteen the number appointed by President Johnson in 1967, who enjoyed a Senate controlled by his own party.

In five years as the chief executive, President Nixon had appointed more federal judges than any previous president. He named 230 judges to the federal judiciary, nineteen more than President Roosevelt in his twelve years of office. Every Nixon appointment was deemed at least qualified by the American Bar Association. President Kennedy, by the way, appointed seven judges and President Johnson appointed four who were considered "not qualified" by the American Bar Association.

One area of comparison that should be made is that of the appointment of blacks to the federal judiciary. Racism, as it existed in the United States for over a hundred years following the abolition of slavery, has left its imprint on every aspect of our political, cultural, and economic society. The federal judiciary is no exception. President Truman was the first president to appoint a black to a lifetime position as a federal judge. In 1945 he appointed a black to the U.S. Customs Court and in 1949 a black to the U.S. Court of Appeals for the Third Circuit. President Eisenhower, in his two terms of office, made only one such appointment. President Kennedy appointed only three, one being Thurgood Marshall to the U.S. Court of Appeals for the Second Circuit. President Johnson, however, was the first president to make a significant contribution to this neglected area. During LBJ's presidency, Thurgood Marshall was elevated to the Supreme Court; Judge Robinson, whom he had previously appointed to the federal district court in the District of Columbia, was elevated to the U.S. Court of Appeals for the District of Columbia; Judge McCree, a Kennedy appointment to the federal district court in Michigan, was elevated to the U.S. Court of Appeals for the Sixth Circuit; and Judge Waddy, a Kennedy appointee to the lower District of Columbia courts, was elevated to the District Court for the District of Columbia. Altogether, President Johnson appointed seventeen blacks to the various federal courts.

The record of the Nixon administration does not suffer by comparison. President Nixon appointed nineteen blacks to the federal judiciary—six to lifetime judicial positions and thirteen to the lower-term courts in the District of Columbia. Had that number been doubled, it would still have been too small.

Barrington Parker of the District Court for the District of Columbia well exemplifies the difficulties a president encounters when he attempts to redress the imbalance of blacks on the federal courts. Since there are no senators for the District of Columbia, an opportunity existed for the president himself to nominate a black to a vacancy that occurred in that court in 1969. Judge Parker was an outstanding lawyer, and had the backing of the community. He was also a Republican. I thought his nomination would sail through the Senate without difficulty. However, the Republican national committeeman who had previously assured me of his support for Parker, had undertaken to persuade Strom Thurmond, a member of the Senate Judiciary Committee, that Parker was not qualified for the position. This fact came to my attention one afternoon when I received a call from Chairman Eastland to come to his office. When I arrived, he and Senator Thurmond were together in his private office.

"Tell Strom what you think about Barrington Parker," Eastland said, opening the conversation.

When I finished my presentation, Eastland turned to Thurmond. "Does that satisfy you, Strom?"

Senator Thurmond responded in the affirmative.

Shortly thereafter, Barrington Parker took his place on the federal bench. He is best known to America by the able way in which he conducted the sensitive and difficult trial of John Hinkley, the would-be assassin of President Reagan. I relate this event for two reasons. First, it illustrates the difficulty presidents face in nominating and appointing blacks and other minorities to the federal courts. Second, it highlights the fairness and open-mindedness of both Senator Eastland and Senator Thurmond.

The ground rules established by Eastland and the Nixon Department of Justice continued through the presidency of Gerald Ford. However, there was one exception. Of the sixty-five judges appointed by President Ford, one nomination was of a person who, the bar committee had determined, was not qualified. Perhaps President Ford was mindful of his prior confrontation with me and concluded that in at least one instance he was going to be president in fact as well as in theory. He appointed his own man.

Senator Eastland retired from the Senate in 1978 and was succeeded as chairman of the Judiciary Committee by Senator Kennedy of Massachusetts. A more striking contrast could not exist. Eastland carefully maintained a low profile, was an authentic representative of the traditions and culture of the Deep South, was a "senator's senator," and was regarded by the public as a conservative as to the federal judiciary. Kennedy, of course, harbors national political ambitions, is a liberal from New England, and, in keeping with his political aspirations, proclaims himself a liberal as to the federal judiciary.

As one might expect, Kennedy used the first meeting of the Judiciary Committee under his chairmanship to make a political statement addressed to his national constituents. On January 25, 1979, five days after the inauguration of President Carter, the new chairman read to the full Judiciary Committee a proposed statement that, naturally, was released to the press on the same day. After prefacing his remarks with appropriate observations about the significance of the federal judiciary in our great country, he then addressed himself to the customs of the Senate with respect to appointments to the lower federal courts. These, he proclaimed, "have been of special interest to individual senators" and "likened to a rubber stamp" by some critics. At the conclusion of his remarks he met the real question head-on: "Finally, we face the question of what to do about the longstanding practice of the one-member veto—or the blue-slip process—which in general has allowed a senator from the home state of the nominee to veto that nominee without any public discussion. . . ." He then pledged that he would "not unilaterally take a nomination simply because a blue slip is not returned by a colleague." But, he added, *"I cannot, however, discard cavalierly the tradition of senatorial courtesy, exception-riddled and outdated as it may be"* (emphasis supplied). He then promised the following new procedure: if a blue slip was not returned within a reasonable time, he would let the full committee determine whether it wished it proceed to a hearing. Thus, he concluded, "The committee, and ultimately the Senate, can work its will."

Whoever wrote these words for the senator from Massachusetts undoubtedly received a high grade in high school civics. The pertinent question, however, is what actually happened thereafter.

The actual practice was really not much different from that before. If a senator did not object to a nomination within seven days, the committee could assume that there was no objection and proceed with the nomination. If, however, a senator did object, that would be the end of it. "Senatorial courtesy," thus, "outdated as it may be," lived on.

Senator Kennedy must have had his tongue in his cheek when he read his statement because he was well versed in the exercise of his right to senatorial courtesy. One of the most controversial incidents in recent times involved the nomination in 1965 by Edward M. Kennedy of "family friend" Francis X. Morrissey as a federal district judge. Even though the nominee was deemed not qualified by the American Bar Association, the Judiciary Committee, at Kennedy's insistence, voted 6 to 3 to send the nomination to the full Senate. Only because heated opposition to the nomination developed did the Senate send the nomination back to the Judiciary Committee. The senator from Massachusetts then withdrew the nomination.

Because the "Eastland system" remained essentially in place after Eastland left the Senate, President Carter can claim credit for the appointment of more federal judges than any previous president. In 1978, two years after Carter's election, a Congress controlled by his party created 152 new federal judgeships. These new positions, together with the normal vacancies, permitted President Carter to nominate and appoint a record number of 265 judges. Only one of these appointments was deemed not qualified by the American Bar Association; that person is a black who now sits as a federal district judge in one of the southern states.

The record is not in, of course, for President Reagan. By the end of his first term, however, he had appointed 167 federal judges, including Sandra Day O'Connor to the Supreme Court. It should come as no surprise that Senator Thurmond of South Carolina has continued to follow the essential ground rules of James O. Eastland when he became chairman of the Judiciary Committee in January 1981. As of this writing, every "nomination" by President Reagan has been deemed qualified by the American Bar Association.

I met James O. Eastland in January 1969. Before then, I would have selected him as the one member of the U.S. Senate with whom I would be the most incompatible. My perception of Eastland was gained, naturally, from the media. He was, I believed, a Mississippi senator who had led the fight to prevent blacks from voting, from using public facilities, and from attending integrated public schools. How could I, with my beliefs, ever have a relationship based upon mutual respect with the like of him?

I left the Department of Justice in mid-1973. Long before then, James Eastland had my respect and friendship. The first thing I quickly discovered about the chairman was that my beliefs were my affair, his beliefs were his affair. Jim Eastland was concerned more with whether a person was honest and sincere in his beliefs than with what those beliefs were. A person's word was everything. He always kept his word and he expected others to do likewise. Keeping truth was the cornerstone of his life, and for it, he gained the respect of his colleagues in the Senate. How often other senators would say to me: "You might disagree with Jim Eastland, but you can always rely upon his word."

Eastland's early counsel made me realize what kind of a person I would be dealing with: "Dick, I want to tell you something. In my position in the Senate, friends of mine from time to time call me to intervene for them with the Department of Justice. When they do, I'm going to call you. You use your own judgment. If you believe it is a proper request, fine; if you don't, just tell me."

I remember but one incident when he called and that was for a status report. He was really trying to say he wasn't going to interfere with the conduct of the Department of Justice. And he never did.

Next only to his country, it was to the institution of the Senate that Senator Eastland gave his loyalty. He recognized that it was in that body that the essential interest of any minority group would find its ultimate protection. The art of compromise is the great strength of a body composed of two members from every state in the Union. His understanding of that art made him the influential and effective chairman of the Judiciary Committee that he was acknowledged to be.

As to the function of his committee in the constitutional process of appointments to the federal judiciary, he was guided by two fundamental principles. Every president, Democrat or Republican, should be treated the same way in the discharge of his responsibility, and every senator, Democrat or Republican, should be accorded the same courtesy in the application of the rules of the Senate Judiciary Committee. He didn't pretend to tell presidents whom they should appoint, nor did he tell other senators what they should do. In short, he saw to it that his committee fairly and evenly did what it was supposed to do in this vital process—nothing more and, to be sure, nothing less.

The federal courts of the United States consist of hundreds of able, dedicated men and women. Most give up lucrative law practices to become federal judges. Most, if not all, undertake the great responsibility as a commitment that will continue for the remainder of their lives. Why? Because of their compelling belief in the rule of law in a free society. To point out one federal judge and say he is the best example of the federal judiciary is impossible. But Roger Robb of the United States Court of Appeals for the District of Columbia typifies to me the best of the best.

Various characteristics are needed if a person is to be considered a judge of the highest caliber. Many come to mind: integrity, intellect, a general education, knowledge of the law, broad general experience, experience in the practice of law, belief in the equal application of the law to all persons, belief in the Constitution of the United States, a basic liking for people, courage, self-confidence, decisiveness, humility. Roger Robb, in my opinion, has more than his share of these and other qualities that, in combination, produce a great judge.

Judge Robb began the practice of law in Washington, D.C., in 1931 after his graduation from Yale College (Phi Beta Kappa) and the Yale Law School. Until his appointment to the federal bench in 1969, he was engaged in a broad general practice of the law. For seven years he was an assistant U.S. attorney and was charged with the enforcement of the law. In his private practice he specialized in civil litigation, trials, and appellate practice. His clients were businessmen, government employees and officials, senators, writers, publishers, lawyers, and an educational institution.

As a trial lawyer he did not restrict his clients to particular segments of society. For example, in 1950 he successfully represented Earl Russell Browder, the former secretary of the Communist party, when he was indicted on sixteen counts for contempt of Congress. In his book *Contempt of Congress,* Browder praised Robb's services and complimented him for his "pride of his profession"—notwithstanding Robb's political values, which Browder characterized as "reactionary." A few years later, Judge Robb was designated by the U.S. Atomic Energy Commission to present to it the evidence that led to its denial of a national security clearance to Dr. Robert Oppenheimer. In another case, the judges of the U.S. Court of Customs and Patent Appeals retained him to appear before the Supreme Court to establish that the Customs Court was a constitutional tribunal. Robb prevailed. The American Bar Association also retained Robb to appear before the Supreme Court on its behalf. The decision of the Supreme Court substantially agreed with the contentions made in Robb's brief. He personally represented Senator Eastland in a suit in which the plaintiff asserted that Eastland, as chairman of the Internal Security Subcommittee of the Senate Judiciary Committee, had conspired with state officials to seize his property by unlawful means. He won the case in the lower federal courts and before the Supreme Court. The Committee on Admissions and Grievances of the District of Columbia Bar Association retained Robb in a case in which it was established that when a lawyer embezzles funds of a client, he should be disbarred as a matter of course. A concluding example of the variety of Robb's clients was Barry Goldwater, whom Robb represented in Barry's libel action against *Fact* magazine and its publisher, Ralph Ginzburg. The case was important as a test of the extent to which men in public life are protected against false and defamatory statements. During Goldwater's 1964 bid for the presidency, *Fact* characterized Goldwater as "emotionally unstable, paranoid, immoral and Hitler-like." A New York City jury awarded sizable money damages to Senator Goldwater.

Roger Robb's civic activities have been similarly broad. It is revealing, however, that for several years he served as a trustee for the Legal Aid Agency for the District of Columbia, as a member of the D.C. Commissioner's Committee on Police Arrests for Investigation, and as a director of the Bureau of Rehabilitation, an organization whose function is to assist prisoners upon their release from confinement.

This is but a sketch and therefore unfair to Judge Robb. It serves, nevertheless, to give an adequate insight into the measure of the man. Student, lawyer, concerned citizen. Courage to represent an unpopular defendant. The professional skill by which the rights of private citizens and public officials are protected. Response to the call to uphold the integrity of governmental institutions. Personal counselor to high public officials. Loyal friend. Distinguished judge.

Thanks to our Founding Fathers, and to the like of James O. Eastland, many Roger Robbs are dispensing justice from the benches of our federal courts.

8
Petersen
Watergate

The world's biggest "law firm" comprises the lawyers in the Department of Justice. They are found in the several litigating divisions, each of which is headed by an assistant attorney general who is appointed by the president with the advice and consent of the Senate. Each litigating division is responsible for the enforcement of a distinct set of laws. Thus, there are, or have been, an antitrust division, a tax division, a criminal division, and a similar division for land and natural resources, civil rights, internal security, and civil matters. The office of Legal Counsel is the small shop of lawyers' lawyers who furnish legal opinions for the other divisions as well as for the executive branch.

The lawyers of the department are also found around the country in the offices of the same ninety-four United States attorneys. The U.S. attorney is appointed by the president with the advice and consent of the Senate.

Notwithstanding the obvious political ramifications of the presidential appointive role, the "law firm" is not only the biggest in the world, but the best. Perhaps this statement was not always true, but for the last thirty years it has been.

When Herbert Brownell became President Eisenhower's attorney general in 1953, he brought with him as his deputy attorney general William P. Rogers. Brownell and Rogers came to the department from prestigious law firms that understood the advantages derived from the employment of young lawyers who had excelled in law school. Why, therefore, shouldn't the biggest law firm be the best? They answered that question by implementing what became known as the Attorney General's Program for Honor Law Graduates, a program which exists today. Each year the litigating divisions of the department recruit from law schools throughout the country young men and women in the upper ten percent of their graduating classes. By 1972, when I was the attorney general, over sixteen hundred top third-year law students had made applications under this program. Only ninety-seven attorneys were selected. Sixty-five law schools and thirty-two states were represented.

Many of those lawyers remain with the department for but a few years and leave to take positions in private firms. They take with them not only excellent training but also a knowledge of how the system works. This benefits both the private and public sectors. In our adversary system of law, an understanding of the role of the lawyer on the other side cannot help but facilitate the application and enforcement of the federal laws.

Most of these lawyers, however, remain and become the career lawyers of the department. As a general class, they constitute the best of "government bureaucrats." I say this for two reasons. First, their intellectual credentials and years of experience cannot be challenged. More important, they are professionals and thus understand the necessity of changing enforcement priorities arising from the policy changes of a new president. Hence, if a Ramsey Clark as a matter of policy chose not to enforce the court-ordered electronic surveillance procedures of the 1968 Omnibus Crime Control Act, so be it. If a John Mitchell chose to do so, well enough. Each new attorney general, however, can depend on this small army of dedicated professionals to enable him and his president to enforce the laws of the land.

I suppose it serves no real useful purpose for a former attorney general to select one or two career justice lawyers as examples of the best of the best. There are so many who fit the description and each attorney general might differ in such a selection based solely on his own experience. For whatever it is worth, I have two selections. One is Mary Lawton (see Appendix A). The other is Henry Petersen.

I met Henry for the first time in November or December 1968. I came to Washington, D.C., from New York City several times to interview prospective candidates to become the assistant attorney general for the criminal division. I had not been a criminal lawyer in private practice in Phoenix, but I believed that the new administration would be better served by one who was not a part of the political process. Nixon had made law and order a campaign issue. Vietnam and the dissent it produced were everywhere. Drugs and their abuse were a national nightmare. Organized crime could at last be challenged with the weapons provided by the 1968 Omnibus Crime Control Act. If vigorous law enforcement was to be a focal point of the new administration, let it be spearheaded by a person who could not be charged with partisan political motives. I was persuaded that the possibility of abuse in the enforcement of the criminal laws existed more readily if the top prosecutor had ambitions for political office. I was thus determined to find a candidate to recommend to Mitchell who would be at once an aggressive, competent professional and a nonpolitical—a straight arrow, if you will.

Petersen was suggested by everyone I talked to as the best person to be found to satisfy these dual requirements. This wasn't a bit surprising to me. I had a summary of his career in the department going back to 1947, when he was employed as a messenger and tour guide while attending law school at night. He was admitted to the District of Columbia bar in March 1951 and immediately transferred to the antitrust division of Justice. In December of that year he transferred to the criminal division and for seven years was engaged in enforcing the liquor, narcotics, gambling, and labor racketeering laws. He was appointed deputy chief of the organized-crime section in 1958. In 1966 he was appointed chief of that section and soon thereafter initiated the highly successful strike-force concept, which to this day provides the Department of Justice with the framework for its efforts against organized crime.

Impressive credentials they were then, December 1968. But the competence of Petersen would become even more impressive in the days of Watergate.

The personality of Petersen equally impressed. One look at him and a few minutes of conversation revealed a rare individual. A quiet modesty based upon self-confidence marked him. I had no doubt as to his character and integrity when he looked me straight in the eye as he spoke. I was soon to learn of his independence too.

At the end of a rather long interview, I said, "Henry, I don't know what your politics are and I don't really care; however, if you are a registered Democrat, would you have any problem changing your registration to Republican?"

"Mr. Kleindienst," he shot back, "my politics are none of your damn business. I'm not saying how I'm registered, but if I had to change it to get this job, then you can take the job and do you know what with it!"

I laughed, terminated the interview, and said to myself, "This is the guy for the job."

The next day I walked into Mitchell's office in the Pierre Hotel and announced that I had found the ideal person to manage the criminal division.

"Don't even bother to mention his name. Senator Tower of Texas has persuaded the president-elect that Will Wilson, the former Democratic attorney general of Texas, now turned Republican, is just what we need. Wilson is on his way to New York City right now and I've arranged for him to meet with you in your hotel room when he arrives tomorrow morning."

Will Wilson knocked at my door early the next morning. He had obviously been up all night but I was nevertheless impressed by his zeal and sincerity. Since the decision had already been made, it wasn't really necessary to have a long conversation. Just as he was leaving, however, he said something that rather astounded me and that I thought was quite naive. "Let me have this job and I'll guarantee you that organized crime in America will be gone in six months!"

I reported the remark to Mitchell later that morning. He laughed and said, "The distinguished former Texas attorney general has a big surprise in store for him."

I think Wilson soon discovered that controlling crime on the national level was a little more difficult than doing so in Texas as the elected attorney general. Fortunately, he followed our suggestion that Petersen be designated the deputy assistant attorney general.

Not long after assuming office, I began to look to Petersen for advice on a daily basis. This was not entirely fair to Wilson, but I needed the help of a knowledgeable professional. A new deputy attorney general had much to learn in a short period. Henry Petersen was the most patient and understanding teacher I ever had.

Wilson learned about the politics of Washington, D.C., and what can happen to a public figure there with a previous political career. That he found it necessary to resign his position of assistant attorney general because of what became known as the Sharpstown scandal in Texas has to be the most agonizing experience in his otherwise illustrious career.

Before seeking public office in Texas, Wilson was a private lawyer and had a client by the name of Frank Sharp. Sharp purchased the controlling stock of National Bankers Life Insurance Company from a former Texas governor, Allan Shivers. Wilson handled the legalities of the purchase. Sharp borrowed the money needed to pay cash for the insurance company stock. The economy tightened up and Sharp was pressed to repay the money he had borrowed. He turned then to his own bank and borrowed money from it to repay the first borrowing, using stock from the insurance company as collateral. This transaction came to the attention of the bank examiners, who required him to replace the money he had borrowed from his own bank. In order to do that, he took money out of the insurance company and thereby wound up buying it with its own money.

Those transactions soon came to the attention of the Securities and Exchange Commission in Washington, D.C., and the fat was in the fire. The part that Wilson had played—quite properly—in the original transaction also came to the attention of the SEC and it so advised Wilson. The possibility of a violation of federal criminal laws existed and Wilson—again, quite properly—on November 19, 1970, excused himself as the assistant attorney general of the criminal division from consideration of matters involving Sharp. He did this in writing following a conversation with Mitchell. His memorandum of that date directed that matters relating to Sharp be handled by Petersen under my supervision.

Shortly thereafter, all hell broke out in Texas. The Sharp machinations began to involve many of the former and present officeholders in the state. As possible criminal violations arising out of an investigation by federal bank examiners were being investigated by the U.S. attorney in Houston, the question of a grant of immunity to Sharp in exchange for his testimony against others came up. Anthony Farris recommended such a procedure to me and Petersen. We agreed only on the condition that the specifics of Sharp's testimony be obtained in advance and in writing before a final decision was made. Farris bungled the matter by granting the immunity without our consent and without having obtained the required specific testimony in advance. Thereafter, Sharp pleaded guilty to related but separate charges brought by the SEC and, to the astonishment of everyone, was given probation and a light fine by the sentencing jurist, Judge Singleton. Wilson, of course, had nothing to do with any of this.

Henry Gonzales was a Democratic congressman from Texas. By July 28, 1971, he had made eighteen speeches on the floor of the House of Representatives with respect to the grant of immunity to Sharp and the prior relationship of Wilson to Sharp and his various companies. The essential charge by Congressman Gonzales was that Wilson had used his position to prosecute top Texas Democrats with whom he had had political differences in former days and, in addition, had permitted his former client, Sharp, to go unscathed.

That attack against Wilson produced an untenable situation both for the Department of Justice and for him personally. You just can't tolerate a situation where an assistant attorney general is accused of political prosecution on the one hand and of sheltering a former client on the other. Regardless of the truth or falsity of the charges—the truth or falsity can be established only after the passage of months—the public's confidence in the nonpolitical administration of the federal criminal laws has to be maintained. With a bitter heart, Will Wilson finally accepted the reality of the situation and offered his resignation. Ironically, he was compelled to resign because he allegedly used his office for political purposes.

Out of bitterness he has accused me of the same political motivation, which also was untrue.

That unfortunate incident served one good purpose. It made me absolutely convinced that the assistant attorney general for the criminal division must not be a political person. I believed that in 1968. By fall 1971—when Wilson resigned—John Mitchell was of like mind. Henry Petersen was appointed acting assistant attorney general on October 19, 1971, and, on January 7, 1972, became the first career lawyer of the Department of Justice to be appointed by a president to be an assistant attorney general. That he remained in that position until he voluntarily resigned on December 31, 1974, after having navigated a perilous course through the quagmire of Watergate, is the only testimony required to demonstrate the worth of that unique man.

Before describing my participation in a part of the Watergate episode with Petersen, I must return to the end of 1968 and the circumstances in which John Dean became a part of the Department of Justice.

The what-if game is the easiest there is to play. The only skill required is twenty-twenty vision—hindsight, that is. Before we begin to speculate on the question ''What if John Dean had not begun his career in the Nixon administration as a member of my staff in the office of the deputy attorney general, would Watergate have been different?'' we must see how he got there in the first place.

Because it administers the policies of the attorney general, the staff of the deputy attorney general is quite large. Two critical staff positions are the associate deputy attorney general for the office of criminal justice and the associate deputy attorney general for legislation and congressional liaison. The former position is critical because of its responsibility as the think tank for each new administration in the field of criminal justice. The latter is critical because it is responsible for preparing legislation to be offered by a new administration and, in addition, is the eyes and ears of the Department of Justice in the halls of Congress. Obviously, both offices are deep in policy. One doesn't, as part of the incoming

Nixon administration, keep Ramsey Clark's architect for criminal justice programs and ideas, or use an aide of Robert Kennedy to represent the department before the Congress.

Where does one find persons who share the basic philosophy of a new president, who are experienced, and who will leave what they are doing for a berth in the bureaucracy? Moreover, time is short in a transition period. A new administration must be able to function by inauguration day.

Donald Santarelli and John Dean were two bright young men. They came to me highly recommended by Republican members of the House Judiciary Committee. They also had their eyes on a position in the Department of Justice in the new administration. Both had served together as staff counsel for the Republican side of the House Judiciary Committee. Dean left that position to serve on the Commission to Reform the Federal Criminal Code. He held that post for about six months. Their interest and talents, I perceived, ideally suited them for two positions of responsibility in Justice.

Santarelli is one of those rare persons who combine high intellect and ability to conceptualize and birth programs. The department's office of criminal justice fit Santarelli like a glove. I dare say no other associate deputy attorney general has achieved the record of accomplishment in that office that he achieved. It was he who almost single-handedly conceived and brought into being the present court system for the District of Columbia. Today the District has a judicial system equal to that of any state in the Union; but in 1969 one factor contributing to the high crime rate in our nation's capital was its inadequate, antiquated machinery for ministering justice.

Dean, on the other hand, had the personality to deal effectively with the Congress. He was bright, energetic, personable. The position of associate deputy attorney general for legislation and congressional liaison seemed to me to be Dean's cup of tea. I liked him the minute I met him.

One small problem existed. Santarelli had no respect for Dean and he candidly gave me his reasons for his opinions. Since I wanted them both in the department, I dismissed Santarelli's attitudes about Dean as a natural outgrowth of the competition between two able and ambitious young men. As a matter of fact, I met with them both together and admonished them that if they were to serve in Justice, it would be without personal antagonism toward each other. I advised them both that if they couldn't work together, then I would replace them both—no matter who was at fault. Looking back, I view this as my error. I should have taken the time to learn more about Dean. What Santarelli was really trying to tell me was that Dean was so completely opportunistic as to be undependable in a crunch. I didn't take the time and as a result have to accept my share of the responsibility for the role he was to play in the future.

Thereafter, each stayed away from the other and each, in my opinion, performed with great distinction. Eventually the distinct qualities of both caught the eye of the White House. Santarelli finished his career in the Department of Justice as the administrator of the Law Enforcement Assistance Administration.

This was a presidential appointment to an agency charged with providing federal financial and technical assistance to help states and localities reduce crime and strengthen law enforcement.

I'll never forget the afternoon in July 1970 when Dean came into my office and said, "Boss, Haldeman and Ehrlichman want me to go to the White House to be counsel to the president. What do you think?"

"Junior," I replied with a brusque incredulity, "you've got to be kidding. To be counsel to the president you have to be a peer of the president. Presidents aren't the easiest persons to deal with. A counsel has to be able to say *no* to a president in a very adroit way if he is heading down the wrong track. You are a very bright, able young man and you have a good future ahead of you. Forget about being *the* counsel to the president at this time in your life."

Dean looked at me for a moment, smiled, and replied, "I guess you're right."

As far as I was concerned, that ended that. To my surprise, about a week later Dean came into my office late in the day and informed me that the White House was insisting that he accept the position. "I know how you feel about it, Dick, but the honor is just too great. I'm going to do it."

"Don't do it, Junior," I responded with more of a feeling of concern for him than anything else. "You're not going to be counsel to President Nixon. You'll have the title, and a big office and all you'll be is a runner for Ehrlichman. Seriously, John, you'll regret it for the rest of your life if you go there assuming that you will be counsel to the president."

"I'm sorry you feel that way, Boss. The honor is just too great to pass up. I'm going to do it."

After he left my office, I remember asking myself, "Who am I to stand in the way of such an opportunity for this young man?" My feelings of concern were based upon one assumption. I assumed that John Dean was an honest young man with character and dignity. When he began to realize that because of his age and relative lack of maturity he was not the counsel to the president, his idealism would be shattered and the experience would be negative rather than fulfilling.

I am now convinced that my basic assumption was incorrect. John Dean was not the person of character I had assumed him to be and he was not just an idealistic and naive young man who found himself becoming submerged inch by inch in the developing quagmire of the Watergate coverup. Rather, I painfully conclude, Dean took to the White House with him, talents (for duplicity and ambition) that enabled him to implement, if not conceive, the coverup.

And here we come back to the game of what-if. What if I had known in January 1969 the reason why Dean's employment as an attorney with the Washington, D.C., law firm of Welch & Morgan had terminated? If I had known, John Dean would not have become an associate deputy attorney general and, therefore, would not have become counsel to the president. Perhaps another person in that position would have perceived the foolishness of the White House plumbers. Perhaps another person would have had the stature to nip the Watergate break-in in the bud at the outset. Perhaps another person would not have been able to structure the coverup because that person would not have had the prior relationship Dean had with the Department of Justice—a relationship based upon the assumption of confidence, respect, and integrity.

Edward P. Morgan was born and raised in Missouri. When he graduated from law school, he joined the FBI in Washington, D.C., and served in it with distinction until 1947, when he began what became a successful law practice in the nation's capital. He and Vincent T. Welch formed a law partnership under the name of Welch & Morgan in Washington. Morgan maintained close professional and personal ties with his native state of Missouri. A valued friend was Senator Thomas C. Hennings, Jr.

John W. Dean III was born on October 14, 1938, in Akron, Ohio, and later attended law school in St. Louis. He met and married the stepdaughter of Senator Hennings, and thereby became aware of Morgan's friendship with the senator. Dean got his first taste of the Potomac River in 1964 as a law clerk in the Washington law firm of Hellbaugh & Jacobs. With the help of the senator, he became employed as an associate attorney by Welch & Morgan on August 1, 1965.

At the time that firm was in the process of making several applications to the Federal Communications Commission for authority to construct new UHF television broadcasting stations. One application was intended for St. Louis. Dean was directed by Morgan to prepare the necessary papers for the St. Louis application, which Dean agreed to do. Around February 3, 1966, I'm informed, Welch was working late in the evening at the firm's offices. He needed a document that Dean had been directed to prepare and asked his secretary, Janice Swales, to see if she could find it in Dean's office. In looking for that document she found, to her surprise, something else. In the top righthand drawer of Dean's desk was a Xerox copy of a draft of the minutes of the first meeting of the shareholders of the Greater St. Louis Television Corporation. The minutes revealed that Dean was the secretary of the corporation and had also subscribed to shares of its stock. More significant, however, she also found a Xerox copy of an application before the FCC in the name of that corporation for authority to construct a new UHF television station in St. Louis. Dean was shown as the secretary of the applicant, and he, his wife, and his wife's mother, Mrs. Hennings, were listed as shareholders. To say the least, Welch was shocked. Dean, in violation of his trust and instructions as an associate of the firm, had filed an application for a corporation in which he had an interest instead of an application on behalf of Welch & Morgan. When confronted by the facts of the matter the next Monday morning, Dean's response was, "You don't have the right to ask me about that!" Whereupon, he was immediately discharged.

Over a year later, Dean applied for a position with the federal government as the assistant director of the National Commission on Reform of Federal Criminal Laws. The Civil Service Commission on August 30, 1967, directed a routine inquiry to Welch & Morgan as a former employer. Question 5 of the form asked whether the appplicant (Dean) had been discharged, and if so, for what reason. Welch, September 8, 1967, replied that Dean had been discharged for "unethical conduct." By way of further explanation, Welch wrote: "While employed by this firm applicant undertook work, unbeknownst to us at the time, in direct conflict with the interests of the firm and a client thereof." This reply put a temporary end to Dean's efforts to secure federal employment.

I can only speculate, but apparently Dean read the tea leaves projecting the election of Richard Nixon in November 1968 and determined to do anything he could to clear the record at the Civil Service Commission and thereby enable himself to secure a position with the new administration. In any event, he retained the services of a Washington, D.C., attorney, Edward P. Taptich, to approach Welch with the plea that the Welch & Morgan reply of September 8, 1967, to the Civil Service Commission be amended. Welch finally relented and, on October 29, 1968, advised the commission by letter that he wished to qualify the reasons given for Dean's discharge. The letter stated that "a more apt characterization of Mr. Dean's departure would be to describe it as having resulted from a basic disagreement over law firm policies regarding the nature and scope of an associate's activities." Some qualification, indeed.

Dean then became employed by the House Judiciary Committee and soon by the Department of Justice as a member of my staff. The foregoing incident should have come to my attention at that time as part of the routine full field investigation by the FBI of every applicant for a noncivil service position with the department. Vin Welch and Ed Morgan have informed me that no inquiry by the FBI was made of them in 1969 concerning Dean. Only two explanations exist as to why no such inquiry was made by the FBI: John Dean neglected to disclose his prior employment with Welch & Morgan, or the usually thorough FBI failed to make the inquiry if Dean had disclosed the former association on his application to the Department of Justice. It really doesn't make much difference which it was. The important fact is, this information never got to my office.

As an aside, Welch was so outraged when he read Dean's account of the incident in his book, *Blind Ambition* (Senator Talmadge raised the incident during Dean's testimony before the Ervin committee), that he wrote this letter to Mr. Taptich on November 16, 1976:

Dear Ed,

John Dean's explanation in his book, *Blind Ambition,* of the circumstances attending him being fired by this law firm, makes me now very much regret acceding to your request to modify the "unethical conduct" charge which I gave as the reason for his discharge in the Civil Service form.

Sincerely,
s/Vincent B. Welch

It is distressingly unpleasant to play the *what-if* game about John Dean. By his own account of his tortuous role in Watergate, he has come to be, in my estimation, a pathetic figure. My only justification for playing the game at all is to provide a setting for the relationship that existed between us commencing Monday, June 19, 1972, two days after the Watergate break-in had been discovered. Henry Petersen and I dealt in good faith with John Dean in his announced role as the person designated by the president to keep him informed as to the progress of our investigation. Not until March 1973 did either of us have reason to suspect that Dean's role wasn't that of reporting back to the president on the investigation. His role, rather, was to use us in such a way that would aid his coverup activities. Being a very "human" human being, I suppose I shall always harbor resentment for Dean that he took advantage of my trust in him, and liking for, him to further his "blind ambition."

I was sworn in at the White House by the chief justice as the sixty-eighth attorney general of the United States on Monday, June 12, 1972. That was a very happy day for me, my family, and my many friends in and out of Justice. The long confirmation hearing was a thing of the past. The ITT "scandal" had been shown to be a victory for antitrust enforcement. I had the understanding with the White House that I would serve only a year as attorney general and I was eager to begin the implementation of several programs of my own. I reveled in such thought the rest of the week. Until Saturday morning, when the course of my life forever was changed.

The annual member-guest golf tournament of the Burning Tree Club was held on Saturday, June 17, 1972. Bob Mardian was to be my guest. On short notice, however, he had to withdraw. John Mitchell had asked Mardian to accompany him on Friday to California to meet with Governor Reagan and Republican leaders in connection with the forthcoming presidential campaign. Consequently, I asked Bill Olson to substitute for Mardian. Just as I was leaving home for what I expected to be a very pleasant day, Henry Petersen called to inform me that there had been a break-in at the Democratic national headquarters at the Watergate Hotel. He had no information at that time.

Olson and I were having lunch in the dining room of the club when I looked up and saw Gordon Liddy and Powell Moore standing in the archway leading into the locker room. When Liddy caught my eye, he began motioning to me in a very agitated manner. I got up, walked over to them, and said, "What are you two doing here? What do you want?"

"I've got to talk to you at once—where can we talk in private?" Liddy asked.

I knew Powell Moore well. He had been Mitchell's press officer in the department and left with him to become the press officer for the Committee to Reelect the President. Liddy was something else again. I had seen him only once before and that was during a meeting in my conference room in 1969 when I was the deputy attorney general. Liddy was on the staff of Assistant Secretary

Gene Rossides of the Treasury Department. The meeting was composed of the members of the task force of the government involved in Operation Intercept. Operation Intercept was the method by which we were attempting to get the attention of the Mexican government and thereby persuade it to cooperate with the U.S. to control the trafficking of marijuana and drugs across the border. By the day of the meeting, the border had been effectively closed down, to the consternation of business establishments on both sides. Secretary Rossides suggested that Liddy be dispatched to all border communities for the purpose of allaying their apprehensions and explaining that the problem would soon be solved. When I agreed to the suggestion, Liddy left immediately for the Southwest. Within a day and a half he had the border in such turmoil that he had to be recalled. Three years later that incident came back to me in a flash when I looked up and saw Liddy motioning to me.

When I directed Liddy and Moore into a private locker-room area, Liddy blurted, "John Mitchell sent me from Los Angeles to inform you that some of the persons who were arrested last night at the Watergate Hotel might be employed by either the White House or the Committee to Reelect the President, and he wants you to get them out of jail at once!"

I couldn't believe my ears. "What in the hell are you talking about, Liddy? John Mitchell knows how to find me. I don't believe he gave you any such instructions."

I then grabbed a phone and called Petersen. "Henry, I don't know what this is all about, but those persons arrested last night are to be treated just like anyone else." Petersen doesn't recall my mentioning to him that Liddy and Moore were present; however, it is my recollection that I did mention their names. I then turned to Liddy and with the use of certain words that I don't care to repeat now, told him to get out of there before I arrested him. Looking back, I'll always be thankful that Powell Moore was present.

Not only did this incident ruin what was to be a beautiful weekend of golf, it also opened the door a crack into a roomful of horrors called Watergate. I haven't seen Gordon Liddy since. I will never forget him.

That Saturday evening I was at the Statler-Hilton Hotel giving a speech when Petersen called. The conversation had to be guarded, but he was trying to report that documentation relating to a White House consultant had been found at the scene of the break-in.

Early in the next week, on Tuesday morning I believe, John Dean came to my office. When he stated that he was there for the purpose of getting a status report on the investigation for the president, I called Petersen. Our recollection of that meeting is substantially the same and doesn't coincide with the mythology that has become characteristic of Dean's writings.

After Petersen gave a brief status report, he turned to Dean and said, "John, I don't know who I am talking about but whoever is responsible for this is a damn idiot and there is only one thing the president of the United States can do and that is cut his losses and the way that he should do that is to instruct the attorney general publicly to run an all-out investigation and let the devil take the hindmost. And that ought to be done immediately.''

I heartily concurred. As I recall I said something like this: "John, a Department of Justice investigation is like a river. Once it starts flowing it cannot be checked and must take its inevitable course. The president should understand this, and he should also know that if anyone associated with the White House in any way had any connection with this break-in it will be a matter of grave consequence for the presidency and for the country.'' At about this point, I remember, Dean broke in hastily and suggested that since he was about to go to San Clemente and would be talking to the president there anyway he would be willing to convey our recommendation to the president in person. On the assumption that that would be done the meeting ended.

As it turned out, it was my mistake to ask Dean to carry a message of such importance to the president. No such public statement ever came from the president. Time after time, in the following months, Petersen would remind me of the Dean meeting and deplore the fact that nothing ever came of it. The reason nothing happened, however, was made known to Petersen on April 15 of the following year in a meeting he had with the president. Petersen, in his testimony on August 7, 1973, before the Ervin committee, stated that "in my later conversations with the president on April 15, I told him this and he [the president] said, Dean had never come to him, and I said if it occurred again, and I certainly hoped it did not, I would be up there knocking on the door myself.''

This was Dean's first act of deception with Petersen and myself. I suppose it can be said that it began the coverup. Not only did Dean not carry out the promise he made to us but his hindsights kept echoing, with adverse and uncalled-for consequences, in Henry Petersen's life and in mine. The first incident happened during the Ervin committee hearings. One early afternoon I was working at my desk in Justice when suddenly I received several calls of inquiry from reporters. John Dean was then on the hill testifying, and that morning he must have dealt with the meeting at Justice which I have been discussing. His testimony apparently conveyed the impression that Henry Petersen responded with weakness to the Watergate challenge or, by inference, colluded with the beginning of the coverup. (Such suppositions were not true in any way or at any time.) The reporters wanted to know what I knew of the meeting and what I thought of Henry. At this point I stopped them and said, "This was a meeting of three men, wasn't it? I remember it well. You have heard John Dean's version. Before I give you mine I want you to call Henry Petersen in the Criminal Division and ask him what *he* remembers. Then call me back.'' They did so, and I gave my account. Of the three participants, questioned independently, Henry Petersen and I had almost identical recollections. John's was much at variance, so much so that it left a contrary impression. The calls soon ceased. The articles in some of the afternoon papers—I saw a good-sized one in the Washington afternoon paper—about Henry Petersen's weakness as a prosecutor were not followed up. But, simply by raising the inferences, the damage to a fine man named Henry Petersen was done.

The second major consequence of Dean's testimony and writings came to my attention only recently, during research for this book. Because of the sorrow always evoked in my memories of this time in my life—the concern for my friends who were caught up and the sense of loss to so many fine initiatives of the Department of Justice—I had previously read almost none of the "Watergate" accounts. I knew I would be powerless, anyway, in that period of Jacobin fever, to correct any inaccuracies I might find, and I wanted to get on with a constructive life. Therefore I was astonished to read in Dean's *Blind Ambition* (Simon & Schuster, New York: 1976, 108-13) not only his version of our meeting's content but also that he placed me, just before that event at Justice, at a gathering in the White House with Ehrlichman, Haldeman, Mitchell, and himself. I never attended such a meeting. I have no idea whether such a meeting actually did occur. I never, so far as I can remember, ever during all my years in Justice participated in a White House conference which included all those men at once. Nor did I, for the reasons cited above, give John Dean a lift to the Department of Justice that Tuesday morning. (In checking the accuracy of my memory I talked to John Mitchell about Dean's inclusion of me. Mitchell could offer no insight because, as he said, he too had never attended a White House meeting at which Ehrlichman, Haldeman, and Dean were all present at once!)

It is conceivable that, if the White House gathering did occur, one of the participants—perhaps Ehrlichman, who had done this concerning me on at least one other occasion—might have included my name either on his ever-present note pad or on the admission list for the Southwest gate, and then decided or was advised not to invite me. If in fact this happened, such an entry, seen later, may have stimulated John Dean to write the episode, complete with appropriate conversational detail. But in this instance, as well as in certain other of his recollections which involved me, John Dean was writing fiction!

May I offer further corroboration of this fact. In the days of the Special Prosecutor's office I was interrogated frequently about some important meeting about Watergate at the White House. (I discuss this experience in detail in Chapter 9.) I could offer no light—I didn't even understand what the investigators were getting at. Repeatedly I volunteered to undergo polygraph tests by the government on any and all questions with which the prosecutor might be concerned. Most of the time my pleas were not given even the courtesy of a reply. Finally, that office abruptly accepted my offer, and I went to Philadelphia for hours of "breakdown" polygraph examinations by two FBI agents. As I recall, this "White House Meeting" was thoroughly explored in those tests, and I satisfied the agents I knew nothing of it. I thought that at the time and after that ordeal the supposition no longer existed—until in the spring of 1983 I read *Blind Ambition*.

Under Petersen's direction, one of the most intensive investigations ever by the department of the FBI was launched. A short while later, Dean came to my office again and informed me that the president requested that I make available the FBI reports of the investigation to him so that he, in turn, could brief the president. This didn't strike me just right. The president was the head of the FBI and was entitled personally to see anything he wanted. Neither Petersen nor I had any reason to believe he knew about the break-in in advance. Indeed, even to this day, there is no evidence to suggest that he did. To hand over such reports to someone else was a different matter. By habit, when I was presented with such a problem, I picked up the phone and called Petersen.

"Tell him no. If the president calls you up and says I want those reports, you click your heels and say, 'Yes, sir,' or if they want to send out a memorandum, say, from the president and say, 'Send those reports over to X, Y, and Z,' we can do that, but we ought not to give those reports on an oral request to any White House staffer."

I concurred with that advice and related Petersen's comments to Dean. As far as I was concerned, that ended the matter.

Not quite.

By his own admission in his book, Dean, having attempted to get these files from me and Petersen without success, then turned to Pat Gray, the acting director of the FBI. According to Dean, he and Gray discussed the matter while sitting on a park bench overlooking the Potomac River. Gray, according to Dean, agreed to hand over the files on Dean's assurances that the president himself wanted the documents. This amazing feat of duplicity by Dean remained hidden from Petersen and me until February 1973, when Gray testified before the Senate during his confirmation hearing to become the permanent director of the FBI. This and one other revelation about Dean by Gray set the stage for the collapse of the coverup one month later.

I'm not prepared to pass an adverse judgment on Gray for this one incident. He perhaps had ample justification for what he did, assuming, of course, that Dean was what he pretended to be. That was the problem. Dean was able to carry off his pretense only because of his past association with the department. He was known and liked by everyone. No one at that time had any basis to be suspicious of his real role. Having possession of the raw investigative data included in the FBI's 301 files was to Dean what it would be to a burglar to have the combination to the safe he was about to rob.

After Dean had been rebuffed by Petersen and me in his attempt to get the FBI files, he must have concluded that nothing further could be achieved through me or the department by him in his coverup role. I have no recollection of any further contacts with him about Watergate.

The annual convention of the American Bar Association in 1972 was held in August in St. Louis. As the attorney general I was invited to be a guest speaker. The national press and TV media were present in force. I was amazed to discover the disbelief of the media in my repeated assertion that the Department of Justice had set in motion the most intensive investigation in history, with perhaps the exception of the investigation following the assassination of President Kennedy. Some members of the media even laughed out loud when I asserted this fact on my way to the ballroom where I was to deliver my speech to the bar association.

Their reaction was deeply disturbing because implicit in it was the disbelief that an attorney general, appointed by the president, could not or would not fairly and zealously investigate a political crime alleged to have been committed by that president's campaign committee. Too, their reaction again waked my notion that a criminal prosecutor should be nonpolitical. By the time I departed St. Louis for Washington, D.C., I had concluded that I would recommend to the White House that I appoint a lawyer from outside the department as my special assistant in connection with all Watergate-related matters. It seemed logical to me that if a person of impeccable credentials and public acceptance could be found, he or she would deal directly with Petersen and be responsible for every prosecutive decision that had to be made. It seemed self-evident to me that this step would both lend absolute credibility to the efforts of Petersen and his career lawyers under him and assure the public that a political crime was not being handled politically. When I returned to Washington I went so far as to discuss the matter over the telephone with Chief Justice Burger and to solicit from him potential candidates for the position.

I ran my idea by Mitchell and the White House, and it was rejected as being impractical. Henry Petersen was adamant in his opposition to the idea. This, I think, was the only issue over which we ever disagreed. Understandably, Petersen felt that the appointment of such a person would carry with it the implication that the Department of Justice was incompetent to do its job. Henry's deep pride in the professionalism of the department's career lawyers recoiled at any suggestion that they could not be depended upon, even in a matter like Watergate.

I abandoned the idea at that time. The idea of a special prosecutor revived the following year, but in a context and form vastly different from that which I proposed. Taking into account what actually came about with Archibald Cox as the special prosecutor—more of that in Chapter 9—I am convinced that if my proposal had been accepted in August 1972, both ultimate justice and the Department of Justice would have been far better served.

On September 15, 1972, the Justice Department announced the indictments of Barker, Sturgis, Gonzales, Martinez, and McCord—the five men arrested on June 17 at the Watergate Hotel. Gordon Liddy and Howard Hunt were also indicted. They were quickly tried, found guilty, and sentenced to prison. Liddy, who refused to testify, was sentenced to twenty years by Judge John Sirica. This was speedy justice, to say the least, and helped politically to defuse the Watergate matter before the November national election. As far as Petersen was concerned, however, the matter had not been defused in his mind. Every time we got together and no matter the reason, he would shake his head and groan. "We can't prove it yet, but sooner or later one or more of those people at the White House or at the election committee who testified falsely before the grand jury will crack—they just won't be able to stand the pressure forever. When that happens, you're going to have a brand new ballgame!" As later events would reveal, Henry was right. There would be a new ballgame, but, unfortunately, Henry Petersen would not manage the team.

President Nixon was reelected by one of the largest landslides in American presidential politics. Ordinarily such engenders great partisan rejoicing, but Watergate's dark cloud frowned upon the gathering of the faithful in Washington, D.C., on election night. Perhaps I imagined this because of Petersen's forebodings. In any event, as a welcome change I looked forward to my meetings in London, Paris, Madrid, and Bonn for discussions with my counterparts concerning the burgeoning international trafficking in drugs.

I returned to Washington only to be met with the urgent request that I proceed directly to the White House and from there, via helicopter, to Camp David. "What the devil has happened now?" I asked myself repeatedly. I was soon to receive another of those shocks that were to become commonplace in the months ahead.

This was the first of my only two journeys to Camp David. Situated in a beautifully wooded area, it has a rustic charm and quietude ideally suited to refresh a weary president. President Roosevelt knew what he was doing when he established this Shangrila so near, and yet so far from, 1600 Pennsylvania Avenue. My two visits, unfortunately, were anything but restful.

I was courteously escorted to a beautiful wood-paneled room and was asked to sit down at a long conference table. "Would you care for something to drink, Mr. Attorney General?"

"No, thank you."

"Very well, Mr. Haldeman and Mr. Ehrlichman will be with you in a minute."

Exactly one minute later, I think, they entered the room.

Bob Haldeman opened the meeting with the usual amenities, and in a very friendly way. Immediately, however, he became all business. "Because of your absence, you are the last member of the cabinet to meet with us since the election. The president is making substantial changes in the structure of his administration. From here on out, only people loyal to the president are going to be running the government for the next four years."

"That's fine with me, boys," I replied, a bit of perplexity in my voice. "What does that have to do with me?"

"That's what we are going to tell you right now."

To my utter amazement, this is what I was told. First, Haldeman acknowledged that since I intended to resign in August when my term as president of the Federal Bar Association expired, that was agreeable to the president. Second, within ninety days I was required to replace every lawyer and every department head not protected by civil service.

"What in the hell are you talking about, you guys? Are you out of your minds?"

For the first time, Ehrlichman joined in. "Nope—that's the way it is going to be because the president wants it that way. And don't bother to ask to talk to him about it, either. His mind is made up. He is going to have people loyal to him in his government and that's all there is to it." That was Ehrlichman at his best.*

Thereafter a heated exchange took place for at least thirty minutes. I pointed out to them that I considered myself loyal to the president and I also believed that the Department of Justice had, consistent only with its responsibility to enforce the laws, faithfully effectuated the overall policies of the president. I painted our success in getting large appropriations for the Law Enforcement Assistance Administration, and for additional attorneys in every division to aid in the fight against organized crime. It was a mistake, but I pointed out the unparalleled record of the Nixon administration in antitrust and civil-rights enforcement. Such a record of achievement, I stated, had to have made its own contribution to the president's landslide reelection.

Then I came to the heart of the matter. It would be impossible to replace some two thousand career lawyers from the private sector—in ninety days or in nine years. They were the experts on behalf of the government litigating against the experts on behalf of the private sector and for compensation at about one third of that of the private lawyer. "Where in the hell do you think their replacements are going to come from?" I shouted.

These arguments were met with such implacable opposition that I quickly concluded that further discussion by me would be fruitless. "You guys are out of your minds. I don't believe the president really wants to do this. I don't think anybody has thought through the consequences of what you are talking about. As far as I'm concerned, you can shove it!" And with that, in my own inimitable and brusque manner, I got up and walked out.

When I got back to the helicopter I was irate. My first impulse was to submit my resignation the next day. Marnie and I were dinner guests at the home of Senator James Buckley that evening. I was going to be late for it. Tomorrow would be time enough anyway.

Upon arrival at the Buckleys, I got Marnie aside and related the amazing situation to her. With her usual good judgment, she instantly demanded, "You call John Mitchell right now and I mean right now!" When Marnie Kleindienst gets her dander up and demands something—a very infrequent occurrence for her—Richard Kleindienst and her four children comply.

Jim Buckley directed me to a bedroom with a phone and in a minute or two I was relating the problem to Mitchell. When I had finished my summary of the meeting with Haldeman and Ehrlichman, I said, "John, I'm quitting!"

"Kleindienst, just hold on and shut up. Aren't you smart enough to realize that's what those two guys want you to do? They want their own attorney general over there—probably Ehrlichman—and you can't permit that to happen. They'll

---

*His second best occurred when the treatment by Woodward and Bernstein of the *Washington Post* began to heat up. He called to say: "General, the president has directed me to inform you that hereafter no reporter for the *Washington Post* will have access to the executive branch, including cabinet officers!" "John," I replied a little testily, "that's impossible for me to comply with since Sanford Ungar of the *Post* is sitting in my office in front of me right now." Click went the phone. I saw Ungar many times thereafter.

tear the place apart. Besides, Nixon's not going to fire you. Forget about quitting and go back and mind the store. Good night.''

Obviously, that's what I did. Mitchell was right. The subject matter was never raised in those terms again by either Haldeman or Ehrlichman.

Erwin Griswold had previously indicated to me his desire to retire as the solicitor general. He had served with great distinction for many years and had every right to pass the awesome burden of that office to a younger man. Upon my recommendation, a distinguished professor of law at Yale (and now a member of the U.S. Court of Appeals for the District of Columbia), Robert Bork, succeeded him. (We visit him again when he becomes the acting attorney general after the resignation of Attorney General Richardson and Deputy Attorney General Ruchelshaus as a result of the infamous "Saturday night massacre.") Ralph Erickson, my deputy and good friend, also desired to return to private practice and was replaced by Joseph Sneed. Sneed was dean of the Duke Law School. This was President Nixon's law school and I was flattered to have a person of such distinction to serve with me in the department. Joe Sneed is now Judge Sneed of the U.S. Court of Appeals for the Ninth Circuit in San Francisco.

Other departments didn't fare so well. In the Department of Transportation, for example, James Beggs, the undersecretary, was informed by his secretary of his replacement by Egil Krogh, of the White House staff; Beggs' secretary was in turn informed by a secretary at the White House. John Shaffer, the administrator of the Federal Aviation Administration, was replaced in a similar summary fashion by White House aide Alex Butterfield. Jim Beggs is now the administrator of NASA and Jack Shaffer is a successful corporate executive and consultant in the aircraft industry. These two fine men had been loyal and effective lieutenants of Nixon for four years. They are men of stature and great accomplishment. Their replacements were men of a different kind of "loyalty."

"Bud" Krogh—whom I personally liked very much—saw his life go down in ruins when his blind loyalty to the president permitted him to be in charge of the plumbers at the White House. He performed these interesting activities under the watchful and approving eyes of his superior, John Ehrlichman. Butterfield will be conspicuous in political history for decades. It was he who revealed in his testimony before the Ervin committee that it was his responsibility to operate and maintain the mechanisms by which President Nixon taped the conversations with all and sundry in the Oval Office.

Throughout January, February, and the first part of March, 1973, my contacts with Petersen were fairly routine. Nixon's second inauguration, in January, with the usual hoopla, pretty well eliminated January as a productive working month in the government. About all I can remember is how cold it was riding down Pennsylvania Avenue in an open car in the inaugural parade. My little run-in with Haldeman and Ehrlichman in November somewhat tempered the festive event. Based upon revelations that were to come, many participants that day, I suppose, were preoccupied by the heavy burden they had been carrying since the night of June 17, 1972.

I was naturally upset in February by Pat Gray's testimony in his confirmation hearing. Based upon what I then knew it didn't do him much credit and it certainly was uncomplimentary of John Dean. Soon thereafter, as we shall see, I began to know a lot more about both Gray and Dean. To the best of my recollection, I had no contact with Dean in the new year until the evening of Saturday, March 17, at our home. What happened that evening demonstrated not only the extent to which Dean had become mired in his life of deception, but also the extent to which the crushing burden of that bizarre life had begun to wear him down. Moreover, it demonstrated the fantasy he found it necessary to impart to others, even strangers, with respect to his role as the president's counsel.

John Connally had become a rather congenial friend of mine. I was, in fact, one of those who urged that he become a registered Republican. He was aware of my intention to leave the Department of Justice in August and had intimated the possibility of my future association in a Washington, D.C., office of his Houston law firm. He had even mentioned that possibility to the president before a conversation I had with the president at the White House on the morning of February 23. (In that meeting I made it clear to the president that, under the law, I could not negotiate any such relationship while I was in the Department of Justice.)

It came as no surprise to me, therefore, when Connally called me in the early part of the week of March 12 to ask whether Marnie and I would be willing to entertain as a guest in our home a young partner of the Houston office. Apparently, the person in question (whose name now escapes us both) was having an extended stay in Washington by himself. Because of his age, we concluded he might find it interesting to meet with the Santarellis and the Deans. Two better examples of bright, successful young men in government could not be found, it still seemed to me. I also assumed that the prior antagonism between the two had dissipated. In this I was mistaken. Santarelli came by himself, paid his respects to our guest, and departed. I think he used the polite excuse that his lovely wife was ill. Dean looked and acted as if he had the weight of the world on his shoulders. When Marnie expressed her concern, he explained to us and to our guest that he had become completely fatigued in a constant effort to investigate every irresponsible charge made in the Washington press of alleged White House involvement in the Watergate break-in. What worried him most was the fact that the press would not accept his responses that there was no such involvement. His manner was convincing and all of us present were reassured.

Dean also devoted a considerable amount of time relating to our guest the extent to which his official duties necessitated constant daily meetings with the president. At the time, I attributed this posturing to the understandable desire of one young man to impress another with his importance. My understanding had always been that Dean didn't see much of the president, but rather received his directions from Ehrlichman. At the time, I recall thinking this had to be part of the rationalization process John Dean must indulge in to sustain his pride and self-respect. Undoubtedly, this was part of the burden. As indicated in the full text of the submission of recorded presidential conversations to the Committee on the Judiciary of the House of Representatives, Dean was in the president's office only four times in five months—on September 15, 1972, February 29, 1973, March 13, 1973, and, interestingly, March 17, 1973, the very afternoon of the day he found himself at our house.

John Dean had apparently played this game with himself for many months. Marnie remembers a similar incident when she attended the marriage ceremony of Mo and John held at his Old Town Alexandria townhouse the preceding October. I was out of the city and Marnie went by herself. After Congressman Barry Goldwater, Jr., made gracious and thoughtful remarks about the Deans, Marnie approached Dean with her respects and best wishes. When she inquired as to their honeymoon plans, the bridegroom responded with a heavy sigh: "We plan to go to Key Biscayne for just a very short respite. The president has advised me that we have so much to do after the election that he doesn't want me away from his side for a minute. Even for the duration of our short stay in Key Biscayne, a special 'Dean' line to the White House will be installed."

Marnie became concerned about Dean by the time the dinner party had concluded that evening. She is known to everyone as a person of loving concern and compassion. She is also a devout Christian. As the Deans got into their sports car, she asked them to wait a minute. She then ran up to our bedroom and took off the wall a little felt banner that had been given to her by a close friend a year before, when we were agonizing through our confirmation hearing. Returning, she handed it to them both with the parting words, "This will help you both." The banner simply read: "Keep me going, Lord." As the events of the next few days would reveal, very few young men in modern history would come to have so much need for such a simple prayer.

On or about March 22, 1973—five days after I saw John Dean for the last time—Judge Sirica took the unusual step of revealing in open court the contents of a letter he had received from James W. McCord, Jr., one of the convicted and sentenced Watergate burglars. McCord involved the White House in the break-in, revealed the payment of "hush" money, and asserted that perjury had been rife throughout his trial. Future historians, in a more detached environment, might well conclude that the McCord letter was not only the turning point in Watergate but perhaps a turning point in modern civilization as well. At least Henry Petersen instantly concluded that a critical point had been reached. This was just the kind of an event that would crumble the posture of those who had previously lied before grand jury and trial jury.

The political temperature in Washington began to heat up immediately. Senator Eastland announced on March 22 that he was suspending the Gray confirmation hearings. Apparently he had concluded that Gray could not be confirmed by the Senate. Gray was a resident of Connecticut and Senator Lowell Weicker had been a friend and supporter. Whether because Gray's confirmation as the FBI director seemed doomed or because the senator saw the handwriting on the wall after the McCord letter to Sirica, Weicker suddenly became highly visible in his attacks on the White House. A few days after March 22, the senator, in a press release, said he had information tending to show White House involvement in the burglary at the Watergate Hotel. This prompted a call from me to the senator. In substance, I wanted to inform him that our investigation had not revealed any such involvement and that if he had any credible evidence to the contrary he should turn it over to the proper persons at the Department of Justice. I also wrote a letter to Judge Sirica in which I emphasized that the department would continue to investigate the matter and would let the chips fall where they would.

Ehrlichman called me on March 28. His main concern was Weicker. I vaguely remember the call. However, my memory was completely refreshed as I read a transcript of the tape of that call in *The White House Transcript*, published in May 1974 by the New York Times Company. Any negative feelings that I had accumulated over the years with respect to John Ehrlichman were inconsequential compared to the revulsion that overcame me when I learned that he had taped our conversations in that critical period without my knowledge. The call on March 28 and the call on April 14 (more about it in a moment) are the only two which have been published. Considering the context of what was later revealed in Ehrlichman's trial, any fair-minded person would have to conclude that Ehrlichman taped his calls with me for the purpose of making a record by which his own involvement might be concealed.

The March 28 call again prompted me to raise the need for a special prosecutor. Ehrlichman intimated that the president was concerned that John Mitchell might be implicated by McCord. I responded by saying, "When you talk about Mitchell and me that really creates the highest conflict of interest. And we want to give some thought to having, in such event, a special prosecutor." Ehrlichman acknowledged that such a concept of a special prosecutor had always been resisted, but on this day he was quite curious as to how a special prosecutor would come about. He also displayed an interest in the procedure by which a person could be compelled to testify in a criminal matter through the immunization process and thereby be deprived of the protection of the Fifth Amendment. I then had no means of evaluating his sudden concern about such matters, matters, I'm quite sure now, that were but the tip of the iceberg. In any event, Ehrlichman signed off the call with, "Okay, great, that's all I had on my list."

"What the hell is he talking about—the president concerned that Mitchell might be involved?" I murmured aloud as I put down the phone. Was this Ehrlichman giving me the needle because of my close relationship with Mitchell and because of his distaste for us both? Knowing how I felt about having any credible evidence furnished to the department in aid of its investigation, Ehrlichman had not indicated that he had any such evidence but offered only that the president was concerned. I couldn't bring myself to believe that the John Mitchell I knew could be involved in the Watergate burglary. It just didn't make sense. I could believe, however, that Ehrlichman would be willing by suggestions or any other way to discredit Mitchell with me or anybody else. "The hell with him,'' I murmured. ''If he knows anything he'd better cough it up or he could be in trouble himself.'' Of course, I didn't have access to the presidential tapes on March 28, 1973. Had I known what the president, Haldeman, and Ehrlichman were discussing six days before, on March 22, there was indeed cause for concern, not just about Mitchell but about many others as well. The call, nevertheless, was disturbing and added to the darkening clouds on the horizon.

I had another reason to be skeptical about Ehrlichman's motive in making that call. Several days before I met with Ehrlichman at San Clemente. I was scheduled to meet with the president to give him my recommendation of a person to succeed Pat Gray as permanent director of the FBI. This was the one and only occasion I had to visit the San Clemente ''White House.'' I had been attending a conference of U.S. attorneys in San Diego. The top people of Justice, including Petersen, were also in attendance. On the Friday evening before I was to go to San Clemente I took Petersen aside and informed him of the projected visit, the purpose of it, and my intention of proposing him for the position to the president. He replied that he thought that would be foolhardy, considering the revelations brought out in the matter of the papers taken from Hunt's safe and delivered to Gray by Ehrlichman and Dean. He felt that the submission of his name would simply raise that issue anew. He then suggested that I recommend Judge Matthew Byrne, of the federal district court in Los Angeles. That was an excellent suggestion as far as I was concerned.

Matthew Byrne was the U.S. attorney in Los Angeles when the new administration took office on January 20, 1969. He agreed to remain in that position for at least another year to finish handling several important and sensitive matters. I had come to know him well, personally and professionally. He was so highly regarded that, notwithstanding his being a lifelong active Democrat, President Nixon nominated him to be a federal district judge. His appointment to head the FBI under the circumstances would be ideal. A young bachelor of impeccable character and integrity, a Democrat, a former U.S. attorney, a federal judge—what more could be asked?

''I'll do it, Henry,'' I responded with enthusiasm. ''Shall I call Matt first?''

''You shouldn't do that, Dick. He's trying the Ellsberg case, and that would place him in an awkward position and might be misconstrued.''

''Of course you're right, Henry, I understand.''

Early the next morning I flew to Los Angeles, and then took a taxi to the place where a helicopter was waiting to fly me to San Clemente, where I was taken to Ehrlichman's office. He was quite congenial and his open demeanor gave no indication of any concern about Watergate and the ongoing investigation or the suggestion that I was to make to the president concerning Byrne. The president, likewise, thought it an excellent choice. I conveyed this to Ehrlichman after my chat with the president.

''That's great—I'll contact Judge Byrne myself right away.''

''John, you can't do that now. The judge is presiding over the trial of Ellsberg in the Pentagon papers case. Petersen and I feel it would be highly improper and could interfere with his acceptance of the position.''

I don't recall what his exact response was, but I left for Washington satisfied that we had successfully resolved a very difficult situation. What a fine FBI director Matt Byrne would be! Unfortunately, this was not to be. As I learned to my sorrow several weeks later, Ehrlichman did what he was cautioned not to do—he personally contacted Byrne, not just once but twice, and discussed the appointment during the Ellsberg trial.

The month of April 1973 will live in my memory forever. In the early morning hours of Sunday, the 15th, in the living room of my home, I was given the shocking revelations of the Watergate coverup. Two weeks later and again on a Sunday afternoon I would find myself at Camp David, tendering my resignation as the attorney general of the United States to an emotionally distraught president.

Annually the correspondents of the press, TV, and radio assigned to cover the White House have a banquet in Washington, D.C. It is a white-tie affair. They give awards to each other and otherwise congratulate themselves on their contributions to our free society. Attendance by the president and those members of the cabinet who are invited is mandatory. I had been invited and had looked forward to the experience. Receptions are held by many of the leading segments of the media following the formal banquet and I was flattered by invitations from several. I knew I would have a good time jesting and jousting with my good friend Katharine Graham and her "vigilantes" at the *Washington Post*. I attended that reception but didn't have a good time after all.

Around six the evening of the banquet, Saturday, April 14, I was wrestling with the various paraphernalia that compose the obstacle course known as the white tie. The phone in our bedroom that was hooked up with the White House switchboard rang. John Ehrlichman was on the other end and in a few seconds I didn't care if I ever figured out how to get into that white tie. Since Ehrlichman was thoughtful enough to tape this little chat, and in order that a full appreciation of its content may be shared, let me quote the opening salvos:

KLEINDIENST: Hi, John.
EHRLICHMAN: Hi, General. How are you?
KLEINDIENST: Pretty good, how are you?
EHRLICHMAN: How was the golf?
KLEINDIENST: Half good and half bad.
EHRLICHMAN: First half good?
KLEINDIENST: Well, the middle was good and—
EHRLICHMAN: I want to bring you up to date on what I have been doing. For about the last three weeks—well, since I saw you, before I saw you out in San Clemente—the president has had me trying to gather together, as you know, a certain amount of law and facts to be in a position to kind of substitute for Dean, and to advise him on the White House involvement, but even broader involvement, in this whole transaction. Yesterday, I gave him my summary and, admittedly, it was hearsay, but some of it is pretty reliable. And the whole thing fits

together well as, at least, a working hypothesis. One of the things that I told him was that I had encountered people who appeared to be reticent to come forward because they somehow felt that the presidency was served by their not coming forward. So he had me today, in a series of conversations with people, to straighten them around on that point. The first one I talked to was your predecessor. Then I talked to Magruder, and—

KLEINDIENST: It's pretty hard to talk to those two when they have testified under oath before a grand jury.

EHRLICHMAN: Well, as it turns out, I was just a little late in talking to Magruder, because he had just come back from telling everything to the U.S. attorney. He has decided to come clean.

KLEINDIENST: No kidding? Magruder?

EHRLICHMAN: Yep. He had his informal conference minutes before he came in to see me.

KLEINDIENST: Would that be inconsistent with his testimony before the grand jury?

EHRLICHMAN: Dramatically inconsistent.

KLEINDIENST: [Expletive removed!]

EHRLICHMAN: And he implicates everybody in all directions up and down in the Committee to Reelect.

KLEINDIENST: Mitchell?

EHRLICHMAN: Yep, cold turkey. My instructions after I had completed—well, I might say I also talked to a couple of other people who are around here just to pass the word to encourage them to testify, if the only reason they were not testifying was some concern about the presidency. Also, being very careful to say that I recognized everybody had rights, and that I didn't mean in any way to indicate that they should not avail themselves of their full rights. Now, Magruder then—

KLEINDIENST: Let me ask one thing—

EHRLICHMAN: Yep.

KLEINDIENST: As a result of what you just told me, it would indicate there is a substantial case of perjury against Mitchell and Magruder in the first instance.

EHRLICHMAN: Yep. No question.

KLEINDIENST: So, complicity in the overall conspiracy?

EHRLICHMAN: More than just a participation in a conspiracy, Dick.

KLEINDIENST: They would be principals?

EHRLICHMAN: Yes, they are principals.

KLEINDIENST: Uh. I can't believe John Mitchell would have ever known that and let it go on.

EHRLICHMAN: Well, I must say that my conversation with him was reassuring in that regard. He is very steadfast in the protestations of innocence. Well, the Magruder case is not only testamentary, but is circumstantial—is persuasive to me.

KLEINDIENST: But Mitchell denied it?

EHRLICHMAN: I saw Mitchell first. I didn't have all of this Magruder business. Now, here I am a citizen of the United States and the designated inquirer of a body of information. My purpose and intent was to advise you of this when I got finished with this process and tender this information for whatever purpose it would serve, recognizing that up until just a few minutes ago it was almost entirely hearsay. Magruder has just unloaded on me the substance of his conversation with the U.S. attorney—informal conversation. And I find that I now have very little to add to what Magruder had already given the U.S. attorney.

KLEINDIENST: That's not good.

EHRLICHMAN: I felt that I should go forward and at least advise you of this and to—

KLEINDIENST: John, at this point, it seems to me that you are going to have to be very careful.

By way of summary, Ehrlichman then proceeded to discuss other points on his "list." What about a special prosecutor? He suggested Joe Sneed, the deputy attorney general. I didn't like the idea and instead reminded him that the chief justice had given me several names who were not in the Department of Justice. He then allowed that he had been "talking to people for three weeks—I have talked to everybody but the milkman." In view of this startling admission I wasn't overly impressed when he volunteered to supply me with "any of this hearsay of mine that I have collected—I would be glad to make it available."

My instant reaction was not only that the offer was a little late, but also that here was a person who obviously had come into possession of information bearing directly on a criminal investigation then in process by the Department of Justice. I responded, "Yours is a very goddamn delicate line as to what you do to get information to give to the president and what you can do in giving information to the Department of Justice, you know, to enforce the law."

I almost choked when he replied, "Well, you are my favorite law-enforcement officer."

Ehrlichman ended our conversation by advising me that Magruder had implicated, in addition to Mitchell, my friends Bob Mardian and Fred LaRue. I was dumbstruck as I got into my car to be driven to the Washington Hilton for an evening with the fourth estate. The only thing of significance I remember is a brief chat I had with Woodward and Bernstein of the *Washington Post* at the *Time* reception following the program. They wanted to talk to me the next day, a Sunday, and I guardedly suggested they call me at home to find out if that would be possible. I knew at the time it would not be possible, but I was hardly in a position to tell them why.

Shortly after midnight I was located at one of the receptions and was advised that I had a very urgent telephone call. Henry Petersen was on the line.

"I can't talk to you on the phone but it is imperative that I see you at once," he opened, agitated.

"Tonight? Now?"

"I'll be at your house in about an hour. Tell me again how to find it."

Within minutes after I got home, Petersen arrived, accompanied by Harold Titus, the U.S. attorney for the District of Columbia, Earl Silbert, his chief assistant and in charge of the Watergate investigation, and Silbert's two assistants, Messrs. Glanzer and Campbell.

Petersen and Silbert began to unfold the most distressing narrative I had ever heard. They informed me that Silbert and his team had been in communication with Dean and his lawyer since on or about April 6. Dean was seeking immunity for his testimony, and for negotiation purposes was advancing certain information. Their judgment had been not to grant him immunity from prosecution; they did, however, agree with him that any information he advanced before that judgment became final would not be used against him. His proffer of information suggested that there was a very successful coverup carried on in connection with the Watergate matter, and that it might still be under way. Involved in the cover were Mitchell, Mardian, LaRue, Magruder, Haldeman, Ehrlichman, and Parker. They then outlined the specific nature of Dean's information with respect to each of the foregoing. Magruder had also been talking to Silbert and his staff, and his information was likewise outlined in detail.

"What about the president?" I inquired apprehensively. "Is he involved?" To my great relief, I was informed that Dean had suggested that Haldeman and Ehrlichman had erected a shield in front of the president and that he was not implicated in the coverup. U.S. Attorney Titus echoed this belief and stated that he had been so informed by Rose Mary Woods, the president's secretary and a good friend of his.

By now it was after four in the morning. Weary and distraught, I asked, "What do we do now?" The consensus, finally, was that we had no course but to advise the president that his two chief aides, Haldeman and Ehrlichman, had become putative defendants, thereby permitting him to take whatever action he might deem appropriate in the circumstances. All present agreed that I should inform the president immediately.

It was now five o'clock. Everyone departed and I went to bed. I didn't sleep but I did weep. Why? Why? Why? I asked over and over again. Bob Mardian involved—impossible! The John Mitchell I knew—impossible!

At approximately eight o'clock on that dreary Sunday morning I called the White House switchboard and stated that it was imperative that I speak to the president immediately. He soon called me.

"I must see you as soon as possible, Mr. President."

In a calm and reassuring voice he suggested that I attend the White House prayer meeting at 11:00 A.M. and that after it concluded someone would bring me to an office where we could talk. I've had the habit of attending a worship service every Sunday all my life. But this was one Sunday that the words read from the Old and New Testaments made no impression and the speaker's message fell on deaf ears. However, I did pray with all my heart.

It was about one o'clock when I was escorted to the president's office in the Executive Office Building, located to the west of it. This is the first and only time I had been in this office. Indeed, I didn't know it existed. Apparently the president used it as a private study and a place where he could not be disturbed.

It is difficult to summarize a conversation with a president under such momentous circumstances. This president had a tendency to ramble and to interrupt either himself or the other person in the middle of a sentence. While I was completely distraught and on the verge of weeping, the president was quite calm. Petersen, in his testimony before the House Judiciary Committee in July 1974, made a similar observation. He remarked that he "was a little exasperated . . . in consideration of the calm with which he accepted what I thought was shattering information." I don't know why, but for some reason I also believed I was imparting to the president for the first time the "shattering information" I had learned of much earlier that day. In light of Ehrlichman's call to me the evening before, I suppose I shouldn't have had that feeling. According to the tapes, Ehrlichman talked to the president about two hours before my meeting with him and, in connection with my scheduled meeting with the president that day, remarked: "Titus would have told him last night what Magruder said, and so he will, this morning, have, I think, as much knowledge about this thing as we have." No wonder the president could be calm.

My first meeting that day lasted about an hour and a half. To the best of my ability, I outlined the substance of the information I had received in my home that morning. Most of the conversation thereafter centered on two principal topics: Should the president dismiss Haldeman and Ehrlichman before there was credible evidence of misconduct by them? Should a special prosecutor be named, and if so, who?

The president felt strongly in his belief that his two trusted aides were innocent and therefore felt equally strongly that it would be unfair to them to ask that they leave the White House. I couldn't disagree with that attitude, because my information suggested only the possibility of wrongdoing by them.

The conversation concerning a special prosecutor was rambling. I pointed out that I had consulted with the chief justice and Judge Robb and that they both felt some kind of a special prosecutor was warranted in view of my close association with Mitchell and Mardian. The name of Barnabas Sears, a prominent Chicago lawyer and former chairman of the House of Delegates of the American Bar Association, was suggested as a possibility more than once by me. The president suggested Joe Sneed, the deputy attorney general. I opposed that idea for the same reason that applied to me. As the deputy attorney general, he was a presidential appointment and therefore could lend no credibility to what had to be an impartial application of justice. I expressed it this way:

"It seems to me there are two overriding considerations here. One is yourself and your presidency, and second is the institution. Both of which I think have to be protected and preserved by the institution of justice. For me to recuse myself and say the deputy is now making all the prosecution statements, the thing I have against that, Mr. President, is that the deputy is still your appointee. He's my deputy."

I then turned the conversation to the consideration of Henry Petersen. I could "delegate the responsibility for the entire matter to Petersen, assistant attorney general of the criminal division. . . . He's the first career assistant attorney general, I think, in the history of the department."

The president replied: "Petersen would be better than Sneed."

At about this point the tape ran out. I'm sorry it did. However, the meeting ended shortly after that with the understanding that I would get together with Petersen in my office at once and get back to the president as soon as possible.

Fortunately for me—perhaps unfortunately for him—Petersen was home when I returned to my office. Upon my request he came to my office immediately. I then quickly reviewed my meeting with the president. The question of a special prosecutor was central to the first part of the meeting. This came as no surprise to Petersen because he knew that was a position I had held for months. As he indicated in his July 1974 testimony before the House Judiciary Committee, "that was a position [I] had long held." He likewise had long held the position that the appointment of a special prosecutor would cast reflection on the credibility of the department. In substance, I said, "Okay, Henry, then you are going to have to assume the responsibility yourself."

This was a terrible burden to impose on anyone. Henry knew fully what it meant. A lesser person, mindful of his career and the obvious perils that lay ahead, would have politely declined and returned home. With a shrug of his shoulders and with an air of resignation, he agreed. I've thanked God since that he did.

I then handwrote a memorandum to him in which I recused myself from any further participation in the Watergate investigation and delegated to him the full authority in the matter thereafter.

At 3:48 P.M., the president called me in my office while Petersen was there. "May I bring Henry Petersen with me?" I inquired.

"Yeah. I want to ask him to do something."

Again for some reason, the taping machine wasn't operative for the meeting. It lasted for over an hour. I recall suggesting to the president that I should not only recuse myself in favor of Petersen but actually resign. The president asked Henry what he thought of that, and he replied, "Absolutely not!" His reasons were again characteristic of his concern for the department. My resignation would only cast doubts, "not only on Mr. Kleindienst, but on the Justice Department as such." The president agreed.

I also recall that Petersen recommended to the president that Haldeman and Ehrlichman be relieved of their duties. The president wasn't willing to accept that proposal but did ask him to prepare a memorandum on the information he had regarding them. According to the record Petersen did so on the following day, Monday, the 16th. I've never seen it. Petersen also recommended that no action be taken with respect to Dean until the negotiations with his attorney concerning his testimony were concluded.

After this meeting terminated I went home in a state of near exhaustion. Even now, over ten years later, it fatigues me to recall the events that took place between Ehrlichman's call at about six o'clock on Saturday evening, April 14, and when I got home at about the same time the following day. My one consoling thought was, come what may, with Petersen in charge, justice would be fairly and impartially administered and the integrity of my revered Department of Justice would be preserved.

When I returned to my office on Monday, April 16, at my usual early hour, I didn't know it, but because of the events that were to occur, two weeks later I would suffer to hear the president announce on national television my resignation along with those of Haldeman, Ehrlichman, and Dean. That would turn out to be one of the saddest days of my life. The series of events in those two weeks will end this chapter.

When a person such as an attorney general "recuses" himself from a matter, it means that, because of a possible conflict of interest, he should thereafter have no involvement whatever in that matter. Bob Mardian was then, and is today, one of my closest friends. John Mitchell was not only an intimate friend, but also one under whom I had served in the 1968 campaign and in the department as a deputy. Since both had been named by Dean and Magruder it was imperative that I remove myself entirely from the Watergate investigation. In addition, for their protection, I decided that until the whole matter was finally concluded, that I should not communicate with either in any way. Even if I called or wrote to express my feelings of sadness, since Dean and Magruder had implicated them, it could later be asserted that I had revealed information to them. Consequently, and with a heavy heart, I wrote a personal handwritten letter to them both, indicating that until the matter was closed I would not communicate with them in any way. I don't think either quite understood my reasoning. Perhaps I overreacted at the time. However, that both are still the closest of friends makes me feel that even if I did overreact it did not harm either of them as they journeyed through their perils.

Except for one instance, Henry, of course, did not thereafter discuss with me anything relating to Watergate. Because of other ongoing matters I did see or talk to Petersen almost every day. When he would come to my office in the ensuing days, he would invariably moan and groan, "It's horrible; it's horrible."

"Hang in there, ol' boy," I'd commiserate.

On the morning of Wednesday, April 25, however, a haggard Petersen came into my office and blurted, "Look, you are out of the Watergate but you are not out of Ellsberg. I need some help!" He then related the following facts: about a week before, on the 17th, he had received a memorandum from Assistant U.S. Attorney Earl Silbert to the effect that Dean had informed him that Howard Hunt and Gordon Liddy, while employed by the White House, had burglarized the office of Ellsberg's psychiatrist. Petersen then sent the memorandum to Kevin Maroney, the deputy assistant attorney general in the Internal Security Division, and asked him to check it out. Lawyers from that division were then prosecuting

Ellsberg before Judge Byrne in Los Angeles. Maroney reported back that neither his division nor the FBI had any such information. Petersen then asked Maroney to see whether a psychiatrist had ever been involved in their pretrial investigation. Maroney reported back that a Dr. Fielding had been interviewed. Fielding was Ellsberg's psychiatrist and it was his office that had been burglarized. The fat was in the fire.

The U.S. Supreme Court decision in *Brady* v. *United States* had held that exculpatory materials in the possession of the government must be made available to the attorneys for a defendant in a criminal prosecution. For Petersen, the legal question was whether this kind of information came within the *Brady* rule. It was debatable, but Petersen finally decided that the information should be made available. Having arrived at that decision, he then informed the president of the facts and that he intended to make the material available. According to Petersen, the president uttered one of those famous "expletives deleted" and said, "I know about that report. That is a national security matter. You stay out of that. Your mandate is to investigate Watergate."

"Dick, we have to make that information available and you are the one who has to do it. I'm also fearful that the president won't permit it."

"Henry," I replied, "don't upset yourself. If I have to I have to."

I then suggested to Petersen that I would like to consult with Dean Griswold, the solicitor general, and Judge Roger Robb to be absolutely sure before I met with the president.

Griswold and I were scheduled to attend a luncheon that day at the Pentagon to honor the retiring judge advocate general of the army. On the ride over I discussed the matter with him and he felt strongly that I had no other choice than to make the information available. After that luncheon Judge Robb, at my request, visited my office at 2:30 P.M. Since he had had to recuse himself from Watergate because his former law partner, Parkinson, was a counsel in the matter, he agreed to discuss the matter with me and to give me his advice.

"The answer is clear, Dick. You have no choice. It has to be disclosed to the court in California and to Ellsberg's counsel," Robb immediately replied.

"Suppose the president orders me not to do that?"

The judge gave me the answer I would expect of him: "In that event, you will have to resign. No one, not even the president of the United States, can order you to violate your professional duty. Anyway, the president is not going to give you such an order."

I then called Petersen to come up to my office and asked Judge Robb to repeat to him what he had just told me.

As I departed for the White House, I said, "Adios, gentlemen. I might not be the attorney general when I return, but before I cease being such, the materials will be made available to Judge Byrne!"

What occurred with the president was one of those unexpected surprises. Since the president had been adamant with Petersen I expected the same strong reaction to me. I just knew this was my last day in the Department of Justice. Hence,

I decided to inform the president of what I was going to do and the reasons therefor, rather than ask his permission to do so.

"Fine," he said, "if that's what you have to do, go ahead and do it. What's all the fuss about?"

As I got back in my car, I muttered to myself in surprise, "Well, I'll be an SOB!"

Henry was waiting for me, and when I told him what had happened he said the same thing. We both laughed nervously and called it a day. It was, nevertheless, a disturbing, disgusting experience for us both.

"What a hell of a way to live," I said to Marnie when I got home.

During the forepart of that week I had nearly arrived at the conclusion, anyway, that I should resign. How can one be half an attorney general? Particularly when the bigger half was Watergate. Nevertheless, it was a difficult decision to make, and beset with mixed emotions. Those emotions weighed on me so heavily that I had imposed on Barry Goldwater, John Rhodes, Mel Laird, and George Schultz for advice. For different reasons, each had expressed the opinion that I probably should resign. Their advice helped, but I still had to decide when.

What happened on the next day, Thursday, took care of that problem.

In the latter part of the afternoon I was brooding over a scotch and soda at Burning Tree when Max Grullion, the bartender and my devoted friend, came to where I was sitting and whispered in my ear, "The president wants to speak to you."

"What now?" I mumbled to myself as I picked up the phone in a private alcove.

In short, he said that it was now publicized that Pat Gray allegedly had been given some documents from Howard Hunt's White House safe by Ehrlichman and Dean and, at their request, had destroyed them. The president then asked me to get together with Gray and Petersen that evening and get back to him with our advice as to what should be done.

I agreed, put down the phone, and said, "Damn it!"

Henry met me in my office in the early part of the evening. He informed me that sometime during the course of Gray's confirmation hearing, in February, he asked Gray if he had received from John Dean any information that he, Dean, had obtained from Hunt's safe and that had not been made available to the FBI agents. Apparently Earl Silbert had informed Petersen that Dean had given this information to Silbert. According to Petersen, Gray responded that he had not. Silbert again raised the matter with Petersen around April 15, and Petersen told Silbert that Gray had denied the incident. Petersen then went back to Gray again the next day and Gray denied the incident again. Petersen reported this to the president, who in turn expressed the belief that Dean was probably telling the truth. Petersen then went back to Gray the same day. To Petersen's surprise, Gray said, "Yes," he had received such documents; further, he said that they (Ehrlichman and Dean) had implied he ought to destroy them, that he had taken them home over the weekend, and that he had brought them back, torn them up, and thrown them into the burn basket. When Petersen asked him if he had read them, Gray responded that he had not because Ehrlichman and Dean had "just said they were politically sensitive."

"Henry," I exploded, "Pat shouldn't have done that. He's going to have to resign!" We then called Gray and asked him to meet with us in my office. Upon his arrival, Gray then repeated to me essentially what he had told Petersen earlier in the day. I liked and admired Pat Gray very much. I felt so sorry for him that evening. Like Henry, I believed him to have been an innocent victim of the improper conduct of Ehrlichman and Dean. However, I had to advise Gray to resign. On the surface, he had been responsible for the unauthorized destruction of government property and his conduct could have impaired or interfered with an investigation of possible violations of the law. Pat disagreed that he should resign. I then informed him that I had no alternative but to call the president and inform him of my recommendation. The president also liked Pat Gray. He had known him intimately since his vice presidential days when Gray had been the navy liaison officer on his staff. "Dick, let's sleep on it overnight," the president suggested. "Okay, sir, but I don't think that will change my mind." Henry also talked to the president and gave him the same opinion.

I returned to the room where Gray was sitting and reported the feelings of the president. "Pat," I said, "do me a personal favor. Tomorrow morning early, meet with the top officers of the bureau, tell them this story, ask their advice as to what you should do, and then come in and see me."

Early the next morning, Pat Gray came into my office with his resignation in hand. I damn near cried. Here was one of the finest men I had ever known caught up in this horrible mess. I haven't seen or talked to him since that sad morning but he has been in my heart these many years.

After Gray left my office on that Friday morning, I concluded that enough was enough. I had had it. On Monday I would meet with the president to submit my resignation. My resignation was, in fact, announced on Monday but under circumstances beyond even my wildest imaginings on Friday morning, April 27, 1973.

Shortly after Marnie and I had returned from church on Sunday morning, the White House switchboard advised that I should be at the White House at 2:00 P.M. to take a helicopter to Camp David. This would interfere with cutting the grass but I expressed to Marnie the satisfaction I would have in being able to inform the president of my resignation today instead of tomorrow.

Senator Dole of Kansas, then chairman of the Republican National Committee, was awaiting me at the helicopter pad and we flew the short trip to Camp David together.

The president was alone when I walked in. I don't think I have ever seen such a distraught-looking person in my life. The tired man, it seemed, bore the weight of the world on his shoulders. My heart went out to him as I looked into his grief-filled face.

"Hi, Mr. President," I said, with as much cheerfulness as I could muster.

"I don't know why you want to see me, but I'm glad to be here. I was going to see you tomorrow and submit my resignation. I just can't continue on and I'm deeply sorry."

"I can understand how you feel, Dick. I feel the same way and that is why I asked you to come up here this afternoon. I want you to resign. I just can't function with half an attorney general. Elliot Richardson is here and he has consented to succeed you."

That which followed in the next few minutes put me into a state of shock from which I am still not completely recovered. And doubtless never will be.

The president then turned to me and said that what he was about to say would be one of the most difficult things he ever did, and what he was going to ask me to do would be the most difficult personal decision I would ever have to make. I couldn't believe my ears when he informed me that he was going on national television the next evening to announce the resignation of Haldeman, Ehrlichman, and Dean. Then came the blockbuster. As a personal favor to him, he wanted me to agree that he would announce my resignation at the same time.

"Why me, Mr. President? I'm not part of their problem. You can't ask me to do that!" I implored.

This poor beleaguered man then began to sob and intoned that he had to make a clean sweep, that he could appear on national television very seldom, that he wanted to be able to demonstrate a new beginning, and that the announcement of the appointment of Richardson as the new attorney general would be of incalculable help to him in his effort to restore public confidence in his presidency.

"Dick, I'm simply asking you to do this for me as a personal favor. You just have to do it for me."

Almost immediately after I agreed to the president's request, Richardson entered the room. Based upon what he remarked to me on our return to Washington, I have had to conclude that he had been able to overhear the conversation between me and the president.

With perhaps the sole exception of Marnie, everyone who has learned of this incident has offered the opinion that my decision to accede to the president's request was the biggest and most damaging mistake in my life. "You were a damn fool to do so" is the typical reply. Even Elliot Richardson expressed the same sentiment as we flew back to Washington that afternoon in the helicopter. His words still burn in my ears: "Kleindienst, I wouldn't have done what you just did for anybody—and I mean anybody."

Maybe so.

But, as I evaluate *all* the circumstances on that fateful Sunday afternoon—maybe not. Here was the leader of the free world in an almost shattered condition. His sobs and distraught demeanor were, to me, profound and genuine. I did not perceive him as a participant in the burglary or in the coverup that ensued. Rather, I perceived him to be the principal victim of excesses committed by so many of his closest and most loyal aides. Moreover, here was a man with whom

I had voluntarily associated almost twenty years before as he spoke for and became the leader of the Republican party, a party to which I had likewise voluntarily given so much time and energy for nearly three decades. I have no basis to think of myself as a superpatriot or, for that matter, a super anything. Nevertheless, in those few minutes in which I had to make such a momentous decision, I did think of my country. I had been a politician and I was in the government primarily because of my deep convictions about my country. Richard Nixon was president of my country and he was imperiled. If he was imperiled, my country was endangered. I was but one person and not very significant at that. At the time I did what I thought I had to do. Given the same circumstances again I think I would make the same decision. Maybe not.

Whereas Haldeman, Ehrlichman, and Dean concluded their government service on the night of April 30, 1973, I remained as the attorney general pending the confirmation by the Senate of my successor. And that came some twenty-three days later. In light of what took place at 11:00 A.M. the next day at a meeting of the cabinet, those twenty-three days in which I acted as the caretaker of the Department of Justice were not the most pleasant of my life. For at the cabinet session I angrily got up and walked out, and that was the last time I saw President Nixon.

As I understand it, when the president was walking to his Oval Office that morning he observed persons unfamiliar to him standing in front of the door leading to Haldeman's office. When he inquired who they were and what they were doing there, he was politely informed that they were FBI agents and were instructed to prevent anything from being removed from his offices. Apparently, the president was also informed that agents were positioned at Ehrlichman's office for the same purpose. As I further understand it, the president fell into a rage and ordered a meeting of the cabinet to be held without delay. When the president walked into the cabinet room it was obvious to me that he was outraged. Why, I didn't know. I was soon to find out.

Cabinet officers are seated in proximity to the president based upon the longevity in the government of their department. Thus, the secretary of state sits to the right of the president and the secretary of defense sits to his left. The third oldest department, Treasury, finds its secretary sitting directly opposite the president and to the right of the vice president. The attorney general is seated to the left of the vice president.

No sooner had the president sat down than he began pointing his finger at me in an agitated manner. And with an equally agitated tone of voice he began exclaiming—as best as I can recall; I was present for but a minute or two—how terrible and unforgivable it was to station FBI agents before the offices of two fine dedicated men, as if they were common criminals. Something like that would never happen again. There was no doubt in my mind that he was talking to—or yelling at—me and that he thought I was the person responsible. When I attempted to interrupt the president and to disclaim any knowledge of the matter, the finger pointing and tirade continued. Whereupon, I stood up, pointed my finger at the president, and said, "You're wrong about me, sir." Then I walked out.

Present at that meeting was Secretary of Defense and Attorney General–designate Elliot Richardson. I learned later that it was he who had determined, the night before, to station the FBI in front of the Haldeman and Ehrlichman offices. I don't know what happened after I walked out, but I do know that Richardson said not a word while I was there.

The president could not have made a better political decision at the time than to designate Richardson as his new attorney general. If there was in the public's eyes a "great man's great man" in the Nixon administration, it had to be Secretary Richardson. (A graduate of Harvard College and Law School, United States attorney, lieutenant governor and attorney general of Massachusetts, undersecretary of state, secretary of HEW, and secretary of defense—a "great man's great man," indeed!)

In addition, Elliot had another distinct advantage. In those politically troubled times, his confirmation by the Senate should have been quick and uneventful. Why should Kennedy, Bayh, and company choose to oppose the selection of such a distinguished public servant and a person of acknowledged moderate persuasion in the ranks of the GOP? Ordinarily, that judgment would have been sound, but those were turbulent times.

Before his confirmation hearings commenced Richardson made the public statement that "he would, if confirmed, appoint a special prosecutor and give him all the independence, authority, and staff support needed to carry out the tasks entrusted to him." He also stated that, although such a special prosecutor would be in the Department of Justice, "and report to me—and only to me—he will be aware that his ultimate accountability is to the American people."

When I read that statement in the press, I had mixed feelings. I fully shared the necessity of a special prosecutor. He should have independence, authority, and full access to the personnel and facilities of the department. In effect, he would make the basic prosecutive decisions in place of the attorney general and thereby avoid the potential contention that such decisions were motivated for narrow partisan reasons by a political appointment of the president. If this was the object, why then should such a special prosecutor "report" to the attorney general? When I recused myself Petersen not only did not report to me but did not discuss Watergate with me. Was the new approach going to work?

Shortly before May 22, Richardson called me at home one evening to report the good news that he had persuaded Archibald Cox to be the special prosecutor if he was confirmed. "Isn't that a ten-strike? I've announced it to the press."

"Good luck, Elliot," I responded and put down the phone.

In the lore of the power of the government, the swearing-in of a new cabinet officer doesn't readily invite competition from those deemed lesser persons. This would especially be true if the occasion were to commence a new beginning with a new attorney general in an environment like Watergate. Nevertheless, the unsung hero at that swearing-in ceremony was Henry Petersen.

I firmly believe that had it not been for Henry Petersen—who he was and what he did—from June 17, 1972, through May 25, 1973, President Nixon probably would not have been given the opportunity for such a new beginning.

The enduring message of Watergate is not that the system nearly failed because of the abuse of power by a handful of highly placed individuals, but that the system worked as well as it did in spite of such transgressions.

Superficially, it is not difficult to enumerate the many adverse byproducts of this lamentable affair. The list is long and need not be repeated here. Historians and political commentators will be writing about it for decades.

What we tend to forget or ignore is that Watergate is the best illustration we have ever had—save for the tragic Civil War—that the Founding Fathers knew what they were doing when they wrote the Constitution. Having endured King George III they were wise enough to realize that not only could a Watergate occur, but indeed probably would. And at such a time the various institutions of our government would, albeit imperfectly, come into play, the transgression would be eliminated, and the system remain.

First, and foremost, the First Amendment worked. The excesses of elements of the media proved that free speech was a fact of life in America and not to be suppressed by even a strong and popular chief executive. I cannot recall the *Washington Post* or Woodward and Bernstein being "chilled" by the White House in their investigative reporting. In many respects we cannot be proud of what they did, but we can be proud that they were free to do it.

An independent federal judiciary also worked. Remember, John Sirica was a Republican appointee of a Republican president to the federal district court in Washington, D.C. There is some belief that Judge Sirica may have committed excesses in his administration of the judicial affairs of Watergate. Many believe he used his judicial power too much as a prosecutor and too little as a judge. The sentences he handed down on the Watergate burglars were unduly severe. Perhaps he shouldn't have been so joyous to get McCord's letter in March 1973. Perhaps he should even have disqualified himself from the future trials. Notwithstanding, we do know that Dean and Magruder came forward and we do know that public trials thereafter were held. We do know that Judge Sirica was independent of the executive branch. The judiciary worked. Not as well as some of us would have liked. But it worked.

The Congress also worked. Being a highly political assembly of our fellow citizens, it could be expected to act with abundant zeal and fanfare. However, Sam Ervin and Lowell Weicker hardly manifested a fear of repression from the commander in chief of the armed forces as they went about their daily business. The Congress is still there doing pretty much what it has been doing for two hundred years.

The Founding Fathers gave, in their wisdom, however, the ultimate remedy indirectly to the people. If the people decide that they no longer choose to have their elected president serve, he can be impeached. President Nixon resigned because he was informed by leaders of his own party that he would be impeached.

To his enduring credit, he avoided the national trauma inherent in such a confrontation. Nevertheless, the impeachment provision of the Constitution worked.

In short, the system worked. Had Watergate occurred in any other government in the world, a radical change in that government would have been the inevitable outcome.

The one ingredient that binds our system together to enable it to work is, of course, the law. Ours is a system of law and not of men. At the same time, men must administer the law. If in crisis the public can have confidence that the law is being administered evenly and honestly, then it will maintain its confidence in the system.

Henry Petersen, the career nonpartisan professional and the incorruptible prosecutor, was at the right place at the right time. He, with a host of others, administered the law without fear or favor at a critical time in our nation's history. So long as there is a Henry Petersen around when needed, we can rest assured that our system will continue to work. If only for that realization, we can thank those who burglarized Watergate Hotel that Friday evening, June 16, 1972.

PART III

If the end brings me out all right, what is said against me won't amount to anything. If the end brings me out wrong, ten angels swearing I was right would make no difference.

Abraham Lincoln
Washington, D.C., 1862

9

Cox and Richardson

The Special Prosecutor and the Saturday Night Massacre

At 9:30 A.M., Friday, June 7, 1974, I stood before the Honorable George L. Hart, Jr., chief judge of the United States District Court for the District of Columbia. I was there to be sentenced as the defendant in criminal action 0.74-256, as a result of a guilty plea that I had previously made to a violation of 2 United States Code S 192. This section of the U.S. Criminal Code makes it a misdemeanor for a person to refuse to answer fully the questions of a congressional committee. The penalty may be a $1,000 fine, or a one-year imprisonment, or both. The conduct which gave rise to the proceeding was my testimony before the Senate Judiciary Committee in March and May 1972, during my confirmation hearings to be the sixty-eighth attorney general of the United States. The issue was whether the questions put to me required a disclosure of President Nixon's call to me on April 19, 1971, with respect to the ITT antitrust matter, or whether I had a duty to reveal that call.[1]

As I stood there before Judge Hart, I began to sob openly as he rendered the following sentence:

> The charge of which this defendant has pled guilty is a violation of 2 U.S.C. Section 192, refusing to answer accurately and fully questions of a congressional committee. Had the defendant answered accurately and fully the question put to him in this case, it would have reflected great credit on this defendant, but would have reflected discredit upon another individual.

1. Chapter 6 gives a detailed account of those questions and answers.

175

While this was technically a violation of law, it is not the type of violation that reflects a mind bent on deception; rather, it reflects a heart that is too loyal and considerate of the feelings of others.

The presentence report, the Special Prosecutor's report, and the many letters written to the probation office from people in all walks of life, reflect a defendant of the highest integrity throughout his personal and official life; a defendant who has served his country well in war and in peace; a defendant who is considerate of and helpful to his neighbors; a defendant whose family life is above reproach; a defendant who has been and still is universally respected and admired.

It is the judgment of this Court that in Criminal No. 74-256 you be sentenced to one month in the custody of the Attorney General, or his authorized representative, and that you be fined $100. The sentence both as to imprisonment and fine is suspended, and you will be put on one month's unsupervised probation.

Those were kind words by the chief judge and the major reason for my public tears was his kindness. Yet that guilty plea has left an everlasting scar on my family and me. Quite apart from the merit—or lack of merit—of the charge against me was the ironic fact that my standing before Judge Hart came at the insistence of the office of the special prosecutor. Ironic because not long after the Watergate burglary I became convinced that in order for the general public to have confidence in an impartial administration of justice in such a case, a special prosecutor was necessary. I also specifically urged on President Nixon his appointment, even mentioning potential candidates.

At the time the reasons for such were quite obvious to me. I not only was the appointee of the president but also had been politically active in his behalf for many years. Two of the burglars were identified as being connected with the White House staff and the campaign committee organized for the president's reelection. The place burglarized was the headquarters of the Democratic party. The purpose of the burglary was to secure information from the files and papers of the chairman of the Democratic party. All of this added up to something quite different from the usual breaking-and-entering case. This was a political crime—nothing more and nothing less.

If it is assumed, then, that the unusual circumstances of Watergate justified a special prosecutor, just what did that mean? From the very outset, it meant several things to me. First, it meant that I should remove myself from anything to do with the investigation and prosecution of the matter. Next, it meant that I should appoint a person as a special assistant who would make the ultimate prosecutive decisions. So far as Watergate was concerned, he would be, in effect, the attorney general. This person had to have two principal characteristics—experience and a nonpolitical background. Finally, the special prosecutor would then proceed to deal directly with the assistant attorney general of the criminal division, the U.S. attorney, the career lawyers of the department, and the FBI in the usual manner. The result of such a procedure would have been, in my opinion, public confidence in the fair and impartial administration of justice.

What happened, however, was something quite different. Archibald Cox was the wrong kind of person to be appointed special prosecutor in May 1973, and was appointed, by Elliot Richardson, for the wrong reasons.

Because of my own experience with the special prosecutor these categorical statements may invite an immediate response of sour grapes. As fairly and dispassionately as I can, therefore, I shall attempt to illustrate why I make these judgments. My reasons arise both from my personal involvement and from considerable reflection and research since.

My contact with the special prosecutor's office began about September 10, 1973. I had been a private citizen since early summer. Around noon that day, as I was walking east on K Street in Washington to keep a luncheon appointment, I chanced upon a friend, William Hundley. I knew Hundley through Henry Petersen. Hundley had, in fact, been Henry's superior as chief of the organized-crime section at Justice. When Hundley retired in 1966, Henry had succeeded him. I had come to like Bill Hundley and to think highly of him. That John Mitchell retained him to be his attorney in his Watergate trial gives some indication of Hundley's stature as a private lawyer in criminal law.

As Bill and I walked together, he caught me by surprise with the information that, according to the rumor factory, the special prosecutor's office was investigating the conduct of Dick McLaren and Erwin Griswold in connection with the ITT matter.

"That's impossible," I exclaimed. I then told Hundley the story of the president's call to me in April 1971, and that McLaren and Griswold knew nothing about it—even to that day. "Shouldn't I meet with Cox, the special prosecutor, on a confidential basis, for the purpose of telling him about the president's call and that McLaren annd Griswold knew nothing about it? Wouldn't that demonstrate that the ITT settlement was a great victory for the department as a result of the exemplary conduct of both McLaren and Griswold?"

Hundley pondered these questions for a few moments and, as we prepared to go our separate ways, said, "Let me think about it—I'll give you a call either this afternoon or tomorrow."

I gathered that Hundley intended to call James Neal, a top aide to Cox, and an attorney on the staff of the organized-crime section at Justice before he entered private practice in Tennessee.

Apparently Neal was contacted by Hundley and Neal immediately informed Cox of Hundley's call. Cox then called Hundley and indicated to him that he wanted to speak to me personally and that he would be willing to keep in confidence anything that I had to say. Cox also indicated that he would like to see me as soon as possible. When Hundley informed him that I had departed the day before—Wednesday, September 12—for Chicago to attend the national convention of the Federal Bar Association as the outgoing president, Cox suggested the possibility of his flying to Chicago to meet with me. To avoid the necessity of such a flight, Hundley informed him that he would call me in Chicago and arrange for me to call Cox the next day. When I called Cox the next morning, September 14, he repeated to me the same ground rules that he had discussed with Hundley. I then related to him the substance of the call I had received from the president on April 19, 1971. When this conversation ended, we both agreed that I would meet in his office on September 28.

I immediately called Bill Hundley and informed him of what had taken place. His immediate admonition was that I not attend such a meeting by myself and that I should be represented by an attorney. When I challenged the necessity for an attorney being present under these circumstances, Hundley absolutely insisted. As it turned out, this is probably the best advice I ever got.

"Any suggestions, Bill?" I asked.

"Jack Miller, former assistant attorney general for the criminal division under Bobby Kennedy, a great guy, and, incidentally, a Republican," he immediately replied.

"Will you introduce me to him when I get back?"

"Sure. See you in a few days."

That was to be a most fortunate introduction. Jack Miller, his partner John Cassidy, and his former partner Ray Randolph, shepherded me through the upcoming tribulations with the highest professional skill and the deepest of understanding.

When I returned from Chicago, Hundley and I lunched with Jack Miller. I've met a host of people in my life—all kinds. But Herbert J. Miller, Jr. was one of a kind. Vigorous and intelligent, he brought to his profession forthrightness, realism, and an understanding for fellow human beings. Upon being convinced of the justness of his client's course, he became a singularly dedicated advocate.

After I outlined the situation Miller, in what I would learn was his customary direct manner, said two things. "If you think that special prosecutor's office is not going to make you a target for prosecution, you're crazy!" More prophetic words were never spoken. I employed him as my attorney.

Miller, Ray Randolph, and I met with Cox and his aides, Richard Davis and Joseph Connally, on September 28, 1973. This was the first time I met Joseph Connally, who was introduced by Cox as his aide in charge of the ITT matter. My sole purpose in being at that meeting was to reveal the president's call and to discuss it in light of the subsequent settlement negotiations. I wanted them to know that I had refused to obey the president's order, that it was revoked, that the appeals in the ITT cases went forward, and that McLaren worked out the settlement by himself without knowledge of the call and without subsequent interference by the White House. For this I was prepared.

I was not prepared for what ensued. Upon interrogation by Mr. Connally I was asked to go back and recall everything I could about Watergate, from the burglary on Friday, June 16, 1972, to the time I left the Department of Justice on May 25, 1973. I made no objection. I was proud of the conduct of the department and of myself during those difficult days. I was happy to tell that story. Nevertheless, try telling a story like that from memory, without preparation. Generally it will be accurate; specifically, matters will be forgotten. Assistant special prosecutor Connally—whom I came to regard as my special persecutor—would remind me of these specifics in the months to come. When the interrogation was finally concluded, I breathed a sign of relief. As far as I was concerned, the ITT matter had once again been laid to rest.

This happy thought exploded in my face Monday evening, October 29, 1973. Just as Marnie and I were leaving the house for a dinner engagement the telephone rang. The caller identified himself as a reporter for the *New York Times*. As I recall, the man was Seymour Hersch.

"Mr. Kleindienst, we have information that on April 19, 1971, the president called you and directed that you dismiss the ITT cases. In light of your testimony before the Senate in 1972 do you wish to make any comment?"

I was dumbstruck. I garbled a reply to the effect that that call had nothing to do with the ITT settlement, that I refused to follow the president's order, and that he rescinded it. "Thank you very much, sir." Click went the phone.

The next day I was branded a perjurer by the national press and TV. I immediately issued a formal statement to the press. It was not quoted or published. However, on Wednesday, October 31, the *Washington Post* reported the testimony given by Mr. Cox the previous day to the Senate Judiciary Committee. That testimony answered my question as to the undoubted source of the information in the possession of the *New York Times*. Mr. Cox admitted to a Senate committee that he had just revealed my confidential conversation with him to his Democratic friends, Senators Kennedy and Hart, and to members of their staffs.

The reason Mr. Cox found himself before the Senate Judiciary Committee on short notice had to do with his behavior immediately after his departure from office, an event that will live in political history as the Saturday night massacre. On Saturday, October 20, 1973, the president directed Attorney General Richardson to discharge Cox as the special prosecutor. Rather than follow that order, Richardson and Ruchelshaus, the deputy attorney general, resigned. Robert Bork, then solicitor general, became the acting attorney general by the internal rules of the Department of Justice. Bork was in fact, under the rules then operative, the end of the line of succession. Had he also resigned, there was no provision for another officer of the department to become the acting attorney general. Bork did consent to serve and, on orders from the president, discharged the special prosecutor.

Watergate produced many bizarre events, but the Saturday night massacre was doubtless the most bizarre. When the personalities and characteristics of all the players are taken into account, one can sense its preordained certainty. With each participant being true to himself from the beginning to the end, a sequence of events was set in motion from which there was no turning back.

Richardson had apparently concluded, in his own mind, even before his confirmation hearings began that previous May that he would and should, if confirmed as attorney general, appoint a special prosecutor. That position was communicated to the Senate committee, and during the course of the hearings, the specific terms and conditions under which he would serve were clarified. According to Richardson, "The key elements of the charter under which Mr. Cox was eventually appointed embraced, first, full authority; second, independence; and third, support." Cox appeared with Richardson before the committee and participated in the clarifying process.

It is more important, however, to note here that Richardson had had no discussions with the president about the selection of a special prosecutor. This is significant because one of the most difficult problems to be clarified was whether the special prosecutor would have the power to challenge in court the assertion of executive privilege. When Cox's name was made public by Richardson, the president had little recourse but to support it publicly.

The question of executive privilege was also before the president. On May 22, in addition to supporting the Cox appointment, the president made this statement: "Accordingly, executive privilege will not be involved as to any testimony concerning possible criminal conduct and matters presently under investigation including the Watergate affair and alleged coverup."

That statement was issued by the president without consultation with Richardson. Richardson was so encouraged by the statement that on that very day, May 22, he "called Mr. Cox on the telephone to inform him of it and to characterize it as what I considered to be a very positive indication that the problem of executive privilege was likely to be minimal." Cox and the committee apparently agreed because Richardson was confirmed the next day.

The precise words of the president's statement and the differing interpretations of them by the president, Richardson, and Cox were the central issue in the massacre. Note first that the president used the term "testimony." He did not refer to documents or papers. Naturally, he did not refer to tapes since their disclosure was not made until July 16. Note second that the president referred to "matters presently under investigation including the Watergate affair and alleged coverup."

A critical point about which there was also no communication between the president and Richardson was the basis upon which Cox could be discharged. Richardson assured the committee and Cox that he would be discharged only for "gross improprieties." As Cox testified on Monday, October 29, "The attorney general was the only person I heard publicly give any such assurance to this committee." Thus, the question was to be raised by all three participants at the end as to exactly what were the ground rules. Obviously, each would declare a different set of rules at the end.

If the subject matter of the special prosecutor hadn't been already mangled beyond repair, the impact of the sensational disclosure by Alex Butterfield of the White House tapes to the Ervin committee on Monday, July 16, 1973, was the finishing touch. Not only was the country shocked, but White House aides, who had not known they were being taped, were both shocked and hurt. The hurt soon turned to fear. What would the special prosecutor attempt to do about obtaining the tapes? What could he do under the law? The answers were soon forthcoming. The courts held that the claim of executive privilege could not be asserted with respect to any matter that might tend to prove criminal conduct by the president or his staff. That was the answer to their second question. What access Cox would demand by way of furthering his investigation would answer their first question and thereby create the ultimate confrontation between White House and special prosecutor.

Cox had the grand jury issue a subpoena to the White House for the production of nine specific taped conversations between the president and various members of his staff. Judge Sirica enforced a part of the request and, with some modifications, his order was affirmed by the court of appeals. In the absence of a decision by the Supreme Court, the issues arose as to whether the tapes would be supplied and in what form they would be supplied.

In an effort to resolve this issue Richardson intervened. He consulted with Charles Alan Wright (the president's legal counselor at the White House), Alexander Haig, Fred Buzhardt, and other White House aides, commencing Monday, October 15, 1973. By Wednesday, the 17th, he had formulated a plan that met with the approval of the White House. The plan was reduced to writing, titled "A Proposal," and delivered to Cox on that day. The objective of the proposal was "to provide a means of furnishing to the court and the grand jury a complete and accurate record of the contents of the tapes subpoenaed by the special prosecutor insofar as they related in any way to the Watergate break-in and coverup." The means of fulfilling the objective was for the president to choose a verifier, one who would certify the completeness and accuracy of the record. Senator Stennis of Mississippi was identified in the Richardson proposal as the chosen verifier. The verifier would be empowered to paraphrase language to avoid embarrassment to the president. (Expletives were then a matter of considerable concern.) It was projected that after the verifier had completed his work, the special prosecutor and the counsel for the president "would join in urging the court to accept the verified record as a full and complete record."

The next day, October 18, 1973, Cox submitted to Richardson his "Comments on a Proposal." These comments enumerated eleven objections. Since comments 1, 2, 6, and 9 became the focal points of the approaching disaster, I describe them:

> Comment 1—The public shouldn't be asked to confide such a difficult task to one person and, besides he [Cox] should not be put in the position of having to accept such a unilateral choice.

> Comment 2—The idea "of tying a solution into court machinery" was acceptable, but he, Cox, preferred the use of special masters.

Comment 6—A transcript prepared by the verifier for investigation purposes only was acceptable. However, the exact tapes must also be produced (at the time of trial) if the Court so ruled.

Comment 9—The proposal was too narrow and "would not serve the function of the court's decision in establishing the special prosecutor's entitlement to other evidence."

The president's counselor, Charles Alan Wright, on the same day, October 18, replied in writing to Cox's "Comments" on the Richardson "Proposal." At the outset, he stated that the purpose "of the very reasonable proposal that the attorney general put to you, at the instance of the president, 'was to meet the requirements of the subpoena for the nine specific conversations and thereby' put to rest any possible thought that the president might himself have been involved in the Watergate break-in or coverup." He then concluded by informing Cox that his "Comments, 1, 2, 6, and 9, in particular, depart so far from that proposal and the purpose for which it was made that we could not accede to them in any form."

Cox replied to the Wright letter in writing the next day, the 19th. He succinctly restated his views with respect to comments 1, 2, 6, and 9, and concluded his letter thus:

I have a strong desire to avoid any form of confrontation but I could not conscientiously agree to your stipulations without unfaithfulness to the pledges which I gave the Senate prior to my appointment. It is enough to point out that the fourth stipulation would require me to forgo further legal challenge to claims of executive privilege. I categorically assured the Senate Judiciary Committee that I would challenge such claims so far as the law permitted. The attorney general was confirmed on the strength of that assurance. I cannot break my promise now.

Wright responded in writing on the same day. He likewise reargued his position on the points in dispute and concluded with this interesting paragraph:

I note these points only in the interest of historical accuracy in the unhappy event our correspondence should see the light of day. As I read your comments of the 18th and your letter of the 19th, the differences between us remain so great that no purpose would be served by further discussion of what I continue to think was a "very reasonable"—and indeed an unprudently generous—proposal that the attorney general put to you in an effort, in the national interest, to resolve our disputes by mutual agreement at a time when the country would be particularly well served by such agreement.

The contents of this letter had to result from a direct conference between the

president and Wright. This seems evident from the president's short letter of
instruction to Richardson on October 19:

The Honorable Elliot Richardson
The Attorney General
Department of Justice
Washington, D.C.

Dear Elliot:
   You are aware of the actions I am taking today to bring an end to
the controversy over the so-called Watergate tapes and that I have
reluctantly agreed to a limited breach of Presidential confidentiality in
order that our country may be spared the agony of further indecision
and litigation about those tapes at a time when we are confronted with
other issues of much greater moment to the country and the world.
   As a part of these actions, I am instructing you to direct Special
Prosecutor Archibald Cox of the Watergate Special Prosecution Force
that he is to make no further attempts by judicial process to obtain tapes,
notes, or memoranda of Presidential conversations. I regret the necessity
of intruding, to this very limited extent, on the independence that I
promised you with regard to Watergate when I announced your appointment. This would not have been necessary if the Special Prosecutor
had agreed to the very reasonable proposal you made to him this week.

Sincerely,
Richard Nixon

   And so matters proceeded to the final act. Friday, October 19, 1973, has to
be a day to be remembered by the attorney general of the United States. Not
only had he witnessed the demise of what he believed to be a reasonable proposal
to Cox, but he had received the above missive from the president. The turmoil
in which he found himself on the evening of that day can be imagined. A look
at the logs of his telephone calls commencing at about six can do nothing but
arouse speculation as to the content of those calls:

Melvin Laird—to 6:10 (unable to talk; returned call 7:08)
General Haig—from 7:00
Archibald Cox—to 7:30
Bryce Harlow—from 8:30
Archibald Cox—from 9:05
Robert Bork—from 9:10
Archibald Cox—to 9:48

Based upon information I have obtained from some of the participants in those telephone calls that Friday evening, the atmosphere was volatile and uncertain. After Haig talked to Richardson at 7:00 P.M., he instructed Harlow to call all cabinet members that evening and inform them of the president's decision to discharge Cox. According to Harlow, he contacted all cabinet members before he called Richardson at 8:30 P.M., and his contact with Richardson was merely to inform him of what he had done. To Harlow's great surprise—he knew that Richardson had fully participated in all these decisions—Richardson suddenly complained of being "shabbily treated" and indicated he would have no part of the plan. Richardson's changed tone indicates that he must have concluded he had to resign after his 7:00 P.M. call from Haig and before his 8:30 P.M. conversation with Harlow. Perhaps his 7:30 P.M. chat with Cox was the catalyst that he needed. Haig, however, was not able to reach Richardson until after ten, although, as a result of Harlow's report to him, it was imperative that he talk to Richardson. Richardson had two additional conversations with Cox before Haig finally got to him. By that time Richardson had made his decision, which also caught Haig by surprise. Small wonder. According to Susanna McBee, a *Washington Post* staff writer, whose interview of Charles Alan Wright appeared in the *Post* on December 9, 1973, Richardson was present at the White House in the morning when it was decided that Cox would have no further access to presidential papers and tapes. McBee quotes Wright as saying that "if he [Richardson] didn't say it first, he agreed to it."

The next and final day—Saturday, October 20—Richardson wrote two letters to the president. In the first he states that the instruction contained in the president's letter the day before "gives me serious difficulty." He then says that he "regarded as reasonable and constructive the proposal to rely on Senator Stennis to prepare a verified record of the so-called Watergate tapes and I did my best to persuade Mr. Cox of the desirability of the solution of that issue." He then pointed out that his "Proposal" to Cox "did not purport to deal with other tapes, notes or memoranda of presidential conversations." He concluded with the hope that some further accommodation could be made and said that he, Richardson, "would welcome the opportunity to discuss the matter with you."

Richardson's telephone logs for October 20 do not indicate a discussion with the president that day. He did, however, talk to General Haig five times—12:43 P.M., 3:20 P.M., 4:20 P.M., 6:00 P.M., and 7:05 P.M. Undoubtedly, one or more of those conversations necessitated the second letter that day to the president. In it Richardson pointed out to the president that in his nomination hearings he had pledged that the special prosecutor could be removed only for "extraordinary improprieties," and that he "also pledged that the attorney general will not countermand or interfere with the special prosecutor's decisions or actions." Richardson's resignation concluded with this paragraph:

> While I fully respect the reasons that led you to conclude that the special prosecutor must be discharged, I trust that you understand that I could not, in the light of these firm and repeated commitments, carry out your

direction that this be done. In the circumstances, therefore, I feel that
I have no choice but to resign.

In my opinion, Richardson created his own subsequent torment when he
concluded, in his confirmation hearing, that unless he nominated a person like
Archibald Cox, his confirmation would be in jeopardy. On May 7, 1973, two
days before his first appearance before the Senate Judiciary Committee on
Wednesday, Richardson held a press conference at the Defense Department and
announced that he would, if confirmed, appoint a special prosecutor "and give
him all the independence, authority, and staff support needed to carry out the
tasks entrusted to him." As a consequence of his statement, most of the dialogue
between Richardson and the committee during May 9 concerned itself with the
questions pertaining to the functions and powers of the proposed special prosecutor. Of particular interest was Richardson's posture that although he would
delegate to the special prosecutor the responsibility for investigating and prosecuting Watergate and related matters, "he must retain ultimate responsibility
for all matters falling within the jurisdiction of the department."

When Richardson returned to the committee the next day, Thursday, May 10,
he discovered that Senators Kennedy and Bayh were interested in not only the
powers of the special prosecutor but also who that person would be. Senator
Kennedy, by insistent interrogation, was finally able to have Richardson agree
that he would furnish to the members of the committee the names of his four
leading candidates for the position. These names would be listed by way of
priority from the top. Richardson may have supplied that information to some
committee members over the following weekend.

Tuesday, May 15, Kennedy inquired whether the person Richardson intended
to select was examining the prepared guidelines for the special prosecutor.

"Yes, at least one of them is," replied Richardson.

That person was also the one at the head of the list. Kennedy then wanted to
be informed should that person turn down the position "because he does not
feel that the guidelines give him sufficient flexibility." Richardson agreed to do
that but also stated that "that has not been a problem."

The hearing recessed on Tuesday, May 15, and did not reconvene until Monday, May 21, when Archibald Cox appeared with Richardson. Before that appearance, Cox had suggested one change to the guidelines, a change agreed to
by Richardson. The inescapable conclusion from the record is that Archibald
Cox was the only serious candidate for the job.

I became even more convinced of this conclusion when I read the fall 1982
Harvard Law School Bulletin. That issue contains articles about Archibald Cox
written by the dean of the Law School, James Vorenberg, Elliot Richardson,
and Professor Philip Heymann. All three articles are highly laudatory. In his
article, "The Rule in Cox's Case," Richardson makes two comments of significance. After summarizing his past impressions of Cox, he writes: "All of
these impressions came to mind the day it occurred to me—I was still at the

Pentagon—that Archie Cox would be the ideal special prosecutor for the Watergate investigation.'' He then wrote: ''Few Republicans, to be sure, leavened the outpouring of Kennedys at the special prosecutor's swearing-in in the conference room of his old Justice Department office. This, I explained in response to the White House's predictably paranoid reaction, proved nothing. *The Kennedys and the Coxes, after all, were friends''* (emphasis supplied). Because of that acknowledged friendship, I presume to say that Archibald Cox was appointed special prosecutor for the wrong reasons.

I also believe that Archibald Cox created his own subsequent torment by accepting the position. Archibald Cox is an able professor of the Law School. He was one of the best teachers I ever had. Moreover, his superior articulation of the objectives of the liberal wing of a great political party is a matter of record. However, no matter how hard he tried, he could never cast aside the public's perception of a committed partisan political past. No person similarly situated could have survived the debacle in which he ultimately found himself. Precisely because he was who he was, rather than resign as special prosecutor when he found himself in opposition to the president, he instead created a public confrontation with the president in his press conference on Saturday, October 20, necessitating his discharge.

Richard Nixon created his own torment too. Knowing he had been a participant in the rough and tumble of American politics for almost three decades, I could never understand why he did not recognize Watergate for the political bombshell it was. It could have been defused at the outset by the designation of a nonpolitical special prosecutor in the Department of Justice. Instead, the matter had escalated to the point where only by the appointment of a partisan political adversary could the mounting tide be momentarily stemmed. At the end, the president had to squander what little respect remained for the presidency in a desperate effort to preserve the constitutional power of his office.

Back to the aftermath of Archibald Cox's dismissal. On the Tuesday following his discharge Cox was driving his car toward the Capitol when he heard over the radio a report of the new position of resistance taken in court by the White House with respect to releasing the tapes. It caused him such concern that he parked his car and proceeded to the office of Senator Kennedy to find out more about the matter. At that point a meeting was arranged for that evening, to take place at Senator Kennedy's home in McLean, Virginia. Present at that meeting were Cox, Senator Hart of Michigan, Senator Kennedy, and Carey Parker and Bert Wides, aides of the senators. According to Cox, the purpose of the meeting ''was to discuss the forthcoming sessions of this committee, and for me to run through what my testimony might be.'' Since he was no longer in the role of special prosecutor, he ''felt that would be proper.'' Besides, he ''was glad to talk over my troubles with some friends. I had been in a kind of lonely position. I was awfully tired at this time, and my memory really isn't terribly good.''

The reason the former special prosecutor was asked to explain the circumstances of that meeting was an article that appeared in the *New York Times* on

Tuesday, October 30. The article revealed the president's call to me ordering the dismissal of the ITT cases, information I had given to Cox and his staff in confidence. When he learned about the forthcoming article the day before, he volunteered the circumstances leading to his breach of my confidence to the committee. To his credit, he acknowledged his conduct "was an inexcusable breach of confidence" and "was wrong." He also agreed that such conduct, had it occurred while he was the special prosecutor, would have arguably constituted such gross impropriety as to warrant his dismissal as special prosecutor by the attorney general. However, he said that since it had been done under "strain and weariness and exhaustion," he would have hoped that Richardson would not discharge him.

Any person who has found himself in circumstances of pressure can sympathize with Mr. Cox. When we are lonely, tired, and besieged, it is comforting to have friends to whom we can unburden ourselves. The problem he had, however, was the characteristics of the "friends" to whom he turned. They were persons with whom he had been deeply involved over the years in partisan politics. Indeed, Richard Nixon could not have selected two other U.S. senators more opposed to him personally and ideologically than Hart and Kennedy. Presumably, aides Parker and Wides reflected the same strong feelings.

The strong feelings were equally shared by Cox himself. Approximately two weeks before he appeared before the Judiciary Committee as a candidate for special prosecutor, he held a press conference at the University of California following a series of lectures on the Supreme Court. There he acknowledged that he was critical of the Nixon administration in general and of Mitchell and myself in particular. Apparently he didn't think it necessary to discuss that news conference with Richardson when he was in the process of becoming the special prosecutor. As he explained with candor, "I think Mr. Richardson knew in general my political views."

Simply put, Archibald Cox should not have agreed to assume the role of special prosecutor for Watergate. Elliot Richardson should not have induced him to become the special prosecutor. The question is not their high integrity and acknowledged ability, but the objective and dispassionate administration of the criminal laws with respect to political crimes. More than ever, the general public, as well as the accused, must have confidence that the law will be applied with fairness. More than ever, the appearance of fairness is absolutely required. When crunch came to crunch it was almost impossible for the White House and Cox to work out a meaningful solution to a difficult problem. In his testimony, Richardson stated the proposition clearly:

> And so I think that there was a feeling on the president's part that here
> was a guy who was motivated by partisan consideration, who was out
> to destroy his presidency, who was stretching his jurisdiction in order
> to thrash around among presidential papers to see what he could get,
> and that this was a violation of important considerations protecting the

confidentiality of Presidential communications. I think it came to the stretching point when he felt that he had made a major concession which Mr. Cox found unacceptable, and so there it broke.

The attorney general had also put himself in a no-win position, again derived from the impossibility of the situation. As we noted, he worked out the terms of the Cox charter with the Senate Judiciary Committee and with Cox but without consulting the White House. One provision of the charter was that Cox would be discharged only for "gross impropriety." When Richardson submitted to Cox the "Stennis proposal," Richardson considered it to be reasonable. Cox did not. Richardson, however, did not regard Cox's rejection of the Stennis proposal as a gross impropriety and therefore was prepared to resign if he was directed to fire Cox over that point alone. Clearly, the White House, Richardson, and Cox each differently understood what constituted "gross impropriety."

Richardson's dilemma, in my opinion, traced to his concept of a special prosecutor. If the reason for the special prosecutor was to remove a political appointee of the president from the decisionmaking process in the investigation and prosecution of Watergate, all the attorney general had to do was recuse himself in favor of a career officer such as Petersen or by the appointment of a nonpartisan special assistant from the outside. It was not necessary to create a special department of justice. (Petersen and Silbert had the Watergate cases "97 percent" completed after the Dean and Magruder disclosures were made to them.) Richardson, however, didn't really take himself out of the matter. Even though he "started out immediately after confirmation and taking office with a totally hands-off attitude," he "fell into this relationship of a sort of middle man because, as time went on, it seemed to me that I could be useful that way." Unfortunately, he couldn't. He was trying to serve two, perhaps three, masters at once—the president, the special prosecutor, and, perhaps, himself. Ironically, the president asked for my resignation because, as he put it, "I have only one half of an attorney general because you had to recuse yourself." The way it turned out, he wound up with less than one half of an attorney general in Richardson.

Leon Jaworski, who succeeded Cox as special prosecutor, is the kind of person who should have been designated special prosecutor by Richardson in the first place. He was the sort I had in mind immediately after Watergate to be a special prosecutor. As a successful Houston lawyer and as a former president of the American Bar Association, he had a public stature comparable to that of Archibald Cox. He did not, however, have the deep-rooted partisan political background that Cox brought with him to the task.

But this could not be said about many of the staff members that Jaworski inherited from Cox, and retained. As a consequence, the ideal of nonpartisan objectivity in this politically charged atmosphere was never given a fair chance to be established. Again, the question was not the integrity and ability of any individual, but the public's concept of fairness. The following summary should illustrate the point:

James Vorenberg—Cox's first deputy, served in Justice under Ramsey Clark as head of the office of criminal justice; he became an adviser to the 1972 McGovern presidential campaign and participated in the drafting of the 1972 Democratic platform.

Philip Heymann—Special assistant to Cox and his aide when Cox was the solicitor general under Robert Kennedy.

Thomas McBride—Served under Attorney General Robert Kennedy.

William H. Merrit—Former assistant U.S. attorney and former Michigan state chairman of the 1968 Kennedy presidential campaign.

George Frampton, Jr.—Former aide to Sargent Shriver.

Francis Martin—Former aide to Democratic members of the House of Representatives, Dow and Conyers.

Robert M. Witten—Aide to Robert Kennedy in the 1968 Oregon presidential campaign.

Richard Ben-Veniste—Former assistant U.S. attorney under U.S. Attorney Morgenthau in New York.

Joseph Connally was identified by Cox, in his testimony on October 31 before the Senate Judiciary Committee, as one of his "key" people. In his book, *The Right and the Power,* Jaworski described Connally as "thirty-two" and one who "had been a brilliant student." He also said that Connally had been an "assistant solicitor in the U.S. Justice Department and had served on the staff of Secretary of Defense Robert McNamara."

Joseph Connally began his career at Justice on December 13, 1967, under Attorney General Ramsey Clark and resigned on April 27, 1970, when John Mitchell was attorney general. He joined the staff of the special prosecutor in June 1973, following private practice in Philadelphia. If he was twenty-six years of age when he joined the Department of Justice, he had to have been one of those "best and brightest" when he served at an even younger age on the McNamara staff at the Pentagon. This young man headed up the ITT task force in the special prosecutor's office. As Jaworski points out, he "was inexperienced in criminal law."

Shortly after I resigned, the Special Prosecution Force undertook its investigation of the ITT matter and focused particularly on the alleged $400,000 payoff. As the investigation went on, whether because of inexperience or because of the competition with other task forces within the special prosecutor's office, Connally, according to Jaworski, "felt frustrated because the ITT investigation had produced only information and suspicion; no evidence had been uncovered that ITT paid or promised to pay money in exchange for a settlement of the antitrust litigation." The frustration must have existed until just before Cox's dismissal. Ten days later, Mr. Cox testified before the Senate: "I have always thought and continue to think that the terms of the ITT settlement were a perfectly good bargain from the government's point of view, the substantive terms of the settlement, and that is the opinion I get from most antitrust lawyers."

Out of his frustration, or for whatever reason, Connally determined that Richard G. Kleindienst would be prosecuted to the bitter end. That determination began a period of horror in the lives of my family and myself that we will never be able to forget.

My attorney, Jack Miller, began with Joseph Connally a dialogue that continued from October 1973 to April 1974. The position taken by Miller was, of course, that there was no basis for a felony prosecution. There was no "payoff" in ITT; if there was Kleindienst knew nothing about it. In addition, a fair reading of his testimony before the Senate in relationship to the president's call on April 19, 1971, was persuasive of the fact that he had not committed perjury. By way of mitigation, he had refused to follow the order of the president. He had also come forward and volunteered that information to the special prosecutor.

Most important, Miller argued, that call from Nixon and the department's quiet response of rejection occurred *before* Felix Rohatyn contacted the Department of Justice and even suggested settlement negotiations, or, for that matter, had his suggestion taken up by the antitrust division. If, in fact, Kleindienst's refusal to fire Griswold and McLaren, or to influence their decisions on ITT, prompted Rohatyn and Geneen of ITT to think settlement, that was to the benefit of the government's attack on excessive conglomerate extension. (Over 80 percent of all antitrust cases are settled without court action. The aim of the basic law is to keep the marketplace operating freely without such action.)

Finally, Miller reminded Connally that the "inexcusable" breach of confidence by Archibald Cox had publicly cast Kleindienst in the light of perjurer, and the already poisoned Watergate atmosphere prevented anything approaching a fair trial. We met with Jaworski, Connally, and Davis on November 19, 1973, to go over these contentions again. We had the same ground rules as I had with Cox, that is, complete confidentiality. To no avail.

On a late afternoon of a cold Tuesday in February I was in my woodworking shop at home when Miller called. "I've just left Connally and he has determined to indict you on 103 counts of perjury!"

"Oh, my God," I replied and hung up.

I was home alone. How, I asked myself, could such a macabre inversion of the truth occur? How could the most stringent divestiture agreement in American antitrust history and my consistent, voluntary efforts to be open about that settlement lead to this? Apparently most of these unbelievable 103 counts were generated by a minute and malicious comparison of my various verbal testimonies with any divergence in the written files, however small. I sat down and held my head in my hands in utter despair.

When Marnie came home she took one look at me and asked, "What's wrong, dear?"

I told her of Miller's message.

Her response was typical: "We know in our own heart and conscience that we are innocent. If that's the way it's got to be, let's hold our heads up high and fight with everything we have!"

Not long after that call Miller reported another blockbuster. Connally had just informed him that in addition to the perjury counts, he intended to indict me for obstruction of justice. Apparently the grand jury had received testimony to the effect that during my confirmation hearings I had instructed a young assistant of McLaren's to destroy an official document in the ITT Justice files.

"Jack, that's a damned lie! I never destroyed a government document in my life and I never ordered anybody else to do so!" I fairly shouted.

I then did something that perhaps I should not have done. It's the kind of thing that clients are apt to do and that drives their attorneys out of their minds. I called Leon Jaworski personally. In substance, I stated to him that this new charge was false and that as he made his final decision in the perjury charges, I did not want him to be influenced by such a spurious charge. I then asked him to subject me to a lie-detector test to be administered by the FBI on this issue. Appropriately, Jaworski heard me out and the conversation concluded without any significant comments by him.

When I informed Miller of what I had offered, he said, "You've got to be crazy. Have you ever had a lie-detector test? Do you know the risk you are taking?"

"If I'm innocent and if the test is fairly conducted, why should I be afraid?"

"Well, it might be too late, but before the fat's in the fire you are going to take a lie-detector test administered by an outside expert as soon as possible. If you flunk it, then we'll go from there. If you pass, it still won't make any difference to Connally."

The use of a polygraph, as I soon learned firsthand, is rapidly growing in this country. With vastly improved techniques and with high standards established by the American Polygraph Association, it is now possible to establish an almost exact relationship between certain physiological reactions—such as pulse rate, blood pressure, muscle tension, respiration rate, and galvanic skin response—and the telling of truth, or falsehood. Empirical data taken from thousands of tests have convinced qualified experts of the reliability of the polygraph. The polygraph examination is helpful for investigative and law-enforcement purposes, and many courts permit its use as evidence if both parties so stipulate.

Out of extreme caution, Jack Miller insisted that before I submit to a polygraph examination by an examiner selected by the special prosecutor's office an examination should be administered by an independent expert. It didn't take him long to find out that Victor C. Kaufman of New York City was a leading—if not the foremost—expert in the country. He had been a member of the New York City Police Department for over twenty years and was a charter member of the American Polygraph Association. In addition, he was the author of numerous articles published in professional journals and security periodicals. By February 14, 1974, when he examined me, he had personally conducted more than ten thousand polygraph examinations for business, industries, law-enforcement agencies, and attorneys.

With an expert like Kaufman, much time is consumed in reviewing the facts of the case. If the right questions are not asked in the right way, the reliability of the test is diminished. The questions must be susceptible to a yes or no answer and the subject should know in advance the areas the questions will cover. Apparently, the very fact that you anticipate a relevant question will cause you to build emotionally toward it and, if you intend to falsify your answer, to react even more emphatically when it comes.

One technique Kaufman uses to alleviate fear and nervousness in the innocent, and to promote fear of detection in the guilty, is the stimulation test, which he uses before the actual examination. He asks the subject to write his mother's name on a piece of paper. He then asks him to name five females, including his mother. I gave him the names of Elaine, Margaret, Jane, Mary, Gladys, and Ann, in that order. I was then directed to answer no to each name as the name of my mother. The machine showed that I lied when I responded that Gladys was not her name.

The process of being "wired up" to the polygraph machine is a frightening experience. A blood-pressure band and cuff are wrapped around the upper part of the left arm with the bladder centered over the brachial artery. The bladder is then inflated to a point approximating one's arithmetic mean blood pressure to record a continuous indication of the pulse rate, and relative blood pressure. A corrugated rubber tube is fastened around your chest and stomach area to record the respiratory pattern. Finally, an insulated sealing for two protruding electrodes is fitted on the right hand to register changes in galvanic skin response.

This done, the examiner begins. He uses a carefully regulated low voice, and is unseen during the examination. At first, meaningless questions are put, like name, age, birthplace. Then one or two germane queries are asked, followed by irrelevant questions. The theory, of course, is that if one is lying about the relevant questions, the polygraph machine will pick up variations of heart, pulse, blood pressure, respiration, and sweat glands from answers to the irrelevant questions.

To the relief of Miller and Cassidy, I passed the damn test. I derived no satisfaction from the experience at all. It was a humiliation that had to be endured to confirm what I already knew—that I had not ordered the destruction of a government document.

The determination of Connally to indict me had convinced Miller that he should make every effort with Jaworski to work out a solution to my case short of a "shotgun" indictment and a prolonged trial. I could not bring myself to believe that I would ever be indicted, but Miller was wise enough about contemporary reality to believe the contrary. He believed that a Washington, D.C., jury in such an inflamed atmosphere would probably find me guilty. That I could not bring myself to accept.

"Listen, my friend, if I can get an agreement with Leon to dispose of your case by a plea to a misdemeanor of some kind, I'm going to do it for your sake. Do you understand?"

"I guess I understand." But I really didn't.

This, then, was the posture of the dialogue between Miller and Jaworski when the Kaufman polygraph examination was concluded. Miller immediately informed Jaworski of the examination and offered that I would be available for a polygraph examination by a competent examiner "across the board."

Thereafter and on March 21, Cassidy had the opportunity to discuss with Jaworski my offer to submit to a comprehensive polygraph examination and that he was trying to talk to Connally about it. According to Cassidy, Jaworski seemed pleased to know that Cassidy intended to discuss the matter with Connally, because, as Jaworski stated, "the boys over there believe that Kleindienst has information which he has not divulged with respect to the reasons for the ITT settlement, which information Kleindienst is reluctant to divulge because it might involve a friend or acquaintance such as Mitchell."

Cassidy then had a long conversation with Connally in the late afternoon of the same day. Connally's attitude was completely negative. He disputed Kaufman's credentials and manifested little or no interest in submitting me to an extensive examination by an examiner of his own choosing. That seemed to be the end of that.

However, immediately following March 25, Connally did an about-face. For this reason. According to documents from the special prosecutor's office released in January 1978 pursuant to requests made under the Freedom of Information Act, Jaworski on March 25, 1974, advised his staff that he had concluded to accept from me a one-count plea to a misdemeanor. Connally vehemently opposed this decision. Apparently, when the frustration and anger had subsided, Jaworski was persuaded by the staff to withhold notifying Miller and, instead, to require me to submit to the polygraph examination I had previously volunteered to take. The reason is simply stated in the report: "If he failed the test we might convince Mr. Jaworski to change his decision." Accordingly, Connally called Cassidy on the same day, March 25. By agreement, the examination was to be given on April 2 at 10:00 A.M. in Philadelphia.

On the day of the test, Miller and I appeared at the FBI offices in Philadelphia where the test was to be administered. Victor Kaufman met us there. After the preliminaries I was directed to enter a room and to sit in the chair adjacent to the machine. The room was perfectly square and starkly painted in an off-white. There were no windows. The floor and walls were bare. The polygraph machine and my chair starkly contrasted to their surroundings. I sat down expecting something to happen immediately. Instead, I sat in that chair looking at that blank wall for at least fifteen minutes before the examiners entered the room. They were grim and all business. No amenities. Methodically, I was strapped to the machine; then, to my amazement, the examiners departed, leaving me in that state for several more minutes. When they returned the examination began. Many questions were meaningless; a few related to the destroyed document question; but most pertained to my relationship and dealings with ITT going back as early as April 1969. When the process was concluded, the examiners took the testing paper out of the machine and departed without a word.

To the best of my recollection, I sat strapped to that machine for at least thirty minutes before they returned.

The chief examiner opened the conversation with these horrifying words. "Mr. Kleindienst, everyone in the bureau admired you as the attorney general. We always appreciated your support. We want to do everything possible to help you and to make your situation as easy as possible. If you come clean now and tell us the truth about many of these matters, we'll do all we can to see that you are treated with leniency."

"What in the hell do you think you are talking about?" I shouted in rage. My blood pressure must have gone through the roof. My heart began to pound and I could hardly breathe. "Something's wrong with that f—— machine of yours. As soon as I calm down, run the damn thing again. I'm not a liar and I haven't lied to you today."

All of a sudden the atmosphere changed. The two examiners began to smile and became friendly. "We know you haven't been lying, General. We deeply apologize for putting you through this last few minutes, but we had to do it. This is the last sure way we have of determining whether a person is proper subject matter of a polygraph test. A pathological liar who is immune to the test will usually confess when he is confronted the way we just confronted you. Again, our apologies. You're a great guy and we admire you." I stumbled out of the room and Cassidy and I took off for Washington with the understanding that I would return the next day for one more session.

The session of April 3 was even more far reaching than that of April 2. The visit by Gordon Liddy at my golf club the Saturday morning following the Watergate burglary started it off. To my surprise, and consternation, however, I was interrogated about a meeting I allegedly attended at the White House on June 30, 1972, with the president and Haldeman. I had no recollection of any such meeting—the kind a person wouldn't forget. Yet, according to the White House records I was there. The polygraph machine came to my rescue and convinced the examiners that I had not in fact attended that meeting. After almost two hours of interrogation, the session ended and I again felt that the ordeal was over. But two days later, on April 5, Connally called Cassidy and requested that I be available for one more session.

Cassidy and I arrived in Philadelphia on Good Friday, April 12, at 10:00 A.M. for what we believed would terminate the interrogation. What occurred, instead, was a yelling contest, first between Cassidy and Connally; then, by telephone to Washington, D.C., between Miller, Cassidy, and Connally; and, finally, between me and Connally. By the time all the yelling had concluded, I was so emotionally disturbed that the polygraph examination had to be postponed.

The dispute arose over who was responsible for leaking to the *Washington Post* information that I was involved in "plea-bargaining" with the special prosecutor's office. I hadn't. (I had no information with which to plea-bargain.) If I was to be indicted and if I had to face trial, nothing more damaging or prejudicial to me could have happened. Yet Connally accused *us* of the leak. This infuriated Cassidy. Then Miller was called by Cassidy and he expressed similar sentiments to Connally. The explosive point was reached when Connally demanded that I be questioned about the incident on the polygraph machine. Miller and Cassidy without hesitation agreed—provided that Connally would also agree to be questioned on the machine about the matter. This he steadfastly refused to do. He then turned to me and accused me of lying about the source of the leak, because Miller and Cassidy insisted that he take a polygraph test also.

I think this was the first and only time during this ordeal that I completely lost control of myself. Suddenly all the pentup frustration and resentment of the preceding months exploded and I lunged at Mr. Connally across the conference table. I was immediately restrained by John Cassidy and the FBI examiners, and escorted from the room. My heart again was pounding, my bood pressure hit the roof, and my rage was so intense that I could hardly breathe. I simply could not understand the manifest hatred of the young assistant special prosecutor for me. "Why me, John? Why me, John?" I groaned as we left the building.

Even though Cassidy is a Roman Catholic, his friendship permitted him to sit with me in a nearby Episcopal church for a part of the Good Friday service. In a few minutes I had regained my composure and we departed for Washington.

On Wednesday, April 17, Cassidy and I returned to Philadelphia for what was to be, at last, the final session. It was expressly understood in advance that Connally would not be physically present in the same room with me and the FBI examiner during the pretest preliminaries. As a result, the testing proceeded without interruption and the chief examiner made a comment to the effect that "there's got to be an end to this sometime; we don't need anything more; we don't think it's going to be necessary to ask you any more questions." For me, a grueling and humiliating experience had finally ended.

We were, of course, unaware that Jaworski had decided on March 25 to dispose of my matter by a plea to a one-count misdemeanor. Miller was convinced that Connally still intended to indict me on as many felony charges as he could persuade the grand jury to return. The results of the polygraph sessions seemed to make no difference to him. Miller and Cassidy were also convinced that a fair trial in the Watergate atmosphere would be impossible. That Archibald Cox had caused a leak to the press of the president's call on April 19, 1971, and that the special prosecutor's office had leaked to the press that I was engaged in "plea-bargaining" had poisoned the public mind to such an extent that my "guilt" was virtually established. Finally, both Miller and Cassidy were convinced that, because of all that had happened to me since the night of the Watergate break-in, I was physically and emotionally drained to the point that I very likely could not undergo the rigors of a trial.

As far as Miller was concerned, the polygraph examinations provided an ideal setting within which to persuade Jaworski that a plea to a misdemeanor was an acceptable solution. He pointed out that section 192 of Title 2 of the U.S. Code made it a misdemeanor for a person to refuse to produce papers or to refuse to answer questions before a congressional committee.

"It is not a perjury statute, but rather a contempt-of-Congress enactment,"

Miller advised. "You could be fined up to $1,000 and imprisoned up to one year, but I don't think you would be sentenced to prison. It's my sad duty to strongly recommend that you do so if it can be worked out."

I left his office with a heavy heart.

How does one make a decision of this kind? Every human emotion imaginable is involved. Disgrace. Self-pity. Wife, children, family name. The beloved Department of Justice. Imprisonment. Disbarment. Innocence. Resentment. Financial ruin.

I searched my soul for an answer. Praying to God was a part of my life, but I never prayed so much for guidance as I did in the next few days. I counseled with everyone whose opinions and friendships I valued. In the end, three persons convinced me of the course of action I had to take—Marnie, Judge Robb, and Trixie Landsberger, my secretary and friend of many years. They felt I could not physically and emotionally survive such a trial.

Looking back over the years since I stood before Judge Hart on May 16, 1974, pleading guilty to a refusal to answer pertinent questions before the Senate Judiciary Committee, produces the same mixed emotions I've always had about the plea. At the time and under all the circumstances, I suppose I really had no other alternative. Yet, I've always had the deep belief that even a Washington, D.C., jury in that horrifying atmosphere would have judged me innocent. Hadn't I refused a presidential order? Didn't he rescind it? Wasn't the ITT case a victory for Justice? It hasn't made such a difficult decision any easier to have so many good friends later express the opinion that my plea to that misdemeanor was the greatest mistake of my life.

If Watergate proved the enduring validity of our institutions of government and liberty, the lessons learned about special prosecutors will be of enduring value. Being essentially a trespass upon our political institutions, Watergate necessitated a special prosecutor. The concept was correct from the beginning. Archibald Cox might not have been the right person, but he was a special prosecutor in every sense of the word. The American public was thereby assured that there was a means by which persons in high positions could be held accountable for their conduct.

Not infrequently, however, valid concepts can become hostages to the turmoil of the times. This happened I believe in the special prosecutor's office. With experience as the best teacher, Congress eventually enacted fairer laws for regulating conduct. In 1978 Title 28 of the United States Codes was amended by the adoption of Chapter 39, "Special Prosecutor." Henceforth, a fair and balanced means would exist for determining whether persons in high positions had violated the law, and if so, what was to be done about it.

Under this statute, the attorney general is required to conduct an investigation whenever he is informed that a high government official has violated any federal criminal law. Those subject to the statute include the president, the vice president, cabinet officers, top staff of the White House, top officers of the Department of Justice, the director of the CIA, the commissioner of Internal Revenue, and any officer of the principal national campaign committee of the presidential candidates. Those categories include all areas of Watergate.

Within ninety days after the attorney general has commenced his investigation, he is required to report his findings to the special court created by the statute. If he finds that there is no substance to the charges, that ends the matter. If, on the other hand, he finds that the matter warrants further investigation, he is required to apply to the special court for the appointment of a special prosecutor. That court is then required to appoint a special prosecutor. Thereby, a prosecutor independent of the executive branch comes into being. His jurisdiction is defined so that no fishing expeditions by an overzealous prosecutor are possible.

Upon appointment, the special prosecutor has full power and independent authority to exercise all investigative and prosecutorial functions and powers of the Department of Justice. Most important, he also may decline to prosecute, and thereby publicly exonerate the official involved. Moreover, he may appoint his own staff, but he also has access to the full resources of the Department of Justice.

As might be expected, the statute requires the special prosecutor to make full reports of his activities to the Congress. The statute also sets forth precise ground rules for the removal of a special prosecutor. Only the attorney general has the power to remove him and then only for extraordinary impropriety, or for physical disability or mental incapacity.

The special court consists of three judges who are assigned to a division of the United States Court of Appeals for the District of Columbia. It should surprise no one that Judge Roger Robb of that appeals court was designated the first presiding judge of the special court.

It took a national scandal to bring us to this point.

Ours is not a perfect system of justice. It depends upon human beings, and they are imperfect. Our system, however, is as near to perfection as any yet devised. Our criminal laws have continually progressed, albeit slowly and pains-takingly. We have fine judges. Our juries in the main return fair verdicts. But it is the lawyer upon whom the system, in the last analysis, depends. The lawyer is the advocate of the accused. Combining his knowledge of the law with skills acquired over many years, the lawyer is the glue by which the entire system is held together.

Jack Miller and John Cassidy are lawyers in every sense of the word.

10
Clifford and Harlow
The Presidential Counselor

Aside from his resignation, that which most strikingly differentiates the Nixon presidency from others is the kind of literature that appeared, especially that authored by those sentenced by Judge Sirica. The typical book by a former presidential counselor extols the virtue of his president, lauds the accomplishments of his administration, and not so humbly describes the contributions of the author. Not so the writings of John Ehrlichman, Charles Colson, John Dean, and Jeb Magruder. The common thread linking all ensures that their works will occupy a unique place in America political history. That thread, perhaps, provides a good part of the answer to the Watergate question: Why?

John Dean, the young counsel to the president, tells us in his book *Blind Ambition:*

> For a thousand days I would serve as Counsel to the President. I soon learned that to make my way upward into a position of confidence and influence, I had to crawl downwards—through factional power plays, corruption and finally outright crimes.

Jeb Magruder, the young staff aide, in his book, *An American Life,* confides:

> I had a job I loved, one that might be a springboard toward unlimited success. "Jeb," I told myself, "you're not going to screw this one up. You like this job and you're going to do what they tell you."

Charles Colson, then the ruthless hatchetman for the president and now a follower of Christ, reveals in *Born Again:*

I had always followed Nixon's order.
—getting the job done for the President whatever the cost. . . .
"Yes, sir, it will be done" in response to Nixon's orders with respect
to Ellsberg— "I don't care how you do it, but get it done. . . ."
Our fortress mentality plunged us across the moral divide, leading to
"enemy" lists. . . .
We had set in motion forces that would sooner or later make Watergate,
or something like it, inevitable.

It is from John Ehrlichman, however, that we are given the deepest insight.
At the request of *Parade* magazine, in September 1982, he painfully articulates
his answer to the question "What have I learned?"

I should have gone to the U.S. Attorney with [my findings]. . . .
My legal obligation was to inform the authorities of those crimes. . . .
At times I think that, if I'd been wiser, I might have deflected the course
of history by persuading or forcing Richard Nixon to come clean early
in the episode. I'll never know for certain. . . .
The prerequisites which attach to presidential power are both delightful
and seductive. . . .
If the President was for me, who could stand against me?. . .
He [Nixon] was my mentor in all matters of government and politics. . . .
When the President declined to "come clean" with the American people, I did what I had been doing for five years: I fell into step with his
decision, rather than to chart my own course by my own ethical
compass. . . .
I intend never again to abdicate the moral judgments I am called upon
to make. . . .

Do these sad, even tragic, admissions tell us only about those who made them
and about Richard Nixon the person? Or do they tell us about the institution of
the modern presidency as well? I'm inclined to think that they tell us more about
the presidency than about Nixon himself.

The political process by which our presidents are selected and the complexity
of our society engender complex presidents. Only by experiencing the grueling
demands of a presidential campaign can one appreciate the diverse qualities a
candidate must possess if he is to emerge victorious. Leaving aside the requisite
physical durability, the presidential aspirant must be strong in his entire person.
He must be strong of ego and fortified by supreme self-confidence, otherwise
he cannot impart to others his convictions and command their support. To ac-
commodate the competing interests of a complicated nation, he must be a skilled
politician. That requires thinking like a politician, and the political mind is often
tangled. Every human emotion is experienced and endured—exhilaration, frustration, despair, loneliness, fatigue, exasperation, resentment, anger, rage, joy,

gratitude, and idealism. No matter his humble appearance when he swears the oath of office on inaugural day, the person with his left hand on the holy Bible and his right hand half raised is no ordinary human. He is president of the United States, and became so only be virtue of extraordinary talents.

The strengths needed to win that office, however, pale by comparison with those needed to discharge its responsibilities. President Truman's sign "The buck stops here" is more than a platitude. The president not only makes but is alone when making the ultimate decision. That's reality. And every decision an American president makes is ultimate. Think too of the range of decisions; imagine deciding in one day matters on unemployment, the interest rate, the appointment of ambassadors, the selection of persons to manage the bureaucracy, the passage of programs by the Congress, his political party, the intentions of the Kremlin, a visit by a head of state, the press, labor, the farmer, the stock market, his family, the environment, a pardon, the budget, the deficit, the forthcoming congressional elections. . . .

In short, he needs astute and trustworthy help.

Being a counselor to a U.S. president is an inestimable responsibility. The rewards for success can be high, and the penalties for failure severe. The sad literature of Watergate chronicles the failures of a few who counseled a president and the penalties they paid.

For contrast, we'll examine two exemplary presidential counselors. Democratic presidents since Harry Truman and Republican presidents since Dwight Eisenhower have been able to call upon two unusual men for counsel—the Honorable Clark M. Clifford and the Honorable Bryce N. Harlow. Superficially, they are as different as two men can be. But both have similar properties of character; both are wise.

Clark Clifford has the most commanding presence of anyone I have ever known. Tall and erect, with a countenance projecting strength and wisdom, he makes an indelible impression on anyone who has ever been in his presence. His full head of wavy hair and his expression of kindly concern have marked him since shortly after his birth in Fort Scott, Kansas, on Christmas Day 1906. His contemporaries in St. Louis expected that he would establish a record of achievement. He did not disappoint them.

For nearly fifteen years, after his graduation from law school in 1928, he had the kind of law practice that would prepare for the challenges to come. Unlike the specialists of today, the young lawyer in 1928 was required to be familiar with the whole range of legal skills. The mark of a good trial lawyer is his ability to marshal facts and advocate a cause. The mark of a good business lawyer is his ability to analyze a problem and present a solution.

By the time Clifford was commissioned a lieutenant (jg.) in 1943 in the U.S. Navy Reserve, he was well prepared to apply his skills of advocacy and analysis to the burdens of war. The skills were first tested in 1944 by the staff of Admiral Ingersoll, who was the commander of the Western Sea Frontier. Clifford and another young officer were assigned the critical task of visiting some thirty naval installations on the West Coast and submitting a comprehensive report as to their adequacy and the problems of procurement in wartime. After reading the report himself, Admiral Ingersoll placed Clifford on his personal staff, where he remained until spring 1945.

Bryce N. Harlow entered the world in 1916 in Oklahoma City. Since his youth, he has never lost his zest for life. As he wrote to me on July 21, 1982, "Well, it has all been such fun, Dick. I have known such grand people, such marvelous times. Imagine—it all happened to that Great Plains Lilliputian, Harlow, of all people!"

Harlow is a Lilliputian in physical dimensions only. That five-foot-five frame, with its piercing eyes, slightly impish smile, and indomitable will, has housed a rare sort.

When he was eleven he landed his first paid job as a greasemonkey at the Oklahoma City dirt airport. There he met Col. Charles Lindbergh, then triumphantly touring America, and serviced his *Spirit of St. Louis*. It is characteristic of Harlow that while at the dirt airport he flew and worked with, and became a friend of Wiley Post; he also met Frank Hawkes, Amelia Earhart, Jimmy Doolittle, and most of the other greats of embryonic aviation. With becoming modesty, he tells us, "Yes, from those exhilarating days until my physical retirement fifty-one years later, I just plugged on. I thank the Lord for seeing that I also plugged up."

Plugged on and up he did.

Ten years after Clifford earned his law degree from Washington University, Harlow, in 1938, departed the University of Oklahoma for Washington, D.C. He took with him bachelor's and master's degrees, and a Phi Beta Kappa key to boot. If he could become a close friend of Wiley Post before he was fifteen, small wonder that at twenty-two, as the assistant librarian of the U.S. House of Representatives, he would quickly establish a personal friendship with most in that chamber, including majority leader Sam Rayburn and majority whip John McCormack. Those friendships enabled the young man to attend several receptions and press conferences of Franklin Delano Roosevelt at the White House.

When war came the Lilliputian from Oklahoma City was known and respected by one and all. He was assigned to General George C. Marshall's staff after Pearl Harbor. For nearly five years he was top aide to the chief of legislative liaison between the War Department and the Congress. Every congressional inquiry to General Marshall, Secretary of War Stimson, Undersecretary Robert Patterson, and other officials was sent to Harlow for reply, a critical responsibility for an officer still in his twenties. In 1946 he returned to civilian life as a lieutenant colonel in the U.S. Army Reserve, accompanied by the Legion of Merit Medal on his breast and a special commendation for his wartime service from the secretary of war.

As might be expected, something was happening next door in the U.S. Navy in 1945 to Lt. Comdr. Clark M. Clifford. Something, indeed. Clifford, as a successful lawyer in St. Louis, had for a client James K. Vardeman. Mr. Vardeman in spring 1945 just happened to be naval aide to President Harry Truman and was preparing to leave with the president for the Potsdam Conference. Vardeman had followed the remarkable service of Clifford as the special assistant to Admiral Ingersoll, the commander of the Western Sea Frontier. What better person to have in charge of the naval aide's office in the White House during his absence than his friend and lawyer! The Potsdam Conference between Truman, Churchill, and Stalin made its mark on modern world history. By bringing Clark Clifford to the White House, Potsdam indirectly left its imprint on modern American history.

Judge Samuel Rosenman was counsel to President Roosevelt and, because of his ability, experience, and wisdom, was asked to remain in that position by Truman after Roosevelt's death. The young assistant naval aide came to his attention while Truman was at Potsdam. During this interim the overworked Rosenman found in Clifford a willing volunteer for long hours of labor. Later, with Vardeman back in his White House office as the president's naval aide, Clifford soon found himself in the role of assistant to Rosenman and thereby under the tutelage of one of the great presidential counselors of modern times. As a result, the assistant naval aide was able to begin a personal relationship with the president.

When Rosenman resigned in January 1946 to return to New York and when Vardeman was appointed shortly thereafter to the Federal Reserve Board, Clifford was designated naval aide to the president, with promotion to the rank of captain. Naval aide might have been his official title, but Clifford, for the next five months, functioned as counselor to the president. That relationship between Truman and Clifford was formalized in June 1946 when Clifford left the navy to become special counsel to the president.

For four years Clark Clifford counseled his president. They were momentous years, to say the least—the beginning of the Berlin airlift on June 26, 1948; the enunciation of the Truman doctrine on March 12, 1947; the implementation of the Marshall Plan in June 1947; the formation of the NATO alliance on April 4, 1949; the creation of the state of Israel on May 14, 1948.

President Truman gradually perceived that the communist philosophy of the Soviet leaders made peaceful coexistence difficult between communist and capitalist nations. In June 1946 he directed Clifford to devote the entire summer if necessary to preparing a comprehensive summary of American relations with the Soviet Union. Clifford consulted with the secretary of state, the secretary of war, the attorney general, the secretary of the navy, Fleet Admiral Leahy, the Joint Chiefs of Staff, Ambassador Pauley, and the director of Central Intelligence and other persons who had special knowledge in the field.

On September 24, 1946, Clifford delivered the original "Top Secret" summary personally to the president. Eleven additional copies were securely locked in Clifford's office. According to Clifford, the president read the document that evening. At seven the next morning Clifford received a call at home from the president, who, somewhat agitated, wanted to know how many copies of the document there were. When Clifford informed him there were eleven, he was directed by the president to deliver them immediately to him. The president feared that if the document was ever leaked to the press, the "roof would be blown off."

Some twenty years later the Clifford summary appeared in public for the first time, as an appendix to the memoirs of Arthur Krock, *Sixty Years on the Firing Line* (New York: Funk & Wagnalls, 1968). Krock, intimate friend of presidents from Theodore Roosevelt to Lyndon Johnson, three-time winner of the Pulitzer Prize, and for more than thirty years Washington correspondent of the *New York Times,* was a close friend of Clifford. The significance of Clifford's document is evinced in Krock's words:

> The memorandum, which reached a total of nearly a hundred thousand words, was a fundamentally important American State paper for a number of reasons. Not only did it supply the new President with every past detail of the wartime relationship with the U.S.S.R., it charted the postwar prospect with startling prescience in which the shape and thrust of Truman's subsequent great programs—the Greek-Turk aid program, the Marshall Plan, the North Atlantic Alliance (including NATO), and what later became known as the "Truman Doctrine"—were outlined. [p. 224.]

It would be a disservice to Clark Clifford for me to attempt to say more. If Clifford had hung up his governmental hat following his outstanding achievement as counselor to President Truman, his mark on history would have been made. Not so with him. I think he'll never hang up that hat.

Understanding the basic policy of the United States vis-à-vis the Soviet Union requires its own rare talents. Being recognized, however, as the principal architect of the unification of the armed services in 1947 shows Clifford to be a person of the broadest talents and understanding. At the direction of President Truman, Clifford for two years worked with every relevant part of the government—the War Department, the navy, and the Congress—to achieve a goal that had eluded presidents for decades. A squabble between partisans in the Congress is a church supper compared to the intense rivalry that existed between the armed services after World War II. Only a person of exceptional ability and determination could have done the impossible.

By coincidence, a congressional reorganization and the unification of the armed services were the events that returned Bryce Harlow to government in 1947, a year after his departure from the office of the Army Chief of Staff.

In November 1946 the Eightieth Congress was elected. For the first time since 1930, both houses were composed of a majority of Republicans, and for the first time, congressional committees were served by their own "professional staff members." By unification the old Military Affairs and Naval Affairs committees were merged into one Armed Services Committee. Its brand new professional staff, provided by the new congressional reorganization statute, was selected entirely nonpolitically by Chairman Walter G. Andrews, Republican of New York, and by unanimous committee vote. Harlow was then in Oklahoma City with his family publishing business but appeared as the number one or number two choice on five different selection lists. Consequently, Chairman Andrews prevailed upon him to return, at least temporarily, to Washington to help the new committee get started. Carl Vinson of Milledgeville, Georgia, a Democrat, had been chairman of the House Committee on Naval Affairs for decades, and because of his seniority, became the ranking Democrat on the new Armed Services Committee. As we Republicans sorrowfully recall, the Republican Eightieth Congress was routed by Harry Truman's 1948 campaign against it as the do-nothing Congress. In January 1949, Carl Vinson became chairman of the Armed Services Committee.

Ordinarily, when a major committee of the Congress changes its majority composition, the new chairman of the opposite party selects a chief of staff who is of his own party. But the Armed Services Committee was no ordinary committee and as a result what ordinarily happened did not happen. Chairman Vinson designated nonpolitical Harlow as his chief of staff. As Harlow recalls, for three years he did everything for the chairman—chief of staff, special assistant to the chairman, personal aide, chief clerk, preparation of speeches and articles, legislative analyses, and the handling of major pieces of legislation before the committee. This notable achievement becomes even more remarkable when we are reminded that Carl Vinson was not just an ordinary Democratic congressman. He was first elected to the Congress in 1913 and took his seat three months after Sam Rayburn of Texas. When he retired in 1965, he had served longer in the House than any other person in our history. (The record still stands.) To the day of his retirement he was universally regarded as the most powerful member of the House, except for Speaker Sam himself.

The confidence Vinson reposed in Harlow is therefore meaningful to us for at least three reasons. First, it tells us something about Harlow himself. Next, the legislation that Clifford did so much to create was the constant preoccupation of Harlow on Capitol Hill during the first critical years of its life. Finally, the stature Harlow achieved in the eyes of members of the Congress enabled him to serve President Eisenhower for eight years at the White House with unparalleled distinction.

But back to the remarkable Clark Clifford. The years 1947–50 were stormy for Harry Truman. The election of the Republican Eightieth Congress in November 1946 set the stage for the expected recapture of the White House by the Republicans in 1948 after a sixteen-year absence. So they believed. The political attacks against Truman by the Congress were incessant. Richard Nixon gained national recognition by pursuing the disreputable Alger Hiss. Joe McCarthy made us believe that a communist was under nearly every bureaucrat's bed in the State Department. The economy shuddered as it endeavored to go from war to peace. The presidency was under siege to an extent almost comparable to that of Lincoln in the early 1860s. The president needed the best advisers he could get, desperately.

To the credit of Clark Clifford, he stayed with his president during those troubled years. Clifford could have returned to private life, laurels safe in hand. President Truman was a man of strong emotions. He needed a quiet, wise, and able counselor like Clifford in those turbulent times. When you serve a president who often quoted Mark Twain's admonition to "always do right and at the same time . . . surprise a good many and astonish the rest," something more than ordinary skills are required. We can just imagine how many times Clifford had to rewrite the speeches of "Give 'em Hell, Harry" to satisfy Truman. But presidents called upon Clifford for more than speeches.

James Forrestal was the first secretary of the new Department of Defense. Dean Acheson was the secretary of state. Strangely, perhaps, those very different men were close friends of Clark Clifford. The relationships provided the secretaries with a daily means of communication with the White House and therefore with a burdened president. It wasn't long before Truman began to realize that Clifford was adroitly relaying to him the messages of his secretary of state and secretary of defense. Truman thereupon included Clifford in the numerous White House meetings with his secretaries. Counselor to the president, indeed!

By spring 1950 Clifford had concluded that his time had come to leave the White House. The fatigue that inevitably predominates in that environment of pressure eventually produces its own diminishing returns on efforts expended. Besides, after two years in the navy and five at the White House, it was time to provide for his wife and children. Clark Clifford began in 1950 perhaps the most successful law practice ever seen in the nation's capital. One of his clients came to be a young senator by the name of John Fitzgerald Kennedy.

After twenty years of depression and war, America cried out for a man like Dwight David Eisenhower. If he were to succeed, Eisenhower would need persons like Bryce N. Harlow.

Eisenhower came to the presidency as the hero of the free world. Although accustomed to command, Ike was a stranger to the arcane ways of Congress. Perhaps Sam Rayburn or Carl Vinson did not have the right to possess the self-esteem of a five-star general, but possess it they did. The circumstances thus required one who had earned the respect of the imperious leaders of Congress and who at the same time could be a loyal and effective lieutenant at the White House under a strong-willed president. That Bryce Harlow served this unusual president for eight years as his administrative assistant, then as his special assistant, and, finally, as his deputy assistant for congressional affairs, tells us what kind of a person Harlow was.

Because of his self-effacing manner and because of the esteem in which he was held by the Congress and by Chairman Vinson, Harlow was able to secure the passage of the president's vital defense-reorganization bill. Through Harlow, the temperamental Vinson and an equally temperamental Eisenhower were able to conduct confidential negotiations. At one point in the process the president became infuriated with what he perceived to be the stubbornness of the congressional chairman. When Harlow came to the defense of Vinson, Ike retreated. Because of personality conflicts between Secretary of Defense Charles Wilson and Vinson, another impasse was reached. Harlow then personally testified before an executive session of the committee and the bill was passed.

Speaker Sam Rayburn often told of the time he had to get Eisenhower's position on a matter pending in the House before the session ended. He called Harlow at two in the morning to get the desired information. In a few minutes Harlow called the Speaker back, saying he had waked the president and had the answer. Rayburn had absolute confidence that Harlow had done exactly what he said and the matter was settled. The president and the Speaker paid Harlow the highest tribute possible—both trusted him implicitly.

An anecdote which Harlow recalls tells us something about the temperaments of strong-willed presidents. President Truman was never reluctant to express his feelings of antipathy toward President Eisenhower. (I've always suspected that one reason for those feelings was Ike's decision to seek in 1952 the Republican instead of the Democratic nomination, which would have been his for the asking.) And Eisenhower, being human, let fly a few uncomplimentary things about his predecessor. Harlow, however, felt that the president should bury the hatchet before he left office by inviting the Trumans to spend a night at the White House as guests of himself and Mrs. Eisenhower. The difficulty was that most senior staffers lacked the courage to broach the delicate matter to the president. Harlow therefore marched in to do it himself. At that point he didn't know but that his White House tenure would abruptly end. The president greeted Harlow's proposal silently and with cold eyes. Harlow argued on and the president grudgingly gave in. Harlow then produced a draft of a telegram for Ike to send to the Trumans; it urged that they stop over in Washington on their way to Europe. "Send it," barked the president. Truman declined the invitation but Harlow had made his point. And in so doing, he remained true to himself and to the president by having the courage to say what he thought was right.

Later he engineered another invitation to the Trumans. Again it was declined. Oddly, Truman maintained that he had never been invited to the White House by his successor.

John Kennedy was elected president in 1960. Like Clark Clifford ten years before, Harlow welcomed the opportunity to return to private life and direct his attention to his wife, Betty, and their children.

Immediately after Kennedy received his party's nomination for the presidency he invited his friend and lawyer Clark Clifford for breakfast. The two talked alone until late afternoon. Every detail of Truman's 1948 campaign was discussed. As Clifford was departing, Kennedy expressed his belief that he would be the next president of the United States. He also told Clifford that he did not want to be met with surprises the morning after the election. Clifford was then asked if he would be willing to devote the next three months to preparing a document that would outline for Kennedy the procedures necessary to take over the executive branch. Clifford agreed.

The 1960 presidential election was a squeaker. Nixon came close. The newly elected Kennedy called Clifford on the morning after the election to inquire if the document had been prepared. Within hours the Secret Service had picked up twenty copies and delivered them to the president-elect. Shortly after, Clifford spent four days in Palm Beach, Florida, with Kennedy discussing the contents of the document. He returned to Washington, D.C., as Kennedy's official representative in the transition period involving the takeover of the executive branch from the Eisenhower administration. Thereafter, and for the thousand days that John F. Kennedy occupied the Oval Office, Clark Clifford served as his unofficial counselor.

When the steel industry broke what Kennedy believed to have been its agreement not to raise prices, Clifford met with the leaders of the industry and persuaded them to rescind their action. Only a person of the stature of a Clifford, and armed with the full authority of the president, could have persuaded a proud Roger Blough of U.S. Steel that a price rollback would be preferable to a head-on confrontation with this young president. Again, the day after the abortive Bay of Pigs disaster, it was Clifford to whom Kennedy turned. The president had the wisdom to admit that he had made a bad decision. At the same time, he was also acutely aware that he had received bad advice because of bad intelligence. By the time his meeting with Clifford had concluded, the concept of a Foreign Intelligence Advisory Board was formulated. It was composed of distinguished persons from the private sector. Dr. James Killian, president of MIT, was its first chairman. Clifford, an original member, succeeded Dr. Killian as chairman in April 1962, when Killian resigned because of ill health.

The day after President Johnson returned to Washington, D.C., from Texas following the tragic assassination of that graceful young president, Clifford was at the White House for a lengthy visit. Johnson and Clifford had had a long association, its roots being the fortnightly poker games that Clifford arranged for President Truman on the presidential yacht. The players included Clifford, Chief Justice Vinson, Senator Kerr of Oklahoma, Senator Anderson of New Mexico, presidential counselor George Allen, and Senator Lyndon Johnson of Texas. There are many ways by which we learn about people. One of the surest is poker.

Throughout LBJ's presidency Clifford would walk the two blocks from his law office to the White House to advise Johnson, and on the same informal basis that obtained in Kennedy's reign. To have such a relationship with two starkly different presidents tells us more about Clifford than about Kennedy or Johnson.

Johnson, like Kennedy, used Clifford well. In 1965 Clifford visited the Far East in his capacity as chairman of the Foreign Intelligence Advisory Board. In 1966 he served as an adviser to President Johnson at the Manila conference. In 1967 Clifford and Gen. Maxwell Taylor visited a number of Southeast Asian countries as personal emissaries of the president.

The albatross around the neck of Lyndon Johnson, however, was Vietnam. Its satisfactory conclusion continued to slip through his fingers like mercury.

Out of near desperation he prevailed upon Clifford to leave his lucrative law practice and rejoin the government as secretary of defense. Nominated on January 19, 1968, Clifford was unanimously confirmed by the Senate on January 30.

Clifford undertook his duties for a president he had known intimately for twenty-three years and with the conviction that our policy toward Vietnam was correct. After all, the Congress had authorized the president to engage in war by passing the Tonkin Gulf Resolution on August 7, 1964. The vote was 412 to 2. After an exhausting month in the Pentagon, however, Clifford arrived at the conclusion that our Vietnam policy was wrong. He concluded that Vietnam was not communist aggression but civil war. It was a bitter pill for Lyndon Johnson to swallow, the day Clifford came to his office and said, "Mr. President, you are wrong!"

The debate over Vietnam and whether Clifford was right or wrong will continue for decades. But that is not the point here. The point is that the same person who was the hawk when he handed President Truman, on September 24, 1946, the document describing the nature of the communist threat to the free world, was the same person who had the courage to tell a Lyndon Johnson that he was wrong. President Johnson never quite forgave Clifford for his Vietnam advice. That he never lost his respect for him, however, is perhaps best illustrated by the fact that President Johnson took Clifford into his bedroom on Sunday afternoon, March 31, 1968, and had him go over the language LBJ would use that evening in an address to the nation stating that he would not seek reelection. That Clifford did not walk away from a difficult, if not impossible, task is illustrated by the fact that he continued to serve as secretary of defense until January 20, 1969, the day Richard Nixon took his oath of office as president.

Whereas Clifford concentrated on his law practice during his "off" years between 1952 and 1960, Bryce Harlow found himself tossed into the stratosphere of big business between 1961 and 1968, first as director of the Washington office of Procter & Gamble, and then as its vice president for national government relations. In other words, he was the corporation's ambassador to the United States government, to the executive branch and the Congress. Like Clifford, he was a lobbyist.

To many Americans, the word *lobbyist* conjures up negative reactions. Isn't he somebody who wields undue pressure on congressmen, senators, and bureaucrats to further the special interests of big business? Shouldn't there be a law to prevent lobbying?

In truth, the Washington lobbyist and lawyer are to government what scientists are to technology—experts without which a complex government like ours could not function. If you seek to hire Clark Clifford as a Washington lawyer because you believe he has influence, he will reject the employment. If, on the other hand, you seek his counsel because of his knowledge of our government, he will accept the employment.

The skilled lobbyist is not quite like a lawyer. But, in a sense, the function performed is similar. The lobbyist usually acts on behalf of one employer—corporation, labor union, or special-interest group. Once a person has established his credentials as a trustworthy and knowledgeable lobbyist, it is not uncommon for the congressman, senator, or bureaucrat to seek out his advice.

Bryce Harlow laid the groundwork in professionalizing lobbying and was directly involved in establishing the Business-Government Relations Council and the American League of Lobbyists. Because of his integrity, and his knowledge of the federal government, not only did he represent the essential interests of a great corporation, but he also advised many in business and in government.

Richard Nixon knew all about the Great Plains Lilliputian. For eight years they were in contact—one as vice president and the other as special assistant to a great president. Like John Kennedy after his nomination in 1960, Richard Nixon was convinced that he would be elected after he was nominated in 1968. That conviction enabled him to persuade Harlow to take a leave of absence from Procter & Gamble in September 1968 and lend his considerable talents to the campaign.

After the November election—when Secretary of Defense Clifford was dealing with the transition representative of the new president—Bryce Harlow was occupying an office in the Pierre Hotel in New York City, along with other advisers to the president-elect. Because I had an office in the Pierre to assist John Mitchell in organizing the Nixon Department of Justice, I came to know this little dynamo for the first time. Recognizing me for the neophyte I was, he was always ready with a reassuring smile and welcome advice. "Just remember, Dick, those in Washington, D.C., came from the boondocks and they put their trousers on one leg at a time, just like you."

More important, however, he endeavored to share with those who would occupy positions in the White House the benefit of his experience. Years later, Dwight Chapin, the young and able appointment secretary to President Nixon, would come to Harlow with tears in his eyes and exclaim: "Our greatest mistake was not having listened to you before we came to the White House!"

Harlow warned the Nixon White House staff-to-be about the pitfalls ahead. He reminded them that Richard Nixon was just a little bit different from most presidents. His political battles over more than two decades had left their scars and bitter enemies. As a consequence, his administration "would attract scandal like a dog would attract fleas. Everything you do and say will be watched to find an opening for attack. Each of you must be as Caesar's wife was alleged to be. Because of the boomerang quality of government in Washington, D.C., learn to know the limits of your power."

Harlow was prevailed upon by the new president to join his staff on January 20, 1969. He served at the White House for the next two years as assistant to the president, then resigned to return to private life. In July 1973 Nixon called him back from Procter & Gamble to be a counselor to the president with cabinet rank. He remained in that high post until April 1974. This was Harlow's only unhappy tour of duty for a president at the White House. Many of those he had sought to advise in the Pierre Hotel in late fall 1968 were no longer there. The Nixon he had known so well since the Californian's election to Congress in 1946 was now a besieged president. With sadness Harlow returned to Procter & Gamble and pursued the arts of his profession until his retirement in 1978, forty years after he first came to Washington at the tender age of twenty-two to be assistant librarian of the U.S. House of Representatives.

In sum, he served for about eight years with Congress, five years in active army duty, eleven years at the White House, and over seventeen years with Procter & Gamble, completing a working career that began as an aviation mechanic when he was eleven years old.

Unfortunately for his presidency, Jimmy Carter did not have before his election the close relationship with Clark Clifford that Presidents Truman, Kennedy, and Johnson had. Indeed, it seems to me that he had no such relationship with any person wise in the ways of the nation's capital when he arrived to take his oath of office. Lloyd Cutler, a Washington lawyer with a stature nearly comparable to that of Clifford, became counselor to President Carter in 1979. For the success of Carter's presidency, someone like Cutler should have been in that position in January 1977.

Jimmy Carter did make limited use of Clifford's talents, however. In January 1977 he appointed him to be his special emissary to Greece, Turkey, and Cyprus. Three years later, President Carter also appointed Clifford to be his special emissary to India.

In November 1980 the mantle of government passed to President Reagan, a Republican. Clark Clifford returned to his impressive law office on the twelfth floor at 815 Connecticut Avenue. Thence Clifford can turn around in his chair and gaze, two blocks south, upon the front portico of the White House. How often he must retrace his steps to the White House to counsel his president. In 1944 Clifford came to the government as a naval lieutenant. He has every right to be proud when, with that kindly twinkle in his eyes, he recalls experiences that for sum constitute a record of service to the nation without parallel.

In a sense, it might be considered either unfair or inappropriate to profile in a single narrative a Clark Clifford and a Bryce Harlow. It is not unlike describing an apple and an orange in one sentence. Two more dissimilar persons did not exist together during their years in Washington, D.C. The physical appearance of the two is a dramatic statement itself. Clifford, six feet two, is imposing. Harlow trots his five-foot-five body down the street with boyish vitality. One is recognized as a greater lawyer of his time; the other is the embodiment of an effective lobbyist. One conceptualized strategic policy and discharged huge responsibilities for his government, whereas the other worked quietly as the intermediary between legislative and executive branches of government. One is a Democrat, the other a Republican. With equal respect and affection I address one as Your Worship and the other as Ol' Buddy.

The highest award a civilian can receive from his country is the Medal of Freedom. It is awarded by the president of the United States. Like the Congressional Medal of Honor, its recipients are few. Clark Clifford was awarded the Medal of Freedom by President Johnson, and Bryce N. Harlow was awarded the Medal of Freedom by President Reagan. Those presidential acts erased the apparent disparities between the two men, even as those acts will preserve the essential similarities between them. Of those similarities, the most important is simply this: each as counselor to his president had the courage to say "you are wrong," and the wisdom to know when and how to say it.

Because of the notoriety accorded to the writings of John Ehrlichman, Chuck Colson, John Dean, and Jeb Magruder, the public has been exposed only to the dark side of a complex president and those few who served him and their country poorly. There were many of distinction who served him and their country well.

We must be reminded that the Democratic senator of New York, Patrick Moynihan, preceded John Ehrlichman as counselor to the president for domestic affairs with full cabinet rank. Before returning to Harvard University to resume his professional post, Senator Moynihan devoted his considerable talents in 1969 to formulating the basic domestic policies that characterized the Nixon presidency. Whereas Ehrlichman tells us he viewed such a position as an opportunity to wield power—"to deal with the Cabinet in the president's place, criticizing mistakes, praising good works, bestowing or withholding favors"—Pat Moynihan quietly departed leaving behind him a record of substantive achievement.

Arthur Burns is one of the genuinely great men of his time. Before becoming chairman of the Federal Reserve Board, he served in the Nixon White House as counselor to the president for economic policy. If he observed a dark side of the president he had the wisdom to ignore it. He benefited his country, not by blindly following the president's orders but by giving him advice. To the credit of President Nixon most of that advice was followed.

Henry Kissinger, who has no modern peer as an international chess player, became assistant to the president for national security affairs in January 1969, and served in that post of awesome responsibility until he became the president's secretary of state in August 1973. Few would doubt that Richard Nixon's greatest achievement as president was his foreign policy. He would have done well in that difficult area without Henry Kissinger; with him he was superb. For five and a half years Henry Kissinger advised Richard Nixon. He not only was the master of his craft but also knew his chief. The world is safer because of it.

Alexander M. Haig, Jr.'s accomplishments eloquently speak for themselves. Not the least of these was his tenure in the White House, commencing in 1969, on Kissinger's staff of the National Security Council. He soon was indispensable to Kissinger—and, therefore, to the president—and became Kissinger's formal deputy. At the beginning of Nixon's second term, Haig left the White House to become vice chief of staff of the army, thereby going from colonel to four-star general in four years. In May 1973, following the resignations of Haldeman and Ehrlichman, he came back to the White House as chief of staff. As he held the presidency of the United States together during those last tragic days, he performed as a presidential counselor a selfless service of patriotism that may never be equaled. I think he did so because—to paraphrase in a negative way John Ehrlichman—he charted his own course by his own ethical compass and did not abandon the moral judgments he was called upon to make.

We think of George Schultz now as the outstanding secretary of state for President Reagan. But back in January 1969 he became Nixon's first secretary of labor. He then headed the Office of Management and Budget. In May 1972 he was appointed secretary of the treasury and remained in that post until 1974. As Nixon states in his *Memoirs* (p. 909), "I considered him one of the ablest members of the Cabinet." He was. Charles Colson, in *Born Again*, tells us that "our fortress mentality plunged us across the moral divide, leading to 'enemy lists,' a new refinement on the ancient spoils system of rewarding friends and punishing enemies" (p. 64). If such a mentality existed, it was not shared by Secretary Schultz or by the commissioner of Internal Revenue, Johnnie M. Walters.

On September 11, 1972, John Dean, counsel to the president, handed Walters a list of those who were either contributors to the McGovern presidential campaign or members of his presidential campaign staff with the request that they be investigated by the Internal Revenue Service. At that meeting Walters received the impression that Dean had been directed by Ehrlichman to make such a request. Walters strongly cautioned against any such use of the IRS and advised Dean that he would discuss the matter with Secretary Schultz and recommend that no action be taken on the request.

On September 12, the next day, Walters informed Schultz of Dean's request. As expected, Schultz advised that the request be ignored. Dean called on Walters on September 25 for a progress report, only to be informed that no progress had been made. Walters informed Schultz of this call; again, Schultz and Walters concurred that nothing should be done about the request. Dean never called back again.

And what about a man like Kenneth Rush? At the time he was appointed ambassador to West Germany in 1969, by President Nixon, he was president of Union Carbide Corporation, one of the world's largest multinational corporations. He served in that capacity until February 1972, when he was appointed deputy secretary of defense. On February 2, 1973, when he left that post to become deputy secretary of state, he was awarded the Defense Department's Medal for Distinguished Public Service. On May 29, 1974, he became counselor, with full cabinet rank, to President Nixon for economic policy. As such, he was the primary adviser to the president for, and the coordinator of, foreign and domestic economic policy. Like Haig, he stayed at this post through the final days of Nixon's presidency and remained as counselor to President Ford. On October 18, 1974, he was appointed ambassador to France and remained in Paris until April 1977, when President Carter's ambassador arrived to replace him. He knows full well what it means to have direct access to a president and, at the same time, the confidence and respect of those with whom he works. As he has so often remarked to me, "Those with whom I worked had to know that their views were being fully and fairly presented to the president and that they had their 'day in court.' "

Moynihan, Burns, Kissinger, Haig, Schultz, Walters, and Rush are but illustrative of the large group of dedicated men and women of distinction and ability who counseled President Nixon without abandoning their own ethical compass.

To the question that has nagged me for a decade I have yet to find a satisfactory answer. Just how could Richard Nixon be served by John Ehrlichman, Charles Colson, and John Dean, who have written as they have, and simultaneously be served by an Arthur Burns or a George Schultz?

To some degree and for varying periods, I came to know most, if not all, of those who became lieutenants of President Nixon. Remarkably, not a single one ever bartered away his position for money. Even more remarkable is the large number of gifted people who willingly experienced sizable personal financial loss to serve their country under the leadership of the president. I am also convinced that even those who failed were idealistically motivated when they began their tenures. But something went wrong.

The most difficult thing for a presidential counselor to do is say, "Mr. President, you're wrong." None of us enjoys being told he is wrong. Presidents detest the notion. After all, he is the president. Why can't he do this or that? Other presidents have. "Besides, you really don't understand the problem." "I'm sick and tired of being hamstrung by some damn career bureaucrat." "I had to make that guy the undersecretary of his department to appease his special-interest group and his loyalty is to it and not to me!" "I was elected to do something about that and, by damn, one way or another I'm going to do it!" For a harried and frustrated president, feelings like those arise daily. Indeed, one of the values of a trusted counselor is that a president can blow off steam in his presence.

There are many "expletives deleted" in the Nixon tapes. I suspect that Harry Truman, Ike, and (most certainly) Lyndon Johnson managed a few, but they were not taped. The real problem, it seems to me, is not whether a president occasionally comes up with a nutty idea or decision, but how the counselor reacts to it.

What he does about it, of course, depends on what he brings to the event. If he is wise in the ways of politics, government, and presidents and is secure about himself—not a dependent on the president—he does one thing. But if he lacks wisdom, and is insecure, thus dependent upon the favor of the president, he is apt to do something quite different.

Let me illustrate. From hearing the tape in question, I recall that Secretary Schultz was sitting in the president's office on April 19, 1971, when President Nixon ordered me over the telephone to dismiss the ITT appeals and fire McLaren. The call was occasioned by my refusing a similar order given me a few minutes before by John Ehrlichman. When the president put down the phone, he turned to Schultz and, in effect, exclaimed that as long as he sat in that chair there would never be another antitrust case filed. Now, that was a ridiculous statement by the president and traced to his temporary frustration.

Two intimate counselors responded entirely differently. Ehrlichman in effect said, Okay, boss, anything you say. Schultz, however, diverted the president's remark by observing that some antitrust actions are justified and some are not. That ended the matter and the president and his counselor returned to the subject at hand. Ehrlichman tells us in September 1982 that he "always fell in step with Nixon's ethical compass." If such was the fact of the matter, then, though I risk being judgmental, John Ehrlichman was loyal not to the president but only to himself. George Schultz, on the other hand, by being true to himself and by understanding the incident for what it really was, was loyal to his president.

H. R. (Bob) Haldeman, until his resignation on Monday, April 30, 1973, was chief of staff to President Nixon from the beginning. Although my contacts with him, during the 1968 campaign and when I served in Justice, were limited, I always liked and respected him. I haven't seen or talked to him since before March 1973, but my respect for him has grown, for two primary reasons. First, he has been willing to admit his own mistakes. Second, as he writes in *The Ends of Power* (New York: Times Books) in 1978, "I am today enormously proud of my service in the White House" (p. 325). He has paid a terrible price for the privilege and yet he tells us that if he was back at the starting point, he would join up again. Bob Haldeman was brusque, and all business. He was also fair, and if the subject matter was important, he would always listen.

Numerous surmises have been advanced as to the reason for Watergate. Nobody, I think, really knows the whole story, and I suspect a few people will go to their graves with knowledge never revealed.* Haldeman's theory as to its genesis makes more sense to me than anything else I have heard or read. It makes sense because of my own knowledge of Richard Nixon in particular, because of my lesser perception of Charles Colson, and because of my own concept of the presidency.

Haldeman, in his book, says:

> The Watergate break-in itself came about as a result of President Nixon telling Charles Colson to get some information regarding Larry O'Brien; of Colson assigning the job to Howard Hunt; of Hunt using Gordon Liddy and the CRP capability and resources to repeat the pattern of their earlier Ellsberg break-in. [p. 317.]

For my purpose, it isn't important to develop that Larry O'Brien was then chairman of the Democratic National Committee and, like Nixon's brother Donald, had been previously associated with Howard Hughes. What is important is

---

Secret Agenda by Jim Hougan (Random House, New York, 1984) with its careful documentation reveals the possible involvement of the CIA and that "Watergate" was considerably more than popularly believed.

what Charles Colson has written about himself: "I had always followed Nixon's orders" and "getting the job done for the president whatever the cost" was all that mattered. If true, and if the president had tossed out the suggestion that he wanted to learn something about O'Brien, may we not expect that Colson would have set in motion the chain of events leading to the break-in at the Watergate Hotel? The president, according to Colson, viewed the conduct of Ellsberg "as nothing less than treason" and instructed Colson to make the truth about him known, stating, "I don't care how you do it, but get it done." Colson responded, "Yes, sir, it will be done," and tells us, "I needed no coaxing." How much, if any, coaxing would be required for a relatively simple operation like Larry O'Brien's telephones and office?

That is only theory. If the man who is now a Christian denies it, I will accept his denial at face value. What matters here, however, is how things can happen when a president makes a suggestion to an aide who, without hesitation or coaxing, will employ any means necessary to implementing it. No excuse exists for the president who makes the improper suggestion in the first place. And if President Nixon made such a suggestion to Charles Colson, he has paid dearly for it. Not only because he made the suggestion, but because he made it to the person to whom he did. There is, likewise, no excuse for Colson pursuing the suggestion—if he did. By doing so, he was disloyal to the president. He fell short of the responsibility imposed upon him as a confidential counselor to a president.

The quandary in which all of those ifs leave me remains. Who is ultimately responsible? The president? The counselor? Both? Or is the nature of the person and of the office such that in any given situation, it could be neither?

There is, however, no quandary in my mind about one thing. When a presidential counselor has the courage to say, "Mr. President, you are wrong," a Watergate will never occur.

Appendix A
Wiretapping and Bugging for National Security

Have you ever had the gnawing feeling in the pit of your stomach that "the government" was listening in on a telephone conversation you were having? Have you ever been at a social gathering only to have someone present assert with absolute conviction a belief that his telephone had been or was being bugged?

If your answer to either one or both of these questions is in the affirmative, you are, unfortunately, not alone. Whether justified or not, too many of us labor under the apprehension that our government does, in fact, listen in on our private conversations. Even if we might secretly admit to ourselves that justification exists for the government to listen in on some people's conversations, it has no right to listen in on you and me. After all, you and I are not spies or crooks. Isn't the right to privacy one of the things that make being an American citizen different from a citizen of other countries? Anyway, isn't there something in the Constitution that protects us against invasions of our privacy by the government?

To me, if the First Amendment contained in our Bill of Rights is sacred, the Fourth Amendment is like unto it. The unreasonable searches and seizures of a tyrannical king were a principal catalyst of our revolution. Electricity and the telephone extended the scope of searches and seizures far beyond the imagination of our Founding Fathers. While I don't believe that I personally have ever been "tapped" or "bugged," I have always been uneasy that others were. I brought this deep feeling with me to the Department of Justice in January of 1969 and I had it throughout my tenure there. Indeed, it was intensified when I had to accept the fact that as the acting attorney general and as the attorney general I was to have the ultimate responsibility for the approval of wiretapping and bugging by the government in national security matters. That responsibility was a heavy burden for me to bear. However, bear it I did. Perhaps this essay will be of interest as I endeavor to trace the history of electronic surveillance by our federal government from its inception to the present time.

The purpose of this appendix is to convince you that as the way things stand now you have nothing to worry about. Your government does not listen in on your conversations. It doesn't do so because your Congress has passed laws that say it shall not do so, save for a very few well-defined reasons under very precisely defined circumstances. This hasn't always been true, however. Indeed, it took almost one hundred years for our Supreme Court and our Congress to reconcile the basic guarantees contained in the Bill of Rights with the realities of the modern age of telephones and sophisticated electronics.

The reason why it took so long is not difficult to understand. In 1791, when the first ten amendments to the Constitution were adopted, the telephone had not been invented and sophisticated electronic eavesdropping devices did not exist. If these devices had existed in 1791, there can be little doubt but that the Fourth Amendment would have been worded in such a way as to embrace their reality.

The Fourth Amendment says:

> The right of the people to be secure in their persons, houses, papers, and effects, against unreasonable searches and seizures, shall not be violated, and no warrants shall issue, but upon probable cause, supported by oath or affirmation, and particularly describing the place to be searched, and the persons or things to be seized.

King George III, through the use of general warrants and writs of assistance, employed dragnet techniques to intimidate the colonists. No one doubts that His Majesty would have readily used the telephone and electronics to secure evidence of sedition and revolution. These colonists had learned through bitter experience that governments are inclined to justify any behavior to protect themselves. After all, the foremost objective of government is to maintain its internal security. If the American revolutionaries didn't appreciate all the benefits conferred upon them by the king and his government then, by damn, their houses would be entered and their papers and effects seized to produce the evidence necessary to prove their treason. When it came time to create their own government, the revolutionaries perceived that their own government might also be inclined to employ similar means of acquiring evidence against anyone who might threaten it. If, then, there was any validity to the adage that "an ounce of prevention is worth a pound of cure," why not ward off the problem before it could occur? Tell this government that its citizens would be secure in their homes against unreasonable searches and seizures! State in unequivocal terms that before their homes could be searched and their papers seized, only a judge could say so and then only if he was satisfied that a crime was probably in the making. The government, under oath, would have to tell the judge the exact place to be searched and the exact things to be seized. No fishing expeditions!

Electronic surveillance is a broad term. Generally speaking, however, it has been understood to refer to both telephone surveillance (wiretap or technical surveillance) and microphone surveillance (by an electronic listening device). The history of the use of electronic surveillance in the United States by governmental agencies is a history of struggle between the government and the individual citizen. The government, as one would expect, sought to use electronic surveillance to gather evidence of criminal conduct against a citizen. The citizen, on the other hand, resisted its use without a proper warrant being issued by a judge as an unlawful violation of his Fourth Amendment rights.

It wasn't until immediately after World War I, however, that the federal government began to use electronic surveillance. In 1919, the Eighteenth Amendment to the Constitution was adopted and Prohibition came into being. The Bureau of Prohibition was created by Congress as a part of the Department of the Treasury. The use of wiretapping or telephone surveillance by the Bureau of Prohibition played an important role in its investigative and enforcement activities. In 1924, however, Attorney General Harlan Fiske Stone prohibited the use of wiretapping by the Department of Justice. This created a perplexing problem. The secretary of the treasury permitted his Bureau of Prohibition to engage in wiretapping and the attorney general banned its use by the Department of Justice. Thus, the problem was merely one of internal governmental policy as opposed to a question of constitutional legality. It was assumed by everyone at that time that wiretapping was lawful. At the outset, the Supreme Court verified the correctness of that assumption.

Some fifty years after the telephone came into use, Roy Olmstead and his confederates used the telephone in what Chief Justice William Howard Taft (a former president) described as a "conspiracy of amazing magnitude" to sell liquor unlawfully. Olmstead's telephone conversations were intercepted by agents of the Bureau of Prohibition and subsequently introduced into evidence at the criminal trial. Although Olmstead objected to the introduction of such evidence on the ground that it was obtained in violation of his Fourth Amendment rights, the federal trial judge nevertheless accepted it. Naturally, Olmstead and his group were convicted. They appealed to the Supreme Court. The question was whether evidence derived from private telephone conversations, intercepted by wiretapping without a proper judicial warrant, violated the Fourth Amendment. The Supreme Court said that it did not. The people have a right to be secure in "their persons, houses, papers and effects," but not in their "conversations." Since the Constitution was silent on "conversations" it was up to the Congress to pass a law prohibiting wiretapping, and this it had not done. So much for Olmstead and his friends.

Notwithstanding the decision of the Supreme Court in Olmstead's case, the Department of Justice, nevertheless, and its Bureau of Investigation (the forerunner of the FBI) continued to prohibit wiretapping until 1931. It was forced to reexamine this position due to the fact that in 1930 the Bureau of Prohibition was transferred to Justice from the Department of the Treasury. It was troublesome enough that two departments had different policies; it was intolerable that two bureaus within one department had different policies. Attorney General William B. Mitchell recognized this in a January 19, 1931, memorandum:

Of course, the present condition in the department cannot have one bureau in which wiretapping is allowed and another in which it is prohibited. The same regulations must apply to all. . . . I think I should give a direction applicable to all bureaus and divisions of the department that no tapping of wires should be permitted by any agent of the department without the personal direction of the chief of the bureau involved, after consultation with the assistant attorney general in charge of the case.

Thereafter, the director of the Bureau of Investigation issued his own regulation that telephone or telegraph wires were not to be tapped without his prior authorization. The attorney general went even further. He issued instructions that no wiretap was to be instituted without written approval of the assistant attorney general in charge of the particular case. In addition, the attorney general specified that wiretapping would be authorized ''only in those cases involving the safety of victims of kidnappings, the location and apprehension of desperate criminals, and in espionage and sabotage and other cases considered to be of major law enforcement importance.'' This directive was followed without change by succeeding attorneys general until 1940.

At this point, it would seem proper to make two observations. Even though the Supreme Court had declared that wiretapping was lawful, there was a reluctance to give it broad and comprehensive implementation. I like to think this reluctance was the result of an intuitive feeling by the attorney general that wiretapping was offensive to an American's belief in his right of privacy even if the Supreme Court had determined that it was beyond the perimeters of the Constitution. The other observation is this. Laudable as the regulation of Attorney General Mitchell was in its limitation of the use of wiretapping, the vagueness of that regulation caused problems. The attorney general, not an independent and detached judge, would decide the question of safety, the question of just what a desperate criminal is, and the question of what it takes to consider a case of major law-enforcement importance.

The Congress must have become jittery about the problem too. In 1934 it enacted section 605 of the Federal Communications Act of 1934. That section made it a crime for ''any person'' to intercept, without authorization, *and* divulge or publish the contents of wire and radio communications. This was pretty good for a starter. The Supreme Court in 1937 upheld the section and also ruled that Congress intended that ''any person'' included federal agents, and thereby precluded the receipt of wiretapped conversations as evidence in judicial proceedings.

The Department of Justice, however, placed its own interpretation upon the 1937 decision of the Supreme Court. It construed the decision as not prohibiting the interception of wire communications *per se* but only prohibiting the interception *and* divulgence of their contents. This interpretation permitted the Department of Justice to authorize wiretapping, but it recognized that nothing obtained therefrom could be used as evidence in a judicial proceeding. This interpretation continued until 1940.

On March 15, 1940, Attorney General—and soon to become a justice of the Supreme Court—Robert H. Jackson rescinded the authority of the FBI with respect to wiretapping and reinstated the blanket prohibition instituted on March 1, 1928, by Attorney General John G. Sargent. Almost two months later to the day, and on May 21, 1940, President Roosevelt transmitted a confidential memorandum to his attorney general directing him "to authorize the necessary investigating agents that they are at liberty to secure information by listening devices directed to the conversations or other communications of persons suspected of subversive activities against the government of the United States, including suspected spies."

Having had some experience in the relationship between a president and an attorney general, I've always been curious as to how President Roosevelt's direction in May 1940 came about. It would appear on the surface that the president had not been consulted by Jackson before Jackson issued his blanket prohibition of the FBI in March. It would also appear on the surface that the president did not consult with his attorney general before he issued his directive in May. I'm only guessing, but I have a hunch that J. Edgar Hoover, the director of the FBI, went directly to the president and complained about Jackson's blanket prohibition. With war on the horizon, Roosevelt was persuaded that his hands shouldn't be completely tied in this vital area. Having come to know Mr. Hoover, I would even go so far as to guess that he carried a copy of the proposed memorandum to be transmitted to the attorney general with him. The memorandum consisted of only one page, but it was nevertheless an excellent political document. The president, in the first paragraph, acknowledged that "under ordinary and normal circumstances wiretapping by government agents should not be carried on for the *excellent* reason that it is *almost* bound to lead to abuse of civil rights." (Emphasis supplied.) He then pointed out that certain nations had been engaged in the organization of "fifth columns" in preparation for "sabotage." He then observed that "it is too late to do anything about it after sabotage, assassinations and 'fifth column' activities are completed." In other words, Mr. Attorney General, when it comes to the defense of the nation for which I alone am responsible under the Constitution, let's get with it!

Even this limited use of wiretapping continued to be troublesome. On October 8, 1941, Francis Biddle, Roosevelt's new attorney general, had a press conference, a good deal of which was consumed in questions about wiretapping. Our nettlesome friends of the fourth estate were poking around in this sensitive area. I don't know what Attorney General Biddle said to the press but it apparently created confusion in Hoover's mind. Had Biddle backtracked on the presidential directive of May 21, 1940? The next day Biddle wrote a confidential memorandum to Mr. Hoover assuring him that he had not. However, he introduced for the first time the specific directive to the FBI that "as a matter of policy, wiretapping would be used sparingly, *and under express authorization of the Attorney General.*" (Emphasis supplied.) So there you have it, Mr. Hoover. Go ahead and do it, but be sure to get my approval in writing before you do it!

For some reason, Tom Clark, when he was President Truman's attorney general, felt it necessary to bring the matter up again and to receive direct presidential authorization. In a letter dated July 17, 1946, to the president, Clark referred to President Roosevelt's May 21, 1940, directive to Attorney General Jackson and recommended that the practice continue in effect in matters involving domestic security. However, he added the recommendation that wiretapping be used "where human life is in jeopardy." President Truman gave his concurrence on the second page of Clark's memorandum. The president wrote in the date, July 17, 1947—apparently one year to the day after the Clark memorandum was dated. Again, I've been curious as to how this came about. Was the Clark memorandum dated in 1946 by mistake? Was Truman's date a mistake? Had the memorandum been sitting around for a year and had something occurred that necessitated action by the president? It just doesn't make any sense. But it does illustrate the imprecise manner in which this sensitive and troublesome matter was dealt with. Everybody concerned handled it differently as he became involved in the problem. Attorney General McGrath—Truman's last attorney general—found it necessary to write a memorandum to Hoover on February 26, 1952, assuring him that he did "not intend to alter the existing policy that wiretapping surveillance should be used under the present highly restricted basis and when specifically authorized by me." But what policy was he referring to? Was it the May 21, 1940, policy pertaining to such matters *or* the July 17, 1947, Truman policy pertaining to such matters *and* "where human life is in jeopardy"? If it was the latter policy, then Hoover could believe that wiretapping was authorized in cases of general crimes—provided only that a human life was threatened. Once again an illustration of the reluctance of an attorney general to come to grips with this nettlesome problem with any degree of precision.

For some reason, Mr. Hoover thought it was necessary to raise the matter with Attorney General Brownell on March 8, 1955, over two years after Brownell had become President Eisenhower's attorney general. On March 16, 1955, Brownell informed Mr. Hoover that the authorization letter of President Roosevelt dated May 21, 1940, would be the policy. He concluded by saying, "I do not think it is necessary to reopen the matter at this time." Why, it might be asked, did he make that rather pointed statement? Had Hoover been putting the pressure on to expand the scope of wiretapping? Again, however, not a very clear and precise way to deal with such a sensitive problem.

Robert F. Kennedy became the sixty-fourth attorney general following the election of his brother, John F. Kennedy, in November 1960. His handling of wiretapping was not only confusing but also rife with contradictions. For example, on March 13, 1962, Attorney General Kennedy, for some reason not made clear for the record, took the unusual step of formally rescinding the March 15, 1940, regulation of Attorney General Jackson. It is to be recalled that Jackson had issued a blanket prohibition of wiretapping. In his formal Order No. 263-62, Robert Kennedy merely stated that the amendment to Jackson's directive was necessary "in order to reflect the practices, which had been in effect since

May 21, 1940," that is, the Roosevelt practices. The Kennedy order then provided that "existing instructions to the Federal Bureau of Investigation with respect to obtaining the approval of the attorney general for wiretapping [be] continued in force." The contradictions emerged, however, because of what Attorney General Kennedy actually did.

In the private office of the attorney general there are locked and secured files containing the wiretapping authorizations of the attorneys general since 1961. These files were carefully examined by top officers of the Internal Security Division of the Department of Justice in 1971, when John Mitchell was the attorney general. He directed the examination as a means of preparation for testimony before the Senate Judiciary Committee. Mitchell was particularly interested in information by which to compare his treatment of wiretapping with that of Kennedy and Ramsey Clark. For some reason the records during the first year of Kennedy's tenure were missing. The Kennedy records that were in the files, however, were quite revealing. As an outgrowth of Kennedy's crusade against organized crime, there were several authorizations to the FBI for wiretapping in organized-crime cases. He had also signed authorizations of telephone surveillances at the home of Martin Luther King and at the headquarters of the Southern Christian Leadership Conference. These surveillances were carried under the heading of "Communist Party USA" which, of course, would classify it as a national security surveillance. From a reading of some of the justifications, it appeared that King was contacted by phone on numerous occasions by Communist party functionaries. The FBI had concluded that the Communist party was trying to use the civil-rights movement as its tool and for its own nefarious purposes.

The reluctance and self-imposed restraint exercised by every prior attorney general were not exercised by Attorney General Kennedy. "Organized crime" was then and is today a menace to our free society. The question so clearly presented, however, is whether its crimes should be exempt from the warrant protection of a judge under the Fourth Amendment. By the same token, what about a person receiving a call from an official of the Communist party? I have no peer when it comes to my anticommunism. No one doubts that the Communist party would offer encouragement to a civil-rights leader if it believed the unrest created by the movement would erode and possibly destroy our government. It should make us feel uneasy, however, if this type of activity should be the object of general electronic surveillance. (I could never quite understand the restraint exercised by our friends of the fourth estate when the Martin Luther King wiretapping became known to the public.) In any event, the Kennedy era dramatically illustrated that the use of electronic surveillance by the government could be extended into areas that went beyond the essential requirements of national security.

President Lyndon Johnson appreciated full well the political implications of the Martin Luther King wiretaps and acted accordingly. On June 30, 1965, he transmitted an "administratively confidential" memorandum to the heads of all executive departments and agencies. "I am strongly opposed to the interception of telephone conversations as a general investigative technique," was the opening sentence. He then recognized that "electronic devices may sometimes be essential in protecting national security." He then declared that their indiscriminate use "could result in serious abuses and invasions of privacy." The memorandum concluded with a specific directive. There would be no wiretapping "except in connection with investigations related to the national security" and then only by "first obtaining the approval of the attorney general." In other words, wiretapping might be legal and beyond the protection of the warrant requirements of the Fourth Amendment, but, as a matter of policy, it shall not be done.

The rather modest publicity given to the Kennedy tenure in the Department of Justice nevertheless began to have its impact. Two years after the Johnson directive, the Supreme Court handed down its decision in the case of Charles Katz, and in 1968 the Congress passed Title III of the Omnibus Crime Control and Safe Streets Act. The telephone, after one hundred years of busy use, would never be quite the same again.

Remember Roy Olmstead and his sale of whiskey by the use of telephone during Prohibition? In 1927 the Supreme Court announced that his conviction, based upon wiretaps, was lawful because the Fourth Amendment was not applicable. Charles Katz, to use the vernacular, was a bookie in Southern California. He found it suited his business purposes if he used a public telephone booth to place his bets. The FBI placed an electronic listening and recording device on the outside of the telephone booth and thereby secured a record of his end of the conversations. At his trial, the government offered the recordings in evidence and Katz was convicted. He appealed his case to the Supreme Court. On December 18, 1967, the Supreme Court did something it very rarely does—it specifically reversed its prior decision in Olmstead's case. It held that when the government electronically listened to Katz's words, it violated the privacy he was justified in relying upon in using the telephone booth and was therefore a "search and seizure" within the meaning of the Fourth Amendment. "The Fourth Amendment protects people, not places," the Court said. When Katz entered his telephone booth he sought to exclude "the uninvited ear" of the government. The government didn't have a warrant and thus Katz did not have "the deliberate, impartial judgment of a judicial officer" interposed between him and the FBI.

Unfortunately, when a bookie uses a telephone booth by which to transmit bets it is not within the realm of national security. In Katz's case, the Supreme Court ducked the national security question in a mere footnote. This is the usual practice of the Court when the facts of a particular case do not permit the consideration of other issues. The Court seemed to invite the opportunity to address itself to this vital question. For nearly fifty years it had been handled as a hot potato by each succeeding attorney general. Sooner or later the potato had to be tossed into the hands of the Supreme Court. As we shall see, a black federal district judge in Michigan, in dealing with the situation of another black by the name of Plamondon, made the critical toss.

If the case of Bookie Katz finally brought the Fourth Amendment into the modern world of electronics, the Congress, on June 19, 1968—six months and one day after Katz's victory—laid out the definitive ground rules for the future use of electronic surveillance. Chief Justice William Howard Taft in 1927 remarked that Congress might, if it so desired, legislate in this field. Since it had not, Roy Olmstead and his friends went to jail. Forty years is a long time in most situations. Quite often, it is par for the congressional course.

By the passage of Title III of the Omnibus Crime Control and Safe Streets Act, the Congress was at its best. To begin with, it described the problem that had been bothering everybody for over fifty years. On the basis of its own investigations and of published studies it made findings. Some of those findings are of interest. Thus:

> There has been extensive wiretapping carried on without legal sanctions, and without the consent of any of the parties of the conversation.

> In order to protect effectively the privacy of wire and oral communications . . . it is necessary for Congress to define on a uniform basis the circumstances and conditions under which the interception of wire and oral communications may be authorized.

> Interception of wire and oral communications should further be limited to certain major types of offenses and specific categories of crime with assurances that the interception is justified and that the information obtained thereby will not be used.

The next thing the Congress did was to declare that, except as specifically provided otherwise, if any person (including federal, state and local law-enforcement agents) engage in electronic surveillance, he "shall be fined not more than $10,000 and imprisoned not more than five years, or both." It is hardly necessary to make the comment that such stiff penalties opened the necessary eyes.

With such an eye-opener, it is almost certain that President Johnson was relieved to read that the act was not intended to limit his *constitutional* power to protect the national security. He signed the legislation and thereby made it law. Three years later, however, the Supreme Court got around to telling his successor, President Nixon, just what his "constitutional power" was.

Being mindful of Roy Olmstead and Charles Katz, the Congress informed all concerned that if there was an interception of any wire or oral communications in violation of the act, "no part of the contents of such communication and no evidence derived therefrom" could be used in evidence. No doubt about it. Do it right hereafter or don't do it at all.

Congress then made its laundry list of what it considered to be major types of offenses, and therefore subject to interception under the ground rules. For the curious, here they are:

Violation of the Atomic Energy Act of 1954, espionage, sabotage, treason, riots, restrictions on payments and loans to labor organizations, murder, kidnapping, robbery, extortion, bribery of public officials and witnesses, bribery in sporting contests, transmission of wagering information, influencing or injuring an officer, juror or witness, obstruction of criminal investigations, presidential assassinations, kidnapping and assault; interference with commerce by threats or violence; interstate and foreign travel or transportation in and racketeering enterprises; offer, acceptance, or solicitation to influence operations of employee benefit plan; theft from interstate shipment; embezzlement from pension and welfare funds; interstate transportation of stolen property; counterfeiting; dealing in narcotic drugs; extortionate credit transactions.

At first glance, this list of major offenses might appear rather broad. Upon closer examination, however, most of the offenses described are the tools of what we generally refer to as organized crimes. While this essay on the Fourth Amendment is not suited for the development of a treatise on organized crime, it is certain, however, that if any class of persons in the United States really had their eyes opened by the Congress it was, indeed, those who fell into that category.

Congress then addressed itself to the most important task at hand. What procedures must be followed to the letter if electronic surveillance was to be used in specific situations? If wiretapping was a "search and seizure" under the Fourth Amendment, was it possible to fashion means by which any such search or seizure would not be unreasonable? Was it possible to devise a method by which judicial warrants could be issued based upon probable cause and describing with particularity that which was to be searched or seized? These questions were answered in the affirmative.

By way of a summary description, here are the procedures that must be followed before an interception of a wire or oral communication can be made by any law-enforcement officer:

1. A written application under oath shall be made to a judge of competent jurisdiction giving the following information:

    a. The identity of the law-enforcement officer.

    b. A full and complete statement of the facts relied upon to justify his belief that an order should be used.

    c. A full statement as to whether other investigative procedures have been tried and failed.

    d. A statement of the period of time the interception is required to be maintained.

e. A statement of all previous applications.

f. If the application is for an extension of an existing order, the reasons therefor.

2. The judge may enter an order authorizing the interception if he determines:

a. There is probable cause for belief that a crime is being committed, has been committed or is about to be committed.

b. There is probable cause that the interception will obtain communications concerning that offense.

c. Normal investigative procedures have been tried and failed.

d. It is likely that the person to be intercepted will use the facilities encompassed by the order.

Having made those findings, the judge's authorization must likewise be specific. Thus, the identity of the person, the location of the facility to be overheard, the communication sought to be intercepted, and the period of time authorized are specifically described.

The most significant provision of the act is that which touches at the very heart of the Fourth Amendment. Within a reasonable time, but not later than ninety days after the filing of an application, the judge may, in his discretion, advise the person intercepted that he was the subject of the application and order. However, this information *must* be supplied to a person ten days prior to his trial.

So there it is. After fifty years of confusion, indecisiveness, and guesswork, the American citizen for the first time was able to answer the question whether, and if so, under what circumstances, the government was listening in on his telephone or other conversations. It was a long time coming, but perhaps that has been to the good of us all. When it did come it was fortified by experience in the marketplace. The Fourth Amendment is secure and, at the same time, we have become more secure as a people because we have the means by which to combat serious crime.

But one problem remained. What is the constitutional power of the president with respect to our national security? Did Congress intend to leave it up to the president and his attorney general to continue to write their own ground rules when it came to the use of electronic surveillance in the interest of national security? The debate on the floor of the Senate prior to the passage of the 1968 Omnibus Crime Control and Safe Streets Act quite clearly demonstrated that the Congress simply did not intend to legislate with respect to national security surveillances. Senator Holland said, "We are not affirmatively conferring any power upon the president." Senator McClellan said, on the other hand, "We are not trying to take anything away from him." Senator Hart said it best in these words: ". . . nothing in Section 2511(3) even attempts to define the limits of the president's national security power under present law, *which I have always found extremely vague. . . .*" (Emphasis supplied.) Amen.

That's precisely the way I felt about it when I entered the Department of Justice as the deputy attorney general in January of 1969. I had heard plenty about Title III of the Omnibus Crime Control and Safe Streets Act during the 1968 presidential election campaign. One of Nixon's campaign promises was that America would have a new attorney general if he was elected. He would have had a new one anyway, but this promise was an allusion to the then attorney general, Ramsey Clark. Clark didn't fit Nixon's idea of a "law and order" attorney general. Specifically, Clark left himself wide open in 1968 when he announced that he would not enforce the Omnibus Crime Control and Safe Streets Act because it entailed the use of electronic surveillance. This produced the expected outcry from the law-enforcement community: "Is he out of his mind? Here is a way finally to come to grips with organized crime and to do it with a warrant issued by a judge!" Quite frankly, I shared that point of view in 1968, and I became more convinced of it after I joined the Department of Justice. A constitutional weapon did, in fact, exist to fight organized crime. But the public posture of Attorney General Clark ceased to make any sense to me when I learned that, as attorney general, he, like his predecessors, had authorized many electronic surveillances in national security cases—without a judicial warrant. Of course, I didn't have to bear the responsibility for national security electronic surveillance until March of 1972, when I became the attorney general. Mitchell reserved two areas of responsibility that he did not share with me. One was his role in advising the president as to pardons, and the other was electronic surveillance. I don't fault him on either ground. The only problem it presented for me was the fact that I had no prior knowledge or experience when I suddenly found myself in the middle of both.

I did, however, bring to the question of electronic surveillance some very definite attitudes. For one, I just didn't like the idea that the government or any person should be listening in on private conversations. Specifically, however, if I was to do so as the government, I was going to do it myself alone and not delegate such a power to others. I further believed that the political responsibility for electronic surveillance should be fixed; therefore, with the valuable assistance of Bill Olson, the assistant attorney general for the Internal Security Division, a precise and completely documented record system was implemented. That record showed why a national security surveillance was authorized or not authorized. Likewise, the same procedure applied in Title III surveillance, even though the act specifically authorized the attorney general to delegate the responsibility to an assistant attorney general.

So much for that.

On February 24, 1972, my devoted friend and able lawyer, Bob Mardian, as the assistant attorney general for the Internal Security Division, argued the position of the government before the Supreme Court in the so-called Keith case. This was one week before I became the acting attorney general. The Supreme Court decided the case on June 19, 1972, exactly one week after I became the attorney general. It was the most momentous decision by the Supreme Court in my some four and a half years at Justice.

Damon J. Keith was a judge of the United States District Court for the Eastern District of Michigan and was conducting pretrial proceedings in a prosecution for conspiracy to destroy government property. One of the defendants was a person by the name of Plamondon. In those proceedings, Judge Keith ordered the government to make full disclosure to Plamondon of his conversations overheard by electronic surveillance instituted without a search warrant. The government responded to this order by filing with the judge an affidavit of Attorney General Mitchell. He admitted that his agents had overheard conversations in which Plamondon had participated. He also stated that he had approved the wiretaps "to gather intelligence information deemed necessary to protect the nation from attempts of *domestic organizations* to attack and subvert the existing structure of the government." (Emphasis supplied.) Judge Keith politely said *no* to the government. The government then proceeded to the United States Court of Appeals for the Sixth Circuit and asked it to order Judge Keith to vacate his disclosure order. The sixth circuit also said *no* and the government then headed for the Supreme Court. At last and for the first time, the delicate question of the power of the president to authorize electronic surveillance in *internal* security matters without prior judicial approval had arrived in the court of no appeals. Be careful to note, however, that just one half of the loaf of bread had so arrived. Mitchell's affidavit referred only to the attempts of "domestic" organizations to attack and subvert the government. And, as one might expect (remember the footnote in Bookie Katz's case?), the Supreme Court restricted itself to this half of the loaf. In the words of the Court: "It is important at the outset to emphasize the limited nature of the question before the Court. . . . There is no evidence of any involvement, directly or indirectly, of a foreign power."

Bob Mardian is an adroit and skillful lawyer. He is also devoted to the rule of law. It didn't disturb him to think that domestic internal security surveillance might be held to be subject to the Fourth Amendment. He shuddered—as did I and many others—that the electronic surveillance of a foreign power would likewise be subject to the precise warrant requirement of the Fourth Amendment. It is generally agreed that Mardian postured this vital case in such a way that the attorneys representing Plamondon found themselves asking the Court to apply the Constitution so that the rights of citizens would be protected. This is precisely what the Court did.

Justice Powell delivered the opinion of a majority of the court. The first problem addressed was whether Title III of the Omnibus Crime Act had conferred any new power on the president. It didn't. Let me offer the following random quotations from Justice Powell's decision:

The price of lawful public dissent must not be a dread of subjection to an unchecked surveillance power.

Our task is to examine and balance the basic values at stake in this case: the duty of government to protect the domestic security, and the potential danger posed by unreasonable surveillance to individual privacy and free expression.

The magistrate ought to judge; and should give certain directions to the officer.

Prior review of a neutral and detached magistrate is the time-tested means of effectuating Fourth Amendment rights.

By no means of least importance will be the reassurance of the public generally that indiscriminate wiretapping and bugging of law-abiding citizens cannot occur.

As I read these lines while sitting in my office on June 19, 1972, I knew what the decision was going to be. I immediately picked up the phone and asked my secretary, Trixie, to locate Bill Olson at once and have him come to my office. Within minutes he was sitting in front of me. Within minutes thereafter, steps were taken whereby six domestic national security electronic surveillances which I had authorized were terminated. I shed a sigh of relief. A troublesome responsibility had been lifted from my shoulders and from the shoulders of those who would follow after me.

All that was left was the use of electronic surveillance without a judicial warrant with respect to national security cases involving a foreign power. This didn't trouble me as long as I remained at Justice, although I continued the practice of complete records evidencing my sole responsibility. I felt so completely committed to this policy that, when I was in Paris in November of 1972 on government business, I required that an FBI agent hand-carry to me an urgent foreign surveillance for my approval.

As we have seen, forty years elapsed between Olmstead and Katz whereby the law of the land declared that electronic surveillance in general criminal cases was within the purview of the Fourth Amendment. Congress responded one year later with Title III of the Omnibus Crime Control and Safe Streets Act. Four years later Justice Powell and a majority of his fellow justices of the Supreme Court brought electronic surveillance in domestic national security matters within the warrant requirements of the Fourth Amendment. Title III was sitting there ready and able to furnish the government with the means by which it could lawfully wiretap or bug an American citizen in a proper case. If probable cause existed that John Doe was getting ready to engage in espionage, sabotage, treason, presidential assassinations and the like, he had better watch out. Every other citizen could go to bed at night secure in the belief that the government wasn't listening in on his conversations, even if such conversations weren't very complimentary of the government itself.

Only one area of conduct, therefore, remained where it was possible that the government would be listening in on conversations without first obtaining a judicial warrant based upon probable cause. That was the sensitive area of foreign intelligence. None of us would be inclined to argue that the use of electronic surveillance by our government directed solely at foreign governments should be hampered by the Fourth Amendment. The Bill of Rights exists for the protection of American citizens. What should we do, however, when an American citizen engages in conduct on behalf of a foreign power which is inimical to our national security? This type of situation was expressly omitted from the scope of Justice Powell's decision in Plamondon's case. This is a difficult question to answer because it presents the ultimate confrontation between the interest in favor of our national security and the essential interest in favor of the protection of the individual citizen. By the passage of the Foreign Intelligence Surveillance Act in 1978, the Congress met the difficult problems presented by this confrontation head on.

The 1978 act said two things. Whether or not the Supreme Court will decide it had the constitutional power to say one or both remains to be seen. Nevertheless, this is what it said.

First, the president, through his attorney general, may authorize electronic surveillance without first obtaining a court order to acquire foreign intelligence information. So far so good. This is a conceded constitutional power and duty of the president. However, when he does exercise that power and when he does fulfill that duty, the attorney general must make a written certification under oath of each such surveillance to the Select Committees on Intelligence of both the House of Representatives and the Senate. The contents of these certifications are precisely outlined in the act. The actual electronic surveillance must adhere to the attorney general's certification and other procedures adopted by him. Moreover, the attorney general is required to report periodically to the congressional select committees his own assessment as to whether his procedures have, in fact, been complied with. In addition, the attorney general is required to file a copy of his certifications with a special court created by the act. Perhaps not so good thus far. Has the Congress overstepped the bounds of its function so carefully delineated in the Constitution? Is the Congress attempting to delegate unto itself a slice of the action in providing for the national defense and security? Or is the Congress merely legislating for the purpose of determining whether the president and his attorney general restrict themselves only to that power and duty contemplated by the Founding Fathers? These are nice questions to be resolved by constitutional lawyers and the Supreme Court. In the meantime, John Doe can derive comfort from the knowledge that a means exists to assure him, in the words of Justice Powell, "that indiscriminate wiretapping and bugging of law-abiding citizens cannot occur."

The second thing the 1978 act said may likewise be simply stated. The president, through his attorney general, may not, without first obtaining a court order, authorize an electronic surveillance to acquire foreign intelligence information if the target of the surveillance involves a United States citizen. Doesn't this requirement of the 1978 act legislate the precise question which the Supreme Court specifically said it was not deciding in Plamondon's case in 1971? It seems to me that it does. The Department of Justice also thought so when it testified before the Congress in hearings prior to the adoption of the 1978 act. Once again, we'll have to leave the question up to those great constitutional scholars on the Supreme Court.

Personally, I come down on the side of the constitutional validity of the act. If John Doe is believed to be acting in concert with a foreign power in such a manner that a crime like treason is in the works, should he not have the protection of the Fourth Amendment before his conversations are electronically intercepted? But what about secrecy? How can the government protect information in such a sensitive and vital area? There are several hundred federal judges. Can each be relied upon to have airtight procedures so that critical information cannot be leaked through inadvertence?

One of the principal reasons why I came down on the side of the act is that Congress made wise and adequate provisions to minimize, if not entirely eliminate, such justifiable fears.

The 1978 act created a special court before which all applications for the authorization of such electronic surveillances must be submitted. This court consists of seven federal district court judges who are publicly designated by the chief justice of the United States. An application is heard by any one of these judges. If a judge denies an application, the attorney general may appeal the denial to a court of review consisting of three judges, all of whom being likewise publicly designated by the chief justice. If the attorney general doesn't like the decision of the review court, he can proceed to the Supreme Court itself. This procedure is good enough for me.

Suppose, however, that an emergency exists and the attorney general doesn't have time to put his papers together. Again, the act responds. In such a case, Mr. Attorney General may institute the electronic surveillance. However, even if it means disturbing the sleep of one of the seven judges, the attorney general must inform him that an emergency surveillance is being employed and that as soon as possible, but in no event more than twenty-four hours later, a formal application for an order authorizing the surveillance will be filed. Fair enough.

Having adequately overcome the ticklish problems of secrecy and emergency, the act then proceeded to borrow from the 1968 Title II Crime Control and Safe Streets Act the procedures to be followed for the issuance of an order authorizing the electronic surveillance. As we have seen from a brief explanation of those procedures, the essential requirements of the Fourth Amendment are more than satisfied.

This, then, is the story of the long journey of wiretapping and bugging by our government of U.S. citizens. It took fifty-one years to complete. Even though former President William Howard Taft, when acting as the chief justice of the Supreme Court, informed Roy Olmstead that his telephone conversations by which he imported and sold liquor in violation of the Prohibition laws could be tapped by the government without a court order, both the public and the government felt uncomfortable. It just didn't jibe with the spirit of the Fourth Amendment. To their credit, all attorneys general from 1927 through 1967 imposed restraints upon the exercise of such an awesome weapon by which to secure evidence of criminal conduct of our fellow citizens. When Bookie Katz was set free in 1967, the end of the journey was in sight. Federal District Judge Keith paved the few remaining miles of the road when he informed the government that it needed a court order to wiretap Plamondon even if Plamondon might have been engaged in a conspiracy to destroy government property. Justice Powell and five of his associates agreed. The Congress then followed through with unusual wisdom and balance. Therefore, you, John Doe, need not have a gnawing feeling in the pit of your stomach that the government is listening in on your private conversations—unless, of course, you are doing something you shouldn't be doing! If, however, you just happen to be, don't be surprised when you hear your voice at your criminal trial under the auspices of the order of one of your favorite judges.

When I became the acting attorney general on March 1, 1972, I had no training to guide me in the authorization of electronic surveillance. The experience was akin to parachuting—why practice when you have to be perfect the first time? When Bill Olson, the assistant attorney general for the Internal Security Division, brought me a comprehensive memorandum outlining the history of the procedures of former attorneys general, I was rather amazed to learn that those procedures were as varied as those attorneys general who preceded me. In most areas of responsibility, such a variance should probably exist. After all, the attorney general is merely an arm of the president and presidential policies and priorities should conform to the changing politics of the times. But the clandestine wiretapping of American citizens upon the sole authorization of the attorney general struck me as a little bit different piece of cake. The very nature of the subject matter precluded it from being involved in the political debate of presidential elections. Moreover, since the authorizations were kept from the public and press, abuse could be tempting. George Bernard Shaw once observed that the reason why marriage is successful is because it combines maximum temptation with maximum opportunity.

Unfortunately, the record of authorizations by preceding attorneys general was almost nonexistent. None existed prior to Robert Kennedy and only a portion of his were in the files. I dare say that he would not have wiretapped Martin Luther King if he thought it would be exposed to public scrutiny. The fact of such exposure had to convince many Americans that the government was, indeed, snooping around in areas of conduct that, at the time, might have been unpopular.

The problem hit me right between the eyes in February of 1973, one year after I began to discharge the duties of the office of attorney general. On February 16, 1973, *Time* magazine published its March 5 issue, which contained the charge that the White House ordered over a period of more than two years the FBI taps on the telephones of several newsmen and a number of White House aides in order to pinpoint a national security news leak in the executive staff. The article stated that the late J. Edgar Hoover, then director of the FBI, at first refused to use the wiretaps but was, nevertheless, ordered by Attorney General Mitchell to follow the White House orders. What really floored me, however, was the charge that, when I was Mitchell's deputy, I wanted Hoover to retire but dropped the issue when Hoover threatened to expose the wiretaps to the Congress. Holy mackerel!

I knew absolutely nothing about any such wiretaps and I had no such contacts with Mr. Hoover. In addition, I had immediately discontinued all domestic national security surveillance the day the Keith decision was handed down by Justice Powell. None of those was connected in any way with reporters or White House personnel. I had to issue a press release at once. Before doing so, I called Mitchell and asked him if he knew anything about the tapes. Based upon his response I included the following sentence in my February 26, 1973, press release: ''I state further that I have the strongest personal assurance from Mr. Mitchell that he never authorized or was asked to authorize the implementation of such devices against reporters on White House order.''

As a matter of fact, however, the wiretaps had been authorized by Mitchell. The subsequent revelations of Watergate brought forth that wiretaps commenced on May 9, 1969, and, in one form or another, continued until February 1971. This was the only time Mitchell had ever been less than candid with me. When I asked him years later why he had misinformed me, his answer highlighted the very problem this appendix addresses. In substance, his answer was that since the wiretaps were instituted to develop leaks concerning vital national security matters, their secrecy, as a matter of policy, had to be maintained. That explanation didn't satisfy me then and it doesn't now.

Another aspect of these wiretaps that disturbs me is the manner in which they were maintained as records. Instead of being filed with Mitchell's other authorizations, they were first kept in the files at the FBI under the scrutiny of the late deputy director, William J. Sullivan. Subsequently, however, at the president's specific direction, Bob Mardian, the assistant attorney general for the Internal Security Division, in July of 1971, obtained the records from Sullivan and delivered them to John Ehrlichman at the White House. They were discovered a few days after Ehrlichman's resignation was announced by the president on Monday, April 30, 1973.

The public attention which Martin Luther King and these wiretappings received led to the long delayed realization in the Department of Justice that a precise procedural standard was needed for the processing and record keeping of national security electronic authorizations by the attorney general.

When Edward Levi was named attorney general by President Ford in 1975, he was quizzed extensively by the Senate Judiciary Committee as to what he would do to stop the "abuses" uncovered by the Church and Pike committees' investigations of intelligence agencies. He pledged to the Judiciary Committee that he would isssue guidelines for the FBI. To fulfill that pledge, in March 1975, he created a committee to draft such guidelines. Mary Lawton, then a deputy assistant attorney general in the office of Legal Counsel, was designated as the chairman of the committee. Among other subjects, the guidelines covered domestic security and foreign intelligence cases and set up requirements for regular department review of these cases and the use of certain techniques. As a consequence, an "investigations review unit" was established for the first time in the attorney general's office.

In the beginning, the unit was not involved in electronic surveillance. Attorney General Levi and one of his personal assistants continued to handle these for a short period of time. Gradually, however, the unit was asked to make the initial review of the requests. This was a great step forward in the standardization of procedures for the authorization of electronic surveillance. The passage by the Congress in 1978 of the Foreign Intelligence Surveillance Act brought about the last needed step.

The creation of the special court to hear applications for national security electronic surveillance necessitated an administrative response by the Department of Justice. Procedures must be formulated without delay to enable the attorney general strictly to comply with the provisions of the 1978 act and with the rules of the new court. These requirements led to the decision that there should be a single focal point for the processing of all intelligence matters within the government. Accordingly, and on February 20, 1980, the Office of Intelligence Policy and Review was created, to be headed by a counsel to be appointed by the attorney general.

The functions of the counsel are comprehensive and clearly demonstrate that the random practices of the past had finally met their long delayed demise. Thus, the counsel shall:

Oversee the development, coordination and implementation of Department of Justice policy with regard to intelligence, counter-intelligence and national security matters.

Participate in the development and implementation of U.S. intelligence policies.

Formulate recommended actions by the executive branch of the government in achieving lawful U.S. intelligence and counter-intelligence objectives.

Supervise the preparation of certification and applications for orders under the 1978 Foreign Intelligence Surveillance Act before the U.S. Foreign Intelligence Surveillance Court.

Monitor intelligence and counter-intelligence activities by all agencies of the executive branch of the government.

Provide a quality control review for all outgoing intelligence and counter-intelligence reports.

The person selected from time to time to perform these critical functions will determine whether it is indeed possible for the United States to provide for its national security and, at the same time, guard the precious liberties of its individual citizens. Is it naive in today's world to believe that the qualifications needed to strike this intricate balance of such competing forces can be found in one person? Where do we find a person who possesses the many exemplary traits of unquestioned patriotism, intellect, legal scholarship, courage, leadership, and perspective?

Mary Lawton is the first person to be appointed counsel of the Office of Intelligence Policy and Review. That she was there at the time and possessed the unique qualities that are hers must have been of great significance in the decision to create the position at the outset.

She was born in Washington, D.C. That was long enough ago to produce a person of mature judgment but not so long ago to deprive the country of energy, spirit and flexibility. Her grandfather started a career in the U.S. government in 1891 and her father had forty-two years of service. Modestly, she suggested that "someday we'll get the hang of it." They did!

Her scholarship is undisputed. Not only did she graduate magna cum laude from Seton Hill College in Greensburg, Pennsylvania, but she was also first in her class at the Georgetown Law Center in Washington, D.C., and was a member of the board of editors of the *Georgetown Law Journal*. These honors were awarded at a time when it was rare for a female even to be a law student, let alone number one.

Upon graduation from law school she entered the Department of Justice under the attorney general's honor program and became an attorney adviser in the office of Legal Counsel. Twelve years later she had become a deputy assistant attorney general in that office of "lawyers' lawyers." I became familiar with her spunk, wit, and independence three years before that distinction came her way. As the primary draftsman of the D.C. Court Reorganization Act and other criminal justice legislative proposals of the Nixon administration, she more than earned that distinction.

During the next seven years as a deputy assistant attorney general, tasks assigned to her provided comprehensive experiences which she must now draw upon in her present vital role. In the preparation of memoranda of law geared to legislative testimony and in the drafting of legislation, she learned about the "ways and means" of the U.S. Congress as few in the executive branch have. In preparing briefs and in arguing appellate cases she likewise became an acknowledged expert in the working of the federal courts.

In 1979 the Corporation for Public Broadcasting induced her to leave the Department of Justice to serve as its general counsel. Such a position is coveted by leading lawyers in the land. That service brought her to the attention of the White House in 1980. In July of that year President Carter appointed Lawton the administrative law officer of the White House. In that post she interpreted and advised in public law and historic precedent affecting the White House and the presidency as continuing institutions. President Reagan asked her to remain at the White House as a member of the staff of the counsel to the president. In 1982 Attorney General Smith appointed her to direct the Office of Intelligence Policy and Review.

The American citizen will sleep better as long as Mary Lawton or someone like her is there.

Appendix B
The Kleindienst Case

On April 23, 1982, the supreme court of the State of Arizona suspended Mr. Kleindienst from the practice of the law for a period of one year. The undersigned represented him in the proceedings that culminated in that suspension. This appendix is a skeletal description of the administrative proceedings of the State Bar of Arizona and the Arizona Supreme Court, which began in 1976 and ended in 1983.

The proceedings were initiated because of a letter from David E. Brinegar, then publisher of the *Arizona Daily Star*, to the State Bar of Arizona, which did not itself allege any wrongdoing by Mr. Kleindienst but which commented on newspaper stories concerning an alleged relationship with one Joseph Hauser and Hauser's associates.

The newspaper stories concerned a lawsuit brought in 1976 by the director of the Department of Insurance of Arizona, as receiver of an Arizona insurance company named Family Provider Life Insurance Company, against several defendants, one of whom was Mr. Kleindienst. In this lawsuit, the director sought to recover funds which the complaint alleged had been wrongfully diverted from Family Provider. The allegation against Mr. Kleindienst was that he or his law firm had received or shared in a $250,000 contingency fee or commission paid to secure a very large piece of insurance business from an entity with the mouth-filling name of Central States, Southeast and Southwest Areas Health and Welfare Fund of the International Brotherhood of Teamsters.

This suit was voluntarily dismissed insofar as Mr. Kleindienst was involved, when Mr. Kleindienst presented the attorney general with the facts concerning the transaction. The allegations concerning Mr. Kleindienst had generated intense publicity in Arizona because of the amount of money involved in the fee or commission, the notoriety of the Teamsters' practices, and Mr. Kleindienst's prominence.

Under the rules which the supreme court of Arizona has promulgated for the governance of the State Bar of Arizona, a bar administrative proceeding is commenced whenever a complaint is made. The first step in such a proceeding is an investigation into the matter by the state bar. In this case, the Brinegar letter was treated as a complaint and, therefore, the proceeding was commenced and an investigation was undertaken.

By the time this investigation was well under way, a United States Senate subcommittee had held hearings concerning the Teamsters' practices, and in the course of those hearings a good deal of testimony had been developed and some documentary evidence had been produced which cast a good deal of light on the operations of Hauser and his accomplices; in addition, depositions had been taken and documents produced in civil litigation resulting from those activities, and the transactions of the Health and Welfare Fund.

Thus, the state bar investigation, while focusing on Mr. Kleindienst's actions in relation to Health and Welfare Fund insurance matters, went beyond circumstances of the fee or commission and inquired generally into his relationship with the Hauser group.

The facts were, and the investigation showed, that because Hauser intended to go after more of the Teamsters' insurance business but needed another insurance company to do so, one of his companies undertook to buy the stock of a New Jersey insurance company, but the owner of the stock of that company would sell it to the Hauser company only as a package with an Arizona real estate development which it also owned. Hauser's plan was to divert the initial premium paid to Family Provider by the Health and Welfare Fund, and use that money as the down payment on these two acquisitions. This plan came close to succeeding, but insurance regulatory authorities in New Jersey became suspicious about representations made to them in order to get approval of the transfer of the insurance company's stock, disapproved the transaction, and alerted the director of insurance in Arizona to the diversion of funds. He ordered that the funds be restored to Family Provider and the divested funds were, indeed, redeposited in banks in Washington and Cincinnati to Family Provider's credit.

Thereafter, since the purchase of the New Jersey insurance company had fallen through (and with it the purchase of the Arizona property), Hauser sought to purchase another insurance company, and in that purchase made a payment of $1,800,000 which was the amount which had been deposited to Family Provider's credit.

The award of the insurance business by the Health and Welfare Fund to Family Provider took place at the end of April 1976. The aborted purchase of the New Jersey insurance company was scheduled to take place at the end of May 1976. The purchase involving the $1,800,000 payment took place in June 1976.

Mr. Kleindienst's firm was engaged, with a Phoenix firm as local counsel, to represent the Hauser company in the Arizona property purchase (but not in the related New Jersey insurance company purchase). It was engaged also to represent the parent company of Family Provider, with Lewis & Roca of Phoenix representing Family Provider, in a hearing before the Arizona Director of Insurance to determine whether the diverted funds had been restored and it prepared the papers for the insurance company purchase which was finally made.

Mr. Kleindienst's firm had no other contacts with the Hauser group.

Although the Hauser group had, up to this time, appeared to Mr. Kleindienst and to others, including other law firms, insurance regulatory authorities, and other companies with whom they had business transactions, to be reputable businessmen, they were in fact a gang of confidence men; and their facade of respectability began to crumble late in the summer of 1976. In Arizona, the director of insurance put Family Provider into receivership. Mr. Kleindienst and Lewis & Roca withdrew from further representation. The SEC and the Senate began investigations. Hauser was convicted of numerous federal crimes stemming from his far-reaching fraudulent activities in the insurance industry. A multitude of other federal crimes were either not prosecuted or dismissed in return for his testimony, and John Boden, his chief accomplice, became a ward of the federal government under the Witness Protection Program of the Department of Justice, was stashed away in Ireland, and was kept on the payroll ready to testify on call in proceedings involving Hauser's activities.

The nature and quite a bit of the detail of Hauser's activities thus became known during the course of the state bar investigation. Therefore, it became apparent to all, including Mr. Kleindienst, that he had indeed been near the scene of several improper transactions. The question was: was he, as he considered himself to be, a lawyer whose client had used and conned him by concealing from him what the client was really up to, while telling him stories which would make him believe he was doing a respectable job of providing respectable legal services to respectable businessmen? Or was he, instead, an insider—one of the perpetrators of the Hauser group's schemes? More than two years after the Brinegar letter, the bar counsel designated to conduct the investigation prepared a nine-count complaint charging Mr. Kleindienst with violating the disciplinary rules prescribed by the Arizona Supreme Court in that he, it was charged, had a conflict of interest in soliciting Health and Welfare Fund insurance business; shared the resulting fee or commission with a nonlawyer; permitted misrepresentation to be made to the director of insurance in Arizona regarding the status of the funds deposited in the banks in Washington and Cincinnati to the credit of Family Provider; and, in a deposition in 1977 in other litigation and in a sworn statement submitted during the course of the state bar investigation, making misstatements concerning telephone conversations with lawyers in the Lewis & Roca firm regarding the deposit of funds to the Family Provider accounts.

In the course of hearings before a local administrative committee of the state bar, the State Bar Disciplinary Board, and the supreme court of Arizona, all of the charges relating to his actions while giving legal advice and representation to the Hauser companies were dismissed because the evidence did not support them. There remained the question of the accuracy of his accounts of his conversations with the Lewis & Roca lawyers. The decision of the Arizona Supreme Court was that this charge was supported by credible evidence and Mr. Kleindienst was suspended from the practice of law for one year.

In my own view, which I freely acknowledge was formed while acting as Mr. Kleindienst's counsel, and which was not sustained by the supreme court, this charge was not substantial. It did not involve the propriety of Mr. Kleindienst's actions as a lawyer during the series of transactions which gave rise to the proceeding. The statements of the other lawyers involved in the telephone conversations contradicted each other and were internally contradictory. The questions asked of Mr. Kleindienst about them were so imprecise as to adduce imprecise answers. The charges included no allegations as to what the real facts were. They related to a matter which was both irrelevant and immaterial. Mr. Kleindienst's testimony concerning his telephone conversations, it seemed to me, reflected an honest effort to respond to confusing questions and to reconcile his recollection with the testimony of others as to the events.

While the administrative proceeding was pending before the supreme court, a state court grand jury returned an indictment charging Mr. Kleindienst with thirteen counts of perjury allegedly committed during the state bar investigation. At the trial on these charges, during which the jury heard at length the testimony in person of many of the witnesses who had given very brief testimony (some only by deposition) in the administrative proceeding, the jury had a far better opportunity to judge Mr. Kleindienst and the prosecution witness than had the local administrative committee of the state bar or the State Bar Disciplinary Board. The jury acquitted Mr. Kleindienst on all counts.

During the administrative proceeding, Mr. Kleindienst, on two separate occasions, voluntarily subjected himself to polygraph examinations concerning all of the matters which he understood to be then pending. As to each of these examinations, the examiner's report was entirely affirmative. The first of these occasions was in 1978. Mr. Kleindienst intended to present the results of this examination at the hearing before the local administrative committee but did not do so because bar counsel, after first agreeing that he would have no objection to such evidence, then made objections which made it logistically impractical for the evidence to be presented. The second of these occasions was shortly before the hearing before the State Bar Disciplinary Board, at a time when the details of the charges as finally formulated were known to Mr. Kleindienst, the local administrative committee hearing had been held, and that committee's recommendations were known. Again, the results were entirely affirmative. They were offered in evidence at the hearing before the State Bar Disciplinary Board, and were received into evidence. Their admissibility was the subject of considerable briefing before the Arizona Supreme Court, but was not touched on in the opinion of that court. In the criminal matter, Mr. Kleindienst offered to subject himself to a polygraph examination by any qualified polygraph examiner selected by the prosecution, the result to be admissible no matter what it was; this offer was rejected.

Mr. Kleindienst accepted with good grace his year's suspension, although he believed (and continues to believe) that it was not warranted by the evidence. Under Arizona procedures, Mr. Kleindienst's reinstatement as a member in good standing of the State Bar of Arizona required a hearing before the Bar Disciplinary Board and an affirmative order of the Arizona Supreme Court. The State Bar Disciplinary Board unanimously recommended reinstatement and the Arizona State Supreme Court unanimously ordered reinstatement. In addition, Martindale-Hubbell, Inc., annually publishes a rating on most, if not all, lawyers in the United States. Its highest rating is "a v." The "a" is the legal ability rating of "very high" and the "v" is a "very high" rating which embraces faithful adherence to ethical standards, professional reliability and diligence, and other relevant factors. Shortly after he was reinstated by the supreme court of Arizona, he requested that Martindale-Hubbell undertake its investigation for the purpose of re-rating him as a lawyer. It is my understanding that the following categories of persons were contacted: most, if not all, living former presidents of the State Bar of Arizona; lawyers in Arizona and Washington, D.C., with whom he had been associated since 1950; judges of the federal courts throughout the country and judges of the Arizona courts. On November 9, 1983, Martindale-Hubbell rated him "a v."

My respect for Mr. Kleindienst's character grew all during these proceedings.

Although I had known him since 1941, and we had been on friendly terms during all that time, we had not been close friends. During the administrative and criminal proceedings, I saw him and talked with him frequently and at length. I became intimately acquainted with his mental processes and with his ethical standards.

I found him to be scrupulously honest, unwilling (and, I believe, constitutionally unable) to fudge on the truth or to try to conceal it.

His respect for the law and the legal process was such that he accepted, willingly and without complaint, the ordeals of the administrative proceeding, the criminal proceeding, and the year's suspension.

> George Read Carlock, Esq.
> Ryley, Carlock & Applewhit, P.A.
> 101 North First Avenue, 26th Floor
> Phoenix, Arizona 85003

Index